HOW THE RURAL POOR GOT POWER

Narrative of a Grass-Roots Organizer

Paul David Wellstone

University of Massachusetts Press   Amherst, 1978

TO MY PARENTS, MINNIE AND LEON WELLSTONE

JS
451
M69
R58
1978

CONTENTS

ACKNOWLEDGMENTS

I met some of the strongest, most determined, most inspirational people I've ever met in my life working with Organization for a Better Rice County. This book is about their work.

Professors Frances Fox Piven and Peter Bachrach were extremely generous with their time in reading, providing invaluable criticism, and supporting my work. I owe special thanks to Malcolm Call, Carol Schoen, and Leone Stein at the University of Massachusetts Press—it has been a fine experience working with them.

Much of this book was written while I worked with the Center for Community Change in Washington, D.C. The staff of the Center, in particular Bruce Hanson, gave me the necessary encouragement.

Sheila Wellstone is a wonderful woman whose support I will always appreciate.

PREFACE

In his constantly instructive and cautionary *The Open Society and Its Enemies*, Karl Popper addresses himself, at the end of a long effort, to nothing less than history itself. He wonders what lessons one can learn from it, and shows, immediately after asking the question, that the very notion of "history" has to be questioned. We have been taught to think of history as a succession of power struggles: the reigns of kings and emperors, the years in which prime ministers and presidents held rule. Meanwhile, the lives of generation after generation of ordinary people go unnoticed, unrecorded, ignored by those scholars who present accounts, really, of a few all too celebrated figures in the name of a portrayal of man's past.

This book is a contribution to quite another kind of history, and is also an expression of one political scientist's willingness to part company with various ideologues in his profession whose way of thinking confirms Karl Popper's suspicions that arrogance and exploitative mischief are by no means absent from academic and intellectual life. All too many political scientists, in our time, have lent themselves eagerly to various "principalities and powers," and for doing so, have been grandly rewarded. All the while, a whole world of important political events, struggles, developments goes unnoticed, unrecorded.

No one very important was involved in the rural organizing effort in the southern part of Minnesota described in the following pages by Professor Wellstone. They were ordinary, hard-pressed, small-town, rural Americans—poor or not so poor, but none too well off, that's for sure. The backbone of the country, I suppose a kind of eastern essayist would say—intent on evoking rural nostalgia as a means of distracting the reader from the grim realities of both country and city living as they are experienced today by millions of men and women. In this book a number of individuals come alive, and with them, a sustained account of what they were struggling to achieve—a more honorable and secure life for hundreds of vulnerable families.

As I read this book, I kept thinking of the community organizers I have known and worked with these past years: the civil rights activists who trudged the dusty Delta roads in the early 1960s, intent on prompting terrribly frightened, suspicious black sharecroppers and tenant farmers to make an effort at registering to vote; the union organizers working with migrants while sheriffs and grower-subsidized private "security men," heavily armed, were always near at hand; or the Appalachian "folk" who tried to organize themselves in the 1960s in hopes of fighting the so-called "war on poverty," rather more quickly abandoned and with fewer misgivings, it seems, than the war we fought in Southeast Asia. Those rural struggles, waged by the poor, always against high odds, were very much like the one Professor Wellstone describes; they were usually plagued by considerable obstacles, and they were not by any means always successful, in the sense that concrete political or economic goals were reached. But slowly, a dazed, or cannily inert, and always deeply fearful people became more active, more forceful, more willing, at times, to take a chance or two—a risk hitherto considered out of the question.

It was, and is, a matter of small victories amid continual resistance and frequent setbacks. It is a matter of gradual, undramatic, localist transformation—arguably the essence of a democratic process, in contrast to a totalitarian one. If only there were, in every county of every state, some of the people and initiatives described in these pages, this would be a better country. And if only there were participant observers around, like this book's author, to record for the rest of us what was done, what was learned, the mistakes made, the achievements managed: our academic life would be less cloistered, less smug and insulated, more in touch with the realities of this life, which also need to be understood and analysed, and which also are sources of intellectual edification, not to mention moral instruction.

Robert Coles

INTRODUCTION

This book is a study of rural poverty and politics. The focus is on the development of a poor people's organization, Organization for a Better Rice County (ORBC). It is the narrative study of an organizing effort in a rural, small-town community in southeastern Minnesota.

The rural poor have traditionally been ignored in our country, even when government activities supported "antipoverty" programs.[1] For most Americans, the terms *slums, substandard housing, joblessness, hunger and malnutrition* call to mind the terms *urban ghetto* and *inner city.* Yet more poverty exists in rural America, proportionately, than in our cities. While less than one-third of the nation's population reside in rural, small-town communities, 40% of the nation's poor, 9.2 million rural people, live in poverty.[2] In 1973, 35% of all nonmetropolitan families, 6.3 million families and 19 million people, had incomes below the Bureau of Labor Statistics lower living standard. This was almost *40%* of the total rural population.[3]

Statistics abound describing the plight of the rural poor.[4] But statistics cannot tell us much *in human terms* of what economic oppression means to millions of rural poor people. Although rural poverty is less visible than its more geographically concentrated urban counterpart, it is nonetheless a cruel reality for many Americans. Mariellen Procopio and Fred Perella, authors of Campaign for Human Development's *Poverty Profile 1975,* put it well: "Rural poverty is no less inhuman than urban poverty. It is just more hidden and more forgotten."[5]

There has been very little research done on rural poverty and politics and certainly not much written from the perspective of the people on the bottom.[6] The experience I've had with Organization for a Better Rice County has caused me to appreciate the extent to which social change often depends on careful research. But there is little research available concerning the factors behind rural poverty and the implications these have for successful citizen organization. Most important, there is little knowledge about various efforts which have been made in rural, small-town communities to construct poor people's organizations.

In rural communities, the political systems and power constraints are different (or modified) from those in urban communities. The rural poor are not heirs of a tradition of political activism and attempted organization, as are many urban communities. Organizing is difficult where there is no expectation for social change and where the assertion of dignity often leads to retaliation. Low-income residents are isolated from one another and from more affluent sectors of the community. They are stigmatized for being poor. Sanctions against rural dissidents can be effectively enforced, for rural, small-town communities lack the more elaborate organizational life and impersonal economy found in urban areas. There are few voluntary organizations to which the poor can appeal. Legal service programs are usually nonexistent.[7] In short, low-income people are extremely vulnerable to economic, social, and physical retaliation. They face many obstacles and restraints in trying to voice their concerns and influence local government.

The critical question which underlies this book is well stated by Bachrach and Baratz in their work, *Power and Poverty*:

> In fact, our approach tends to reverse the basic question. Rather than asking, who rules? it asks, What persons or groups in the community are especially disfavored under the existing distribution of benefits and privileges? It asks, further, To what extent does the utilization of power, authority and influence shape and maintain a political system that tends to perpetuate "unfair shares" in the allocation of values: *and how, if at all, are new sources of power, authority, and influence generated and brought to bear in an effort to alter the political process and in turn lessen inequality in the value allocation?* [Emphasis mine][8]

Bachrach and Baratz analyze "poverty, race, and politics" in the city of Baltimore, but the question they pose is crucial to the study of both urban and rural poverty politics. I have in mind the experience of protest politics in the 1960s. Many of us believed that as the grim details of poverty were brought before the nation, a national conscience would be touched and this would translate into public policy to correct social and economic injustices. There was a great deal of public discussion—numerous reports and books were written about the poor. But the revelations did not automatically set into gear the machinery to deal with the problems. Middle-class reformers, often representing the poor by proxy, ran out of time or energy or interest, and government officials were unwilling to act on the recommendations of their own commissioned studies.[9] There was (and is) a major ingredient missing from our perception of how political changes are brought about; that ingredient is power.

It is important to study political problems through the process of systematic investigation. As a teacher, I certainly believe in this process. But it is a serious mistake to assume that the "correct solutions" will ultimately influence social policy. Michael Parenti makes an important argument when he reminds us:

> There are no correct solutions to social problems: there are different solutions involving conflicting ends and conflicting value positions. What is missing from this approach to the study of social problems is the essence of politics itself—the inescapability of interest and power in determining which solutions are suitable, which allocations supportable, and which problems should even be studied in the first place.[10]

Bachrach and Bennett raise the same issue:

> The heroic call for "a new revolution in political science" by David Easton five years ago was more symbolic than real. For in his appeal to the profession to become politicized, to utilize its expertise to rectify the imbalance between the privileged and the masses, he wrongly assumed that the injection of knowledge in the right places would somehow be effective. Unfortunately, what the poor, the weak, the inarticulate desperately require is power, organization, a sense of identity and purpose, not the rarified advice of political scientists. If our ranks were filled with women and men

who possessed the skills and dedication of the late Saul Alinsky, it would be a different matter. But they are not.[11]

The point is that most reports and studies have not increased the power of the poor, and without a shift in the balance of power, policy and practice will remain the same; that prior to a "reordering of priorities" in America, there must be a reordering of power; that trying to reorder priorities without reordering power is a contradiction. It remains empty rhetoric unless strong and durable citizen organizations are developed to turn this appeal into specific programs backed by political clout.

My work with OBRC has convinced me that citizen organization can play an especially vital role in the lives of rural poor people. A strong organization provides rural, small-town residents with a degree of social support and personal friendship that perhaps is rarely obtained in an urban setting. But the challenge to build for power is a difficult one. The OBRC experience in Rice and surrounding rural counties in southern Minnesota raises some important issues about community organizing as a method of social change. If strong and durable community organizations through which poor people can take positive steps to alleviate their social and economic deprivation are to be developed, we need a better sense of what works, what doesn't, and why. I hope the narrative study which follows contributes to this goal.

The reader should be aware of several methodological issues while reading this book. I never planned to write a book about OBRC until this past year. As a result, I have not consciously viewed the organization from the perspective of a scholar-observer over the past three years. I cannot even claim the role of participant-observer. During the first two years, from the summer of 1972 until the fall of 1974, I was intensely involved with OBRC. I founded the organization, did a great deal of the initial organizing and fund raising, and served unofficially as director.

This past year (January 1974) I was fired from Carleton College and given a terminal one-year contract. After a long and bitter struggle the decision was reversed and I was awarded tenure. "OBRC people" were very active on my behalf. I have been through many fights with the organization. I have deep affection for many OBRC members. In short, I am not without my biases.

My close association with OBRC has also limited the scope of research. Accessibility to county commissioners, city council-men, welfare department employees, and other county officials has been a real problem. The conflict tactics employed by OBRC have not endeared the organization to political and economic notables in the county. OBRC and the welfare department are bitter adversaries. Many of these officials hold me responsible for OBRC actions. It makes little difference that I am no longer active in the organization. It was impossible to obtain "candid" interviews.[1][2]

On the positive side, I have not faced the suspicion or hostil-ity a political science professor might normally expect when studying a poor people's organization. I have had unlimited ac-cess to the organization's documents, and key organizers, lead-ers, and rank-and-file members have generously given me many hours of their time.

Five months prior to writing this book, I phased myself out of OBRC. I used this time to carry out research and reflect about the organization. This break has made it easier for me to gain a perspective difficult to obtain when one is actively involved in organizing efforts. The strongest check on "objectivity" is my deep belief in community organizing; in the importance of build-ing for power to overcome social injustice. The analysis that fol-lows will be critical in perspective.

1

THE STRUGGLE FOR RECOGNITION

Rice County (population 41,582) is located directly south of and adjacent to the seven-county Twin Cities metropolitan area. The greater part of the land is used for agricultural purposes; there are only two cities in the county of appreciable size—Northfield, population 10,235 (including students at Carleton and St. Olaf colleges), and Faribault, the county seat, population 16,595. The county is dotted with fourteen townships and four villages. Until two years ago, the general relief welfare program was administered (with total discretion) by the township boards and village governments.

Thirteen percent of the population (1,175 families) have annual incomes below $4,000; 40% of all single individuals (many over sixty-five years of age) fall below the poverty line as defined by the Social Security Administration.[1] Close to two-thirds of families classified as poor by the census are rural; altogether slightly more than half of all poor people live in rural areas. One in five persons over sixty-five is below the poverty line, and they represent one-fourth of the poverty population (although only one-tenth of the total population is over sixty-five).[2]

Of those low-income families under sixty-five, 85% of the heads of the family are working in the labor force.[3] People are not poor in Rice County because they don't work or work less, and hardly any of them receive any public assistance.

The structure of low-wage industry is pervasive. The major natural resource of Rice County is land. This land is some of the most fertile in the United States. When the area was first settled, the land was used for farming. Early railroads reduced the cost of transportation of raw materials and finished products and enabled manufacturing industries to profitably locate in the county. The development of extensive highways and the growth of the trucking industry post–World War II made it feasible for more manufacturing firms to locate in Rice County. In addition to this decrease in transportation costs, there has been a dramatic decline in agricultural employment due to mechanization. Ex-farm workers form a large labor force for industry.

Food processors and machinery manufacturers are the two most common types of manufacturing industries. The average wage in food processing is two dollars an hour.[4] The work is seasonal. Unions are nonexistent or weak. A migrant labor stream usually fills some of the labor positions every summer. With the exception of the small migrant population, there is no "minority" population in the county. Poor whites are the minority. Many of them hate the Chicanos because they feel the Chicanos take their jobs during the summer and/or depress the wage level for everyone.

The average wage in machinery manufacturing is much higher —$2.69 an hour[5] —but there are several low-wage employers. The operations are labor intensive. The industries threaten to leave if strong unions come in. The employees take these threats seriously. There are few alternative job opportunities available for low-wage workers in industry. Clerical and sales workers, many of whom also work full time for their poverty, are faced with the same limited job-opportunities structure.

In the town of Faribault, OBRC's home base, many of the industries are still family owned. Nutting Truck and Caster Company builds industrial carts. Gopher Shooter and Supply Company is a wholesale distributor of sporting goods. It is also the parent company of the Bonanza factory, which makes reloading equipment for ammunition used mainly by target-shooters. Faribault Woolens makes a variety of products and is especially well known for its woolen blankets. Sellner Manufacturers is the world's only manufacturer of Tilt-a-Whirls.

The owners are determined "never to let the union in." The Faribault Canning Company, a major food processor in the area, also shares this determination. These industries pay low wages and the workers can take it or leave it. Recently, a group of women discovered that they were training men for jobs that paid more than their own. Angered, they went to the owner and told him they would quit unless he did something about the discrimination. He fired the women and immediately replaced them. The bitter lesson that wage earners (whether they be working poor or just above the poverty line) repeat often is "there is no way out." They feel they have no other choice but to accept the situation.

Even in those industries where the workers have union representation, the wages are usually low. Crown, Cork and Seal, which makes bottle caps, and McQuay's, a manufacturer of air-conditioners, pay "good wages"—six dollars and above per hour. But workers in the cheese factory, now owned by Kraft, don't do so well. At Richmond Farms, better known as "the turkey plant," workers are paid little more than the minimum wage. The "nonprofessionals" at the State School for the Deaf, Blind, and Retarded, Faribault's largest employer (close to 1,000 men and women work at the state school), are represented by the American Federation of State, County, and Municipal Employees (AFSCME). Yet, wages are still notoriously low.

It is a difficult environment for the unions. The industries do not face much competition for wages. Little if any industry has come to town in the past decade. The industrialists are the power brokers in town. They control the chamber of commerce, the city council, and the industrial commission. They use this power base to keep higher-paying industries out of town. About a year ago, a glass factory wanted to locate in Faribault. The chamber of commerce sent three representatives to meet with the company: the owners of Nutting Truck and Caster Company and Faribault Woolens and the manager of Faribault Canning Company. The glass factory decided to locate elsewhere—in Owatonna, a town of 16,000 about thirteen miles south of Faribault. The union leadership was furious, but it was powerless to do anything about it.

Because of low wages, most families depend on both husband and wife working in order to make a living. One woman I interviewed told me, "I don't mind talking about Faribault because nobody in town is going to read your book anyway." In a slightly defensive way, I asked her what she meant. She explained that because both husband and wife work in many families, people in town have little time for their own children or their neighbors, much less time for reading. Patti Fritz, an OBRC activist, expressed some of the anger that low- and working-income people feel: "I would like to say this to the big shots. I want my husband at home more with me like your husband. Instead, he has to work all the time. Am I being selfish? Am I being greedy? To want a good family life with some economic security? To be able to pay for groceries, rent, heat, the telephone? I don't think so. There are more of us than them. We should not have to take it."

A senior citizen who spent his whole life in Faribault once described the town to me as "a low-income town that looks down on low-income people." Poor people are deeply resented in town. The local paper religiously attacks welfare programs and includes under this rubric almost all social programs. Faribault, Minnesota, a town run by business interests, a town hostile to unions, a town so deeply principled in conservatism that it refused WPA funds in the 1930s, was an unlikely home for a poor people's organization.

It was not until the late 1960s that poverty was officially recognized in Rice County. In 1967 an official "anti-poverty" program, the Rice-Goodhue-Wabasha Citizens Action Council, was established to "serve the poor." My first introduction to rural poverty and politics was through the Citizens Action Council (CAC).[6] Observing the agency "serve the poor" was quite an experience. This local OEO program was a case study of what the late Saul Alinsky called "political pornography."[7] The agency was controlled by conservative labor and veteran interests, along with the public officials who sat on the policy-making board. There was little meaningful participation by the poor. I once observed the secretary of the board of directors take fifty-five minutes out of an hour to lecture Headstart mothers on the importance of maximum participation by the poor. Whenever poor people spoke out at meetings, they were put down. Once humiliated at a meeting, they rarely came back. The CAC refused to sponsor welfare advocacy or any kind of advocacy program for the poor. Organizing for power was out of the question. The mandate of the agency as interpreted by the director and those who controlled the board was to help the poor as needy individuals. Even this service orientation was qualified by what was acceptable to county officials. One evening during a class I taught on "poverty politics" for Headstart mothers and staff, we had a discussion of Saul Alinsky's book, *Rules for Radicals.*[8] The focus was on applying Alinsky's analysis to rural poverty in Rice, Goodhue, and Wabasha counties. The conclusion reached by the class was that the first organizing project should be to get rid of the director of the agency. Some of the staff seemed hesitant about this strategy, but the mothers were quite unequivocal.

During my one-year appointment on the CAC Board of Directors, I identified a core of poor people from Rice County who were disillusioned with the OEO program. Some came to meeting after meeting to speak out, though the forum guaranteed failure. Some stopped coming to meetings altogether. Some were aides in various service programs, paid less than poverty wages by the antipoverty agency. Some were welfare mothers seeking relief from harassment by the county welfare department. Some were just looking for encouragement and social support to survive a cruel and disappointing life. None were to receive any satisfaction from the agency.

These were strong people, but as individuals they faced sure defeat. I was able to take advantage of my position on the board and later as the professor of the poverty politics class to work closely with several Headstart-welfare mothers. We met and discussed grievances and what could be done about them. We discussed the idea of building an independent poor people's organization *outside* the structure of the Rice-Goodhue-Wabasha CAC, an organization that would challenge the hierarchy of power in Rice County and gain poor people a voice. Everyone thought it was a great plan. The question was whether we could make it happen.

The organizing effort began in June 1972. There were five of us who did the initial organizing: two Carleton students (one of whom was to become a community VISTA), a welfare mother, a Headstart mother, and myself. We received a $2,000 grant from the national United Church of Christ which enabled us to set up a small office with a phone.

The strategy was to build an organization around conflict issues. We knew people who were angry but very discouraged about being able to do anything about their plight. The challenge was to bring people together to *act* on their needs and concerns. If poor people were to get together and win a few victories, we could overcome the legacy of defeat and despair. The organization's first attempt had to be a success. If we grouped people together only to suffer defeat, the organizing campaign would be over.

In the beginning, very little emphasis was put on developing a formal structure to the organization. The "Alinsky model" of pyramiding organizations into a coalition umbrella organization did not apply to rural Rice County. There were few politically active church, union, or neighborhood organizations. There were not any organizations in the county which represented or would represent the poor.[9] We could not call a convention to develop a structure before taking on issues because the concept of a poor people's organization (in a vacuum) would be too abstract to bring people together. Poor whites in Rice County were not affected by social movements in the 1960s. As a result of years of racial oppression many Blacks developed a feeling of group identity, and racial oppression became the basis for unity and group action. Strong welfare rights, tenants' rights, and neighborhood organizations were formed. There was no comparable development among poor white people in the cities or in rural communities.[10]

The decision not to build a formal structure in the beginning meant that OBRC was essentially five organizers who made the decisions about the issues, the strategies, and the tactics. This historical fact would later hurt the organization.

Housing was the first issue. During the winter and spring of 1972, fifty Carleton students worked on several community research projects—housing, food assistance, and health care needs in the county. The work was conceived of as action-research. We wanted to provide analyses of these problems that could be followed up with the kind of social action that would contribute to solutions. The research effort was to provide background information for a yet-to-be-born poor people's organization. Accordingly, the students did not make any policy recommendations in the studies. No presentation of the materials was made to county officials. The idea behind the research was that students could best make a contribution through their research skills. They would document and identify significant problems. It would be up to the people most seriously affected by the problems to reach conclusions about what should be done.[11]

The housing study was comprehensive and quite sophisticated. The state HUD office (Housing and Urban Development) and the state planning agency were very impressed with the study. It was the first solid rural housing study that had been done in the state. In mid-June, HUD turned down the Faribault Housing Authority's proposal for 200 units of "236 housing." HUD argued the housing authority had not provided sufficient documentation of need and insisted the authority use "the Carleton student housing study" as the basis for grant proposals.

Rick Kahn, the Carleton student who directed the housing study, stayed on during the summer to help organize OBRC. The "Carleton student housing study" became the OBRC study. OBRC's monopoly on relevant housing data (a curious turn of events for a citizen organization) gave the two-week-old organization considerable leverage in the housing field.

Five citizens sat on the housing authority—all appointed by the mayor with the approval of the city council. The chairman was manager of the Northern States Power (NSP) utility company office in Rice County. Other members included: two bankers, a retired city official, and the wife of the school superintendent. They were determined to apply for "low cost" housing which would be restricted to senior citizens, the deserving poor, and would be too expensive for the lowest income people in the county.[12] Rick Kahn was a skillful negotiator, and within a one-month period OBRC had changed the proposal considerably. The housing authority applied for 200 units of *public housing*; 175 senior citizen units and 25 four-bedroom units for large families. This was the first time the county (the Faribault Housing Authority was in effect the county authority) had ever applied for public housing, housing which provided the deepest subsidy and which poor people could afford.

People in the county read in the *Faribault Daily News* about this joint effort by the housing authority and Organization for a Better Rice County. The authority linked up with OBRC because it needed OBRC's expertise if it was to get any proposal funded by HUD. OBRC was unknown at this time and did not constitute any threat to local officials. They viewed OBRC as an organization of "do-gooders" from Carleton College. They were not far off the mark. This was good publicity for OBRC. But it hardly represented an action by poor people; it was rather an action in their behalf. We could not be pleased with this dynamic.

The "Carleton student housing study" also provided invaluable background information for active tenants' rights work. In addition to extensive work with census data and interviews with bankers, builders, and real-estate people, the students had interviewed over 100 families in the county. They focused on the housing needs of the poor, and initially this created a serious methodological problem. In rural Rice County, 491 square miles, it was very difficult to determine who the poor were or where they lived. Our methodology (with the help of several community people) was to swipe a list of food-commodity recipients from the local OEO. The food commodities list was not inclusive of all or even a majority of poor people in the county (only 20% of those eligible for commodities participated in the program), but it did give us some basis for drawing a random sample of 100 families to be interviewed for the study.

Many families complained about their landlords. From reading the interviews, we could discern a pattern of slum ownership. We examined the county property records to get a full reading on the property holdings of the major slumlords, wrote up a few hundred copies of tenants' rights booklets, and concentrated on tenants' rights organizing. Minnesota tenant laws were (are) among the most progressive in the country. Several slumlords were in obvious violation of these laws. We felt it would be relatively easy to win some legal victories, if we could group some of the tenants together against their slumlord. The tenants had immediate and pressing concerns; faulty wiring, exposed electrical outlets, rat-infested basements, and other dangers facing their families. A successful organizing campaign would involve the tenants actively working on their problems, and if OBRC could *publicly* take on a major slumlord and win in the courts, then poor people would see "what happens when folks on the bottom stand up for their rights." This was, roughly speaking, the strategy.

We spent six weeks trying to organize fifteen families against the worst slumlord in Faribault–rural Faribault. The tenants were frustrated and angry with their landlord but wary about taking any action. Political organizing of poor people was totally new to this rural, small-town community, and the reaction to our work ranged from cautious to suspicious to hostile. One tenant went straight to the landlord to warn him about "outside agitators" and bargained to get repairs in exchange for information about our activities. Most of the people had never heard of Organization for a Better Rice County, and for a good reason, since we were just getting started. Or, as one man said, "I've heard of your goddamn fucking organization, and I don't want any of your fucking help."

We overcame some of these problems by visiting families several times and spending a great deal of time talking with the people about tenants' rights and OBRC. We left copies of tenants' rights booklets with each family, and all of the tenants were very interested in finding out about laws and protection that they did not even know existed. Most importantly, the people had strong grievances. We finally set up a meeting where the tenants could come together and discuss what action they might take collectively against their landlord. Ten out of fifteen families were represented at the meeting. Peter Schmitz, a highly respected lawyer from Northfield, attended the meeting and agreed to litigate at no cost to the tenants or OBRC. He assured the people that their case was legally sound and promised to write up a legal brief to be circulated to everyone for their approval.

In the end, not one family took legal action. After six weeks of work, we had nothing to show for our efforts. It was painful to analyze the failure. Tenants' rights organizing was a tough place to start in trying to build an organization. We were trapped by housing market conditions. The extreme shortage of adequate low-cost housing gave low-income tenants a weak bargaining position. I remember talking with one man about his decision not to take action against the landlord. He was a disabled worker, the father of five children. His wife worked as a cook at the hospital, and the family lived on her meager salary. We were sitting in the backyard. Looking at the house, he said to me, "It's not much. I'll admit to that. But where else can we live in a house for eighty dollars a month? At least we have a roof over our heads." And then, looking at the crumbling roof, he added jokingly, "At least I think we have a roof over our heads." The tenants were in an impossible position, given the housing market. They feared their landlord would, if put under pressure, walk away from the property or raise the rent to cover substantial repairs to the point where they would be priced out of shelter for their families.

The more fundamental problem was that we were unable to inspire confidence among the tenants. They had never heard of "tenants' rights." They had never heard of OBRC. The landlord told his tenants we were a group of Carleton prelaw students "trying out their training on you." In the early goings, we were vulnerable to such charges. The people worked with us but never with complete confidence—and not enough confidence to take the risks involved in fighting a landlord.

After this setback, we developed a somewhat different strategy. The emphasis would still be on conflict issues. In September we anticipated a major political fight with the country welfare board over the administration of the food commodities program. Before this confrontation, however, a full month would be spent canvassing the county and talking with as many poor people as possible. We had to establish personal contact with as many people as possible.

The canvassing was long, hot, hard work. We learned a great deal from the people we met. Sometimes we were viewed with suspicion and hostility; more often than not, we were royally received. In fact, there was often a real tension between the goal of trying to meet and talk with as many people as possible and the strong desire to spend an afternoon drinking coffee and eating cookies, listening to people reflect on their lives.

We were careful to ask questions about what could be done through collective action, through an organization of poor people. These were agitational questions in that they raised the possibility of doing something about conditions that most people regarded fatalistically. Many people had strong grievances, though they were cautious about "this OBRC." A few people became active right away. Most people were taking a wait-and-see attitude. But the personal contact was invaluable. When people read about OBRC they could say to themselves, "We remember those OBRC people—they came by the house not too long ago. It looks like they're doing pretty well. Maybe we ought to call and find out what is going on." As it turns out, this is exactly what happened.

During the last two weeks of August and for most of September we organized around the food commodities program and made it a major poor people's issue in Rice County. We had used the food commodities list (swiped from the OEO) for the canvassing. And in our conversations with people, food commodities turned up as an important problem-issue. Some people wanted the county to switch to food stamps, though they had little knowledge about the stamps program; others (most) wanted improvements in the commodities program. Especially troublesome to people was the problem of transportation since there was only one food commodities distribution center in the entire county.

Food commodities was an important organizing issue. For all the low-income families we talked with, food was the most basic of issues. Food assistance was a survival issue. Moreover, the food assistance program affected not just the welfare poor but working poor and senior citizens as well. Carleton students had done research on commodities and stamps. This report—now an OBRC report—provided valuable documentation of problems with local implementation of the commodities program. The county welfare board had to make a decision by November 1 whether to stay with commodities or switch to food stamps. They had never in the past asked recipients what they thought about stamps or commodities. Poor people never had any say over what kind of food assistance program the county would have or how it would be administered. We planned a confrontation with the welfare board over this issue. Our goal was that a large number of poor people would directly challenge the county officials as OBRC members and force positive changes in the food assistance program.

The scenario went as follows. In mid-August five copies of the Carleton student research report—now an OBRC report—were delivered to the five county commissioners. The commissioners served as the welfare board (along with two lay members appointed by them). Enclosed with the reports was a note which said, "We at OBRC have done extensive research on the food commodities and food stamp programs. We have found serious problems with the way you, the commissioners, are handling the commodities program. Get in touch with OBRC to learn more about these problems." It was a note calculated to assure they *would not respond.*

It was not until 1969 that Rice County had a food assistance program of any kind. The county ran the commodities program on a shoestring budget. They contracted out the administration of the program to the Rice-Goodhue-Wabasha Citizens Action Council for $5,000 a year. There was one staff person to supervise the program for the entire county. There was only one distribution center in the county, located in Faribault. There was not any "outreach program." For those who knew about the program, knew they were eligible, and had transportation to get to Faribault, there was a long wait, several hours, before they received commodities at the distribution site. There were no chairs for senior citizens and others during this long wait. The implementation of commodities seriously discouraged participation; only 20% of the eligible population was participating in the program.[13]

If the county commissioners had responded to the OBRC research and asked us to come and testify about the food assistance programs, we would have been in real trouble. A few organizers with perhaps a few recipients would make a presentation. The commisssioners might agree with the report; they might not. It would make no difference. Poor people directly affected by food assistance programs would not be involved in this process in any significant and meaningful way. We were determined to develop this issue.

In August and September we sent out a mailing of booklets on food stamps and food commodities. The booklets explained the programs and identified the relative advantages and disadvantages of each program. There were no conclusions as to whether Rice County should have commodities or stamps. The booklets informed people about their rights and focused on the critical question of how best to run a program in Rice County. The question was raised over and over again: Shouldn't the people most directly affected by food assistance programs have the say about what program the county has and how it is run? People were invited to call, write, or drop by the office to express their opinions.

The last week of September we were ready to move on this issue. The county board had not responded to the OBRC report. We had done the necessary canvassing and personal contact. OBRC issued the following press release which was carried on the front page of the *Faribault Daily News* (the county newspaper):

County Commissioners Charged with
Apathetic Food Distribution Handling

Organization for a Better Rice County (OBRC) in a statement today charged that the County Board of Commissioners is apathetic
and negligent in its handling of food distribution programs in the
county.

"Although the board must make a decision by the end of the
fall whether Rice County will have a food commodity or food
stamp program, a decision that will vitally affect thousands of residents, the board has not shown any interest in trying to understand the way these programs really work," stated Paul Wellstone,
one of the OBRC staff members. Wellstone went on to say: "We
spent over 20 weeks preparing a report for the Commissioners but
none of the Commissioners even bothered to contact OBRC to
say they had read it or talk about any of the conclusions. We are
sure most of them did not even bother to read it, and also that
most of them have little understanding about commodities or
stamps."

The OBRC also challenged the way commodities is now run in
the county. OBRC pointed out that around 400 households or
1,500 people now participate in the program, but that based on
1970 census figures 1,865 households or 4,300 people are in fact
eligible. As a result, at the very best, the commodity program is
only reaching 20 percent of the people who are in need of food
assistance.

"These figures are shocking, and there is no way to avoid the
real problem—our neighbors, including the very young and very
old, are going to bed every night without enough food to keep
them healthy," stated staff member Wellstone.

OBRC stated that although the national programs are weak,
the county board is responsible for the failure of the food relief
program in the county. OBRC charged that the commissioners
have been hypocritical because although we have a program, the
lack of money, the lack of staff, not enough distribution centers
(only one center in the whole county—creating tremendous transportation problems for senior citizens), and not enough concern
have all doomed the program to failure. "The Commissioners
have been stingy in their handling of commodities, and everybody
affected by the program knows this," stated Wellstone.

OBRC concluded by stating that the commissioners must hear

from as many citizens as possible before they make their final decision about what kind of program we will have in the county
and how it will be run. OBRC stated that in Wabasha County the
commissioners made their decision without consulting anybody
affected by the program, and vowed that this will not happen in
Rice County.

The organization demanded that the commissioners show its
[sic] concern by setting up public hearings so that it can hear
from residents before it makes any further decisions about commodities or stamps. [Faribault Daily News, September 27, 1972]

The next day the director of the county welfare department
and the chairman of the county welfare board got on the radio
five times to deny the story and denounce OBRC. Whatever
terms they used—OBRC is irresponsible, OBRC is reckless, OBRC
is militant, OBRC is a bunch of agitators—they made OBRC a
household word overnight. The action was in the reaction. OBRC
demanded free radio time and got it. In a thirty-minute interview on prime radio time, we discussed not only the food commodities controversy but the promise and future of OBRC.
There was another two weeks of charges and countercharges in
articles and letters to the editor in the Faribault Daily News.[14]

The conflict generated a tremendous amount of excitement
among low-income people. Some were specifically interested in
the food assistance program. Others who had been treated badly
by the welfare department were pleased with the fight. I was
teaching an evening class for Headstart mothers at this time, and
I remember vividly how several women came up to me with big
smiles on their faces and said, "We don't know much about
OBRC yet. But if Chester Pearson [the director of the welfare
department] hates you guys [you guys is a midwestern expression comparable to you-all] so much, you must be doing something right. We're going to join."

OBRC's next step was to call for a public meeting on food
commodities and food stamps. The meeting was held at the Labor Temple Building, a small meeting hall in Faribault. Over
fifty poor people attended the meeting. The building was crowded with welfare mothers, senior citizens, and the working poor.
It was an emotional meeting, for many people had strong opinions to express. For the first hour, people who wanted the county to change to stamps debated those who wanted the county

to stay with commodities. This was a divisive question which was splitting the people apart. One speaker would oppose commodities because there were bugs in the flour. Another speaker would suggest there were bugs in the flour because the kitchen was probably not clean.

Charles Liverseed, a seventy-two-year-old handyman, broke the deadlock. He asked for a straw vote on how many people favored commodities over stamps. A large majority favored commodities. Liverseed suggested OBRC push for the commodities program for one more year, provided the county commissioners make improvements in administering the program. There was widespread agreement. He concluded with a strong, emotional attack on the county board of commissioners and a resolution demanding they hold a public hearing on the commodities program. The resolution was passed unanimously. A committee chaired by a welfare mother was appointed to appear before the board to request the public hearing.

The OBRC meeting was an unprecedented event in Rice County. Never before had so many poor people come together. Men and women realized there were others "in the same boat." A number of people emerged as strong spokesmen. The confidence was contagious. After the formal business, everyone stayed to chat and to have coffee and all the cakes and cookies which had been brought to the meeting. The meeting was in the best tradition of citizen politics.

The following week the committee appeared before the county commissioners to request a public hearing. A welfare mother who never before had spoken at a public meeting acted as the representative for the group. When she made the request, the commissioners told her she had come to the wrong government body; that the county welfare board, not the county board of commissioners, administered commodities; that she would have to make her request to the right government body at the appropriate time.

Their tactic was devastating. The county welfare board and county board of commissioners were in effect one and the same. But the board was smarting over the OBRC attacks and intended to humiliate the woman—to point out to her and the rest of the OBRC delegation how stupid they were not to know where or how to make the request. As organizers we had made a serious mistake. We had not researched carefully the fine distinction between the county board of commissioners and welfare board. As a result, a woman who had attempted to assert her dignity was publicly humiliated. She dropped out of OBRC and never returned.

Charles Liverseed volunteered to act as spokesman for the OBRC committee. They appeared before the welfare board this time and requested the public hearing. Given the controversy OBRC had generated over this issue, the welfare board had little choice in the matter. The public hearing was granted.

The hearing was held in the third week of October. It took place in the middle of the afternoon, which precluded working people from attending, but there was a strong delegation of poor people who jammed the small meeting room at the county courthouse. The commissioners were confronted with specific demands: (1) Set up another distribution center in the county; (2) Increase the staff to administer the commodities program; (3) Provide chairs for people while they wait in the commodities line; (4) See that people receive more vegetables and meat; (5) Start an outreach program to inform people of the commodities program.

The county board of commissioners had never been confronted by poor people like this before. They seemed confused about the dynamic of this hearing. Poor people were speaking up and some were militant. Commissioners were asked if *they* would like to eat commodities for one month, if *they* would like to wait three or four hours in line, if *they* would like to see their children go hungry because they could not get to the distribution center.

The welfare board agreed to an additional distribution center in Northfield, agreed to provide chairs at the distribution sites, and agreed to get more volunteer staff to administer the program. They rightfully pointed out that they did not control which commodities actually came to Rice County, that responsibility lay at the federal and state levels. They would not spend additional money to develop an outreach program. In fact, they only conceded on the issues that did not require any additional expenditure of county money. But this was an enormous victory for OBRC. Poor people, acting through the organization, had forced the county welfare board into positive reforms of the food commodity program. They had come together around a common problem, had spoken for themselves, and had been successful. Nothing builds confidence like success. Charles Liverseed captured the mood of the meeting when, much to the welfare board's dismay, he gave a five-minute speech at the conclusion of the meeting. His final remarks were, "We here at OBRC have just made a contract with you the commissioners about improving the commodities program. If you don't live up to your word, we're going to come back and make you live up to your promises."

OBRC was now a visible organization in the county. The organization had developed rapidly as a result of the controversy. But it was still an organization in name only. There was no internal structure through which people could participate in decisions and occupy important leadership positions. All the strategy had been the work of a few organizers. We felt it was time to put together a formal organization run by and for poor people. Accordingly, we planned for the first convention.

The "first annual convention" took place in mid-November. OBRC was a five-month-old organization, and we should have known better. The convention was a fiasco. It snowed that day, and the temperature dropped to near zero. More important, OBRC was not ready for a convention. OBRC had involved close to seventy people in the food commodities conflict, but this was a direct self-interest (for some, survival) issue. A convention was another matter. Very few people were ready to make this commitment. Two weeks was not enough time to prepare, not nearly enough time for the person-to-person contacting that is so important in community organizing. All of which is a roundabout way of saying that twenty-five people came to the first OBRC convention.

The one bright spot in the whole evening was the election of Therese Van Zuilen as president. The wife of a small farmer and a resident of Rice County for twenty years, she became a strong grass-roots leader in OBRC. Previously, Therese had worked as an outreach aid for the OEO. She was disillusioned with the agency, and from her own experience as a poor person in Rice County, she was attracted to the idea "of getting an organization together of people who had been downtrodden and whipped and everything else as far as the county officials were concerned."

For the next two years she would play a vital role as a strong leader in OBRC.

The first convention was a keen disappointment. But we had made some progress over the first six months. OBRC's confrontation and denunciation tactics had generated considerable publicity (later on, when OBRC became a real force, the organization would find it difficult to get any newspaper or radio coverage). The large delegation of poor people was a new experience for the Rice County Board of Commissioners. People were curious about "the OBRC." Most of them were suspicious of OBRC's militancy. Some businessmen in Faribault started talk about OBRC being a Communist organization. Some poor people started talk about OBRC being "a damn good organization." OBRC had a long way to go, but it had gained recognition in the county.

Charles Liverseed

You drive out Route 60 five miles east of Faribault. You pass a couple of garages, a few new rambler-type homes, until you come to a driveway that takes you to Charles Liverseed's home. It is an old farmhouse set back a way from the highway. The front entrance to the dull brown-yellow square house is boarded up. Most of the windows are stuffed with cardboard to keep the wind and the cold out. Once upon a time, it must have been a nice farmhouse; a living room, dining room, three bedrooms, a front porch, several barns and a smokehouse in the backyard, with a beautiful view of the countryside. Now, the building is dilapidated and will soon be torn down.

Charles Liverseed lives in two small rooms of the house. There is no heat or wiring in the house—only a small wooden stove. He uses the stove for his heating and cooking. In winter, he sleeps in a sleeping bag next to the oven. When it is less cold, he can sleep in a small bedroom adjoining the kitchen. There is one light, one kitchen table, and two old chairs—that is the furniture. The old refrigerator is stocked with some turtle meat and a little cheese. Charles Liverseed lives in this house alone for a monthly rent of thirty-five dollars.

We sat down at the kitchen table next to the wooden stove and began to talk. It was a cold day in mid-December 1974.

If you bring the children out, see—I want it warm for them. I figure if you do come out with the children sometime—you and the Mrs.—I can get a roast and have the neighbor roast it for us.

You have so little to eat. How will you buy the roast?

I don't know, to tell you the truth. I always got something in the freezer, though. I got two bags of turtle meat right now.

Can you tell me a little bit about your background?

I was born in 1900. I am seventy-four years young. I feel that way. But when I start to work or something, I am done already on account of my asthma is so bad. I was born in Faribault. I went to Lutheran school. Then I went to public school. I was a smart aleck, a very smart aleck. Being a smart aleck, I stayed two years in seventh grade. From there, Dad needed me bad. I worked on our thirty-acre farm—hauling gravel and sand, doing the plowing, planting, and cultivating. I stayed with Dad until I was twenty-one. I went to my sister's farm in Detroit Lakes. I left home with three dollars in my pocket. But I went right on through. I never starved. I always had something to eat. I remember one day going up to Grand Forks. I went up pretty near all day from town to town—it must have been twenty miles. I stopped at a farm. I asked if there were a few chores I could do. I said I was hungry. The man and his wife said, "You don't have to do chores." He gave me an egg sandwich. She came out with a piece of cake. That was the only time I ever had to beg. I was hungry and tired.

I got a letter from my brother in Faribault. They wanted me

to come back home. I think I landed here with $160. I gave my dad $98 to pay the taxes. I said, "Take it—you and Ma raised me, you got it coming." We had a wonderful Christmas that year. Well then, from that time on I stayed home until I was twenty-eight. When I was there I took care of milking, raised cows, and raised a few hogs. We butchered our own stock. I made bacon and hams; I smoked it. We had a little wooden smokehouse. And we usually used maple wood. It was really good. It ain't like the meat you buy now.

Well, then I left home again. I told dad I can get work shocking and threshing. I went off. I walked to St. Paul. I took a streetcar to Anoka. From there I walked and then catched a ride with a farmer and a team of horses. I got back up to Detroit Lakes. I had some more jobs. Worked with a couple of farmers, helped them put their crops in. I left there in 1932 to go back home. I got married back here in 1934. I had a little truck of my own and hauled black dirt and gravel. And I hauled junk to Minneapolis and St. Paul. I made a darn good living for the kids. I had five kids. After I left home there was one more born. He was born in March. I left home the first part of December. And I was gone about nine years. When I came home I went to St. Paul.

Where were you for those nine years?

Uh? I don't want to even talk about it. I got into trouble, that was all. I didn't mean that against you. Them things are past and have been forgotten. I have learned a lesson. I was gone nine years, nine months, and eighteen days. I was in jail. I was in Stillwater.

I went to St. Paul. I worked with the Salvation Army because of the studies I took when I was incarcerated—let's put it that way. Well, anyway, I stayed there five weeks. I heard about two boys in trouble about the time I was—working in the Hotel St. Paul. They were doing good. They got me a job running the washing machine. So I worked there. Anyway, I was there about a month. One morning the foreman—he came in and said, "Charlie, you don't have to come to work tomorrow or Sunday." I thought, gee whiz, I am fired. Anyway, when I got back there Monday my washing machine was gone. All's I could see was just pipes sticking up. Oh no, I says, I must have done something now, blew it up and didn't even know it. They brought in a stainless steel washing machine, the biggest in Minneapolis and St. Paul at that time. I worked there about two years. This one big fella said he's never seen anybody put through dishes so fast as I did. One afternoon I slipped on the floor—the floor was slippery from the soap. I slipped and hurt my back. I suffered. I went to the hospital. Because of the back trouble I could no longer work.

In the spring of 1952 we moved back here [Faribault]. We lived on my social security. I did a little work to make a little extra; made enough for the taxes and our living. Finally, my wife and I could not see eye to eye with each other; we could not agree on anything. She started to bring up the back troubles and throw them at me. She went to a lawyer and got a divorce.

I got in contact with OBRC one month after it started. I think you was at the meeting. My very first meeting. I challenged you, but you got the best of it. OBRC makes a great big difference to me, as much as it does to you, and you are not a man that needs their help. I am there to give and help because if I can help somebody that needs something, whether it is out of my pocket or off the table or through OBRC, I says I am doing a deed. And I will be rewarded. I have been told to leave the OBRC. It is the truth. Somebody in government—they says, "They're no good, it ain't going to amount to anything." They were jealous. They knew if we ever got started, we would find out some of the things they are not doing right. We did demand. We had to demand. Because if we didn't, where would we be today? We would be sitting right back—back where we was ever before we started. I think once the OBRC gets in contact with the right sorts of people to get more help—if we could get the business people back of us, they could do the demanding for us. The people will speak for themselves; that is first. Second is to get the business people to understand. Now, you take a divorced woman with five or six children, maybe only three. That poor woman has to live in a dump. I am living in a dump here, but I am alone and can make it.

OBRC has helped people. The children get a little better clothing. I have been to different meetings, have found out about different organizations. We went to see the governor. We went to see the director of the welfare department. We have got kicked in the face. But we have not stopped. How many times have we been kicked in the face by the welfare or county commissioners? Then we went to the city council [Faribault]—who in the city council is connected to the county commisssioners? We don't know. But there must be somebody, because we got kicked in the face. They did not want to give us any help because they were jealous we would start to tell them what to do if we got in there. That is not our intention; our intention is to ask for help for poor people.

Can I ask you what your income is now?

Social security is $110.00 a month. Rent is $35.00, groceries is $57.00, gas is $11.00, our insurance is $38.00, and the car tax is $15.50. With the welfare I get a total of $146.50. That leaves me $19.50 extra a month after these expenses. I have it figured out right here on paper. I am getting by. But I have skinned myself. I have come here after I have been in the woods chopping wood so damn tired I go in and lay down. Get up an hour after to get something to eat—grab a slice of bread, some meat I slice up. Fix my fire up, get wood in, go crawl into bed. That is what I live on. I am happy.

*Do you take part in the food stamp program?**

I do not take part in food stamps. There is a wonderful thing that I would like to have you understand. You have an awful hard question to answer. I am going to answer it my way. Did anybody ever come to you—the welfare commissioners, city councilmen, bankers, the state school where you worked—and say, will you bring in all your receipts of what it costs you per month, no matter what it is? I am asking you. Well, that is what they want me to do up there at the welfare. Is it any of their

*The U.S. Department of Agriculture (USDA) discontinued the commodities program in 1974.

damn business how I spend my social security money? If I go and get a drink in town or bring a six-pack of beer home sometimes—is that any of their business? They don't tell me what they got, where they go to have their parties, what women they are running around with. I ain't buying me food stamps. And their food stamps is too high. It would cost me thirty-six dollars for forty-four dollars of groceries. You go to the grocery store and say, "I have got food stamps." They tell you what groceries you can get. And that is not fair.

What are your goals for OBRC?

If the people don't get behind us, and get to understand us, to study us out, find out what we're really up to, and we lose out, the city of Faribault, the city of Northfield, and all the cities around is going to be sitting on the rocks. They are not going to give any help to anybody. What does the government know without the people telling them? We have been kicked in the chin goddamn often, we took it on the chin and went right back at them, and we are going to continue. Our organization is strong enough to stick together.

There is a lot of things. If I got anything to say when I go to a meeting and I understand things the way they should be understood in my way of thinking, I want to say something about it, and I think everybody should and I don't think OBRC is going to back down against anybody. It may be that we got to say don't amount to a raw bean. But there may be a little point in there—like a pin or needle you get in close to you and you are going to feel it. And maybe a little point like that in there that somebody will grasp and make something big out of it, and get something out of it. Am I right? That's my opinion.

I am just as proud to be in OBRC as to be saved by the Lord Jesus Christ. They are helping people; they are backing up everybody. They will even help me if I ask them to. If I get into trouble of some kind, if I needed help, if you needed help, or anybody that is connected at all with it, they will support you.

If I get so I can't get around, I would like to hang around the office, and if I can be sent out to do anybody any good—ask them to come to a meeting or explain something maybe they are up against, give them a good feeling so they don't worry too much. There are a lot of people you can talk to that are coming down; they are all disgusted and worried and don't give a damn about anything.

Therese Van Zuilen

This interview took place in the second week of December 1974. Therese Van Zuilen served as president of OBRC for two years. She was one of the first strong leaders in the organization. In November 1974 (at the third annual convention) Therese stepped down from a leadership role in OBRC. She remains an active rank-and-file member.

When I arrived at the Van Zuilen farm early in the morning, she had a big pot of coffee and several *dozen* homemade buns ready. We sat in the kitchen and talked.

Can you tell me a little bit about your background?

I was born in Faribault, and when my folks moved to Ohio I of course went with them. I was six months old and lived there for five years. Our house burned down, and we moved back up north, and we lived under very dire conditions. There were nine of us then and we were scattered all over—different relatives took us, and my folks lived in a small cottage. My dad worked on various farms for relatives so that he could get a little money. Then he bought a farmhouse and we lived there two years, but then dad lost the farm and we moved to Appleton, Minnesota. Dad went on WPA and held a job working as a sexton in the church and working in the mills to support us all.

My husband and I were married in 1946, and we have farmed all of our married life. We have eleven children. We've lived here twenty years. Phil is a psychiatric technican at the state school, which is a big name for the guy who does the daily care of the residents. He makes $279 every two weeks. I have worked as a cook, an outreach aide, and I have done volunteer work in the schools. The farm is eighty acres. We've had five bad years—we had an average income of $1,500 in those years, which is one reason we had to get out and find something else to do as far as supporting our family. We've had medical bills. One child was in a cast for two years, and one child had to have cancer surgery on her eye. That is one reason I started with OBRC. I was always upset when we got turned down for medical help when we needed it. In 1964 Karen had cancer; we had been hailed out—we had ten children. We went to the welfare department for medical aid just for her, which our doctors in Rochester told us to, and they turned us down because Phil carried mortgage insurance. That was stupid because we borrowed the money to pay the insurance that year, and there was absolutely no face value to that insurance policy—we couldn't cash it in. We didn't know where to turn; we were green, it was the first time we had asked for any type of help. We just went about paying the bills the best we could. There were five or six years when the kids never went to the dentist. We did finally get on medical assistance for a year—in 1971—but then we were turned down again because the value of the farm had gone up, they said.

How did you get involved with OBRC?

The first time I met you was when I spoke to that group, the Human Relations Council over there in Northfield. I think the reason the county nurse picked me was as a poor person on the panel. There was a school nurse, two doctors, two dentists, and one or two welfare workers. They were talking about why low-income people don't take care of their medical and dental needs themselves—and I was the low-income person on the panel asked to explain why they didn't. "If the roof is leaking and you have a bad tooth, you know which to fix first—the roof." That's what the dentist had to say about poor people [he was emphasizing the wrong priorities of the poor, the lack of appreciation of good health]. And the young whippersnapper in the audience was Paul. If it hadn't been for you guys, I probably would have said about ten words and then sat down and shut up. I said to the dentist—if you have children in the house sick, you get the roof fixed so more won't get sick.

Dudley [Carleton student; community VISTA] used to use my office for phoning when I worked as an outreach aide for the OEO. I got to talking with him, found interesting what you had in mind of getting an organization together of people who had been downtrodden and whipped and everything else as far as the county officials were concerned. As we talked, we found out we had a lot in common. Later, we appealed my case when the welfare department cut us off medical aid. The evaluation of the farm was supposed to have gone up, and we were supposed to go in and turn in the medical card right then. This was in December of 1972. Phil was sick and I called Dudley. He said, "Let's appeal it." They never before had a welfare appeal in Rice County. They told me at the welfare department I couldn't do that. Dudley said, "Well, you can too," so we did. They were supposed to give me two weeks' notice, and we were supposed to come in and the judge was supposed to come. They called me one Tuesday and told me that I had to be there Wednesday afternoon. Dudley was out of town [Dudley Younkin was the one full-time staff person for OBRC during the first year], and I called Paul Wellstone, got him all shook up. He found out, no, they had to let me know ten days ahead of time. We went in the next morning, and there was all the county commissioners and all the welfare workers they could get on hand down there —they were going to show me which way to go. Anyway, we told the judge [state "fair hearing" official] after she had started talking a little bit that we'd only been given twenty-four hours notice, and she said that she would give me time to get my stuff together and she'd let me know personally when it was time to come down. [The hearing was postponed because of

procedural violations by the Rice County Welfare Department.]
And one of the social workers was very indignant because I was
taking up important people's time. Sometime later we lost the
case but it was worth every minute of it. And from this first
time we kind of gathered more people together that were interested in it, and we've grown into being a fairly good-sized
organization of people for human rights, welfare rights, and
tenants' rights.

*Can you tell me about the time you testified at the state
legislature?*

I got up there. Well, there were a couple of men that were up
there from the town board. Anyway, the welfare says it was the
town board that turned us down for help when our girl had cancer. I don't know. They pass the buck. But there were a couple of
men from town boards up in northern Minnesota that really ac-
costed us. The more they jumped on me when I was speaking, the
madder I got. It was fun and interesting, and it made you feel
good to know that a poor person could get up there and speak
in front of the legislature like that and have a say. I think Phyllis
[Phyllis Hanson] really helped. She was a lot better at just giving
me encouragement to go ahead and speak out because the two
of us were such loony-birds. I got Phyllis interested in OBRC.
We met through Headstart and got active there. I think Headstart is a fantastic thing if you can get the parents involved.

*As long as you talk about Headstart, what is the difference be-
tween the OEO and OBRC?*

The difference in the two is that OEO over in Zumbrota is not being run by poor people for the poor people. It is being run by a group of I don't know what you'd call them. It's always been the same people who have run the board. The idea of the OEO has been a fantastic thing, but it's been taken out of the people's hands.

What are your goals for OBRC?

To grow and do just what we are doing—helping people that don't know where to go. You don't know what it's like, Paul, not to have any idea where to go. I really hope OBRC continues to be a place where people can come.

Does OBRC have power in the county?

Oh yes, I think it does. I think the one reason that there is power is because the city council [Faribault City Council] and county commissioners are afraid of us, and they wouldn't be afraid of us if we didn't have some power. There's power in numbers. We've taken a group of poor people who wanna be able to talk to the government about these issues. And if they don't get through, then we've got leverage power. We can do something about it. We're getting out to other counties to organize, which I think is fantastically interesting. The main thing to do is to first let those people know, "Hey, you can do it, you can organize. You don't have to sit back and let somebody else tell you what to do." I think the main thing we've done with OBRC is to give a voice to the people. I think one of the first things people have learned is how to handle themselves; you know, you can't cry in front of welfare, you've got to get up and stand proud. Another thing I think we've done good, and it probably doesn't sound like much, is the fact we've gotten senior citizens —they've got a place to just stop in and say "hi" or "I'm cold." They respect us. Some of these senior citizens worked for the city as so-called important people. One day one of these men said he thought rebels were all long-haired kids, but he's a short-haired old man who is a rebel 'cause he's working with us. I think senior citizens are a lost bunch of people—as Father McNamara from Campaign for Human Development [the national social action arm of the Catholic Church] said, they're lost in the cracks of society. And most of them have put out good lives and were useful people. Now they're forgotten.

Did you feel you had as much say as you wanted as president of OBRC?

Yeah, I really do. It took me some time to get a few things ironed out, but of course we were all nonprofessional people, the majority of us on the board. Some things I took to the board took a long time to get through, but they finally did and I think we were better for it. I didn't speak too much at meetings and the like. I did feel like the other people in the organization should be involved. This is the reason I didn't even want anything on the board this time—because I really felt it needed younger people—not necessarily young, but new people with younger ideas. I felt I needed some time to sit back and contemplate what OBRC needed, what had to be done or what could be done more, and sometimes if you are not working directly with it every day you see things that can be done easier. You asked if I thought I had enough power as president. The best thing in the world for me was going into that dirty office and scrubbing it every week. That really keeps you down on the level, and it keeps your sense and values where they belong.

I agreed to be president because I was asked to be in the first year. But in the second year it was growing, so I really felt or wished I hadn't been president because I would rather have liked to be out on the field work. The second year being president kind of held me back on some things. I work for OBRC because I have been downtrodden myself for so many years I like to be able to give people a voice, and this is the only way I know how to help them is to get out and work with them. We didn't get any money for the work, but my family grew in understanding—that we weren't the only ones who had problems; the children became interested in it and this is good.

2

WELFARE RIGHTS

Shortly after becoming president of the OBRC, Therese Van Zuilen received notice from the welfare department that her family was no longer eligible for food commodities and medical assistance. The welfare department took the position that the Van Zuilen farm had gone up in value and the family no longer qualified for assistance. The Van Zuilens were told to turn in their medical cards immediately.

Therese felt she had come under close scrutiny because of her involvement with OBRC. OBRC decided to file a welfare appeal for a "fair hearing." This was the first welfare appeal that had ever been filed in Rice County. The first step taken by Therese and OBRC was to notify the department that as a matter of law she was first entitled to a fair hearing before being cut off from medical assistance and commodities. Therese acted as her own spokesperson and received enormous satisfaction from this initial personal victory.

In mid-December (1972), Therese Van Zuilen received a call from the county welfare department notifying her that an official from the state welfare department would be down the *next* day to conduct the fair hearing. She called other OBRC people in "a state of panic." We met Wednesday evening and Thursday morning for the hearing which was to take place late Thursday morning. The OBRC delegation that came to the hearing was well prepared. Therese once again acted as her own spokesperson.

The small room at the county courthouse was packed. It seemed as if everyone from the welfare department was there, along with several county commissioners. Therese had good reason to be nervous. The county officials were relaxed and appeared to be very confident about the outcome.

The hearing was called to order. The Rice County Welfare Department proceeded with its case. But before they could go too far in their testimony, Therese interrupted the proceeding. Acting as her own lawyer, she argued that the Rice County Welfare Department had violated important due-process procedures which precluded her from getting a fair hearing. She rattled off the procedural violations: no written notice ten days before the hearing, no written copy of the procedures to be followed at the hearing, no written statement of her right to be represented by a lawyer, and no written statement concerning her right to use a legal-aid lawyer for her defense.

The state fair hearing officer had no choice but to call the hearing off. She reprimanded county officials for the way they had handled the case. The welfare department employees and county commissioners were humiliated, frustrated, and angry. They had never been faced with a welfare challenge before and were not aware of the laws. There had never been such a thing as "welfare rights" in the county, and there was no need for the welfare department or welfare board to know these laws. They did as they pleased. Several officials protested the OBRC tactics. The head social worker in the department, a man widely feared and hated by recipients of Aid to Families with Dependent Children (AFDC) shouted that OBRC was taking up the valuable time of the state at considerable cost to the taxpayer by demanding a postponement of the hearing. The OBRC delegation responded with a request that it be a matter of public record on the written transcript of the hearing that the head social worker of the Rice County Welfare Department was outraged that a welfare recipient should request due process and fair treatment. The state official was annoyed by the course of events and angrily brought the hearing to adjournment.

The Van Zuilen hearing was an important milestone in OBRC's development. OBRC became a "welfare rights" organization out of necessity—to protect the president against retaliation. Once involved in welfare rights organizing, OBRC and the Rice County Welfare Department would become bitter adversaries. OBRC's leverage with the county welfare department was the tactic of filing numerous welfare appeals and bringing the department under close scrutiny by the state Department of Public Welfare. Over the next two years, as OBRC moved into surrounding rural counties to sponsor welfare rights organizing, the organization would follow the same tactic. In 1971, there was a total of nine welfare appeals in the state of Minnesota *outside* the Twin Cities metropolitan area. Rural counties had a free hand in dealing with recipients and often violated the law. The recipients were without knowledge of their rights, without money to hire lawyers, without legal services help, and without organization.

As OBRC gained strength and visibility, many welfare mothers from surrounding rural counties contacted the organization. Over the years, OBRC welfare advocates, welfare mothers who represented welfare mothers, have filed numerous appeals in rural counties with great success. Other local welfare departments have come under state scrutiny also, the result being that they are forced to adhere more closely to legal procedures.

The personal victory for the Van Zuilens was a critical victory for OBRC. A welfare recipient had worked through the organization and had stood up against the welfare department. OBRC had humiliated the welfare department. The word spread about what had happened at the courthouse. Few recipients had ever heard of the right to appeal. "Welfare rights" was a new concept in the county.

If a sense of timing is crucial to organizing, now was the time to move in welfare rights. We contacted welfare mothers and held several evening meetings to discuss the welfare situation in Rice County. Out of this series of meetings came very real grievances: slum housing, inadequate relief benefits, humiliation and harrassment by welfare officials, and despair over being despised in the community.

Welfare rights posed some serious problems since we were in the early stages of organizing. AFDC mothers were viewed as "white trash" in the community. The organizing was bound to create a backlash. The women were vulnerable to retaliation by the welfare department. It would not be easy to translate the grievances into winning organizing issues. If we failed in the early goings there would be no second chance. Few of the women viewed welfare as a right. Most of them internalized the dominant cultural stereotypes of welfare mothers in the community and viewed themselves as failures. They were on the defensive.

A yearning for dignity and fair treatment brought the mothers together. But only positive action and substantial achievements would keep the welfare mothers together. A failure would bring the whole welfare campaign to a halt.

OBRC first concentrated on the township relief system. In part, this was a question of timing. The Minnesota state legislature was holding hearings on a bill to transfer general relief throughout the state from township boards to county welfare departments. Rice County was one of the few counties in the state which still allowed the town boards to administer the relief program. Therese Van Zuilen and several other welfare mothers had had bitter personal experiences with the town boards and were anxious to see the township system of relief abolished.

We requested an opportunity to testify before the Senate Welfare Committee considering the bill. As the only rural poor people's organization in the state, located in one of the few counties which still had a township system of relief, OBRC had no difficulty in being granted a hearing. A delegation of OBRC people, with Therese Van Zuilen as spokesperson, appeared before the legislative committee to testify against the township system in Rice County. The OBRC testimony received local coverage. The *Faribault Daily* carried a front-page article which read in part:

> St. Paul: Two Rice Countians spoke this morning in favor of a Senate bill that would shift the responsibility for ruling on welfare cases from township to county government. People attempting to receive assistance are forced to undergo the scrutiny of boards unsympathetic to them and extremely concerned about the slightest expenditure of taxpayer's money, Mrs. Van Zuilen, a member of Organization for a Better Rice County, told the committee this morning. Mrs. Van Zuilen told the senators that Organization for a Better Rice County found that many townships had had years with no assistance granted at all. [*Faribault Daily News*, March 7, 1973]

The legislature passed the bill to abolish the township system of relief. Close observers of the legislature knew the bill would be passed without much of a problem, and OBRC took advantage of the situation. For years, liberals in the county had tried to abolish the township system. The last attempt was a referendum where they were beaten badly. The fifteen township boards had considerable clout. Most important, it had always been the League of Women Voters and other well-meaning organizations that had spearheaded these reform campaigns. This time, OBRC, a poor people's organization, took on the issue and was successful. The OBRC testimony may have had only a marginal effect on the outcome at the legislature, but what counted was the dynamic in the county. Not only had poor people testified at the state legislature—the testimony made a difference. OBRC received considerable publicity for this effort, and the organization was widely perceived in the county as being responsible for the demise of the township system. The organization was building up its "political capital." The people were building up their confidence.

OBRC was ready to take on several other welfare issues. The first of these was housing. About twenty AFDC mothers, acting through OBRC, took their case before the Rice County Welfare Board. They presented the board with a statement which was also covered in the *Faribault Daily News* and read in part:

> Housing costs for Rice county recipients are covered up to a maximum of $105, regardless of the family size. When a family is forced to live in a place costing more than $105, it means that money is going to have to come from food and clothing. For children this means an inadequate diet and malnutrition, poor health and poor performance in school. . . .
>
> There is a great deal about the welfare system that a county board can do nothing about, but this issue of housing allowances is one area where you do have the power to act. As set forth in the Public Welfare Manual, VIII–4116: "When housing costs in a county exceed the maximum shelter in effect, a county may request a change."
>
> It is particularly difficult to understand how ten people can be expected to live on the same amount as a single person. There is only one other county in Minnesota on the same scale. In every other county there is some sort of graduated scale.
>
> In preparing this request we have gone to a great deal of effort gathering information about the current housing situation in the county. . . . There are a number of housing units in the county which do cost less than $105, but half of these are inadequate. . . . Units large enough for families are virtually non-existent, and

when they are available, the prices are prohibitive. The welfare board has a responsibility for both the adequacy and the availability of housing for the people it is empowered to serve. . . .

OBRC feels that a request to change to Area IV would be the most appropriate choice. Included in that area are Scott and Dakota counties, which we border, and Blue Earth county, to which we are reasonably close. More importantly the figures on available rental property approximate more closely the allowable rents under that category. This would allow a maximum of $100 for one and two-person households and up to $150 for a household of six or more.

Housing was a strong organizing issue. While the state Department of Welfare determined the flat grant for food, clothing, personal needs and utilities, the county welfare board made the decision on housing allowances. Welfare mothers could organize *locally* around this issue—an issue of great importance to them. The inadequate housing allowance forced welfare mothers and their children into dilapidated housing infested with rats and mice. A higher allowance would not solve the problem of a critical shortage of low-rent housing in the county, but it would give AFDC mothers at least the chance to move if they found decent housing. The housing research by Carleton students was used by welfare mothers to support their grievances. Because the women had access to this carefully documented research, the welfare board was unable to pursue a strategy of delay by calling for a comprehensive study of housing conditions to find out if there was in fact a problem.

This was the first time in the history of the county that welfare mothers had brought their grievances directly before the welfare board. The commodities fight involved the aged poor and working poor as well as the welfare poor. The demand for higher housing allowances by welfare mothers set off a heated debate. One rural commissioner lectured the mothers that rural people often live in bad housing but never complain. He told the mothers that "welfare people have to learn to live within their means." An AFDC mother angrily responded, "Are you telling me that my kids have to live in substandard housing—with frost on the walls? I think they have a right to live in a warm house." It was a lively session. In the heat of the debate, welfare mothers were up on their feet arguing for a higher housing allowance as *a matter of right*. Women who came to the meeting with no intention of speaking were debating the county commissioners for a higher housing allowance.

The meeting ended on a satisfactory note. OBRC could not exact a commitment from the commissioners to raise the housing allowance. On the other hand, the welfare board did not turn down the request. They argued for more time to consider the question and agreed to take up the issue again at the next regularly scheduled welfare board meeting (the welfare board met every two weeks). This would give OBRC time to further develop the issue. We were confident we could involve many more mothers around a strategy of militant protest to force the welfare board to raise the housing allowance.

The optimism gave way to pessimism when the Minnesota Department of Public Welfare announced just one week after the Rice County meeting that it was moving to a system of flat grant payments. Under this new system, each family would receive a flat grant. The level of assistance would be determined by the state legislature. County welfare departments would no longer make decisions about housing assistance or any other individual needs. This made welfare organizing very difficult. We were putting together a welfare rights organization which would have clout at the local county level. The flat grant system, by shifting more of the decision-making power to the state level, undercut this organizing effort. Recipients could not regularly travel 100 miles round-trip to the legislature. And while welfare mothers were in a position to put real pressure on the local welfare department through disruptive tactics of one sort or another, they were without the conventional political resources to become successful lobbyists at the legislature.[1] Moreover, the housing issue was dead. It was no longer up to the Rice County Welfare Board to determine the housing allowance. OBRC could not press the housing issue with the local welfare board.

This was the winter of 1973. Richard Nixon had just been re-elected by a landslide victory. The Department of Health, Education, and Welfare (HEW), reflecting the antipoor posture of the administration, put tremendous pressure on state governments to "reduce the number of errors made in computing AFDC grants." By "errors," HEW meant overpayments of "ineligibles" on the rolls. HEW threatened to cut off federal funds to Minnesota, and the flat grant system was a response to this pressure. Federal welfare policy became increasingly more repressive, and welfare organizing became very difficult in this environment.

OBRC shifted its focus to the flat grant system. The state Department of Public Welfare announced there would be two schedules of flat grant payments—urban and rural. Rice County was classified as rural. To determine the flat grant, the average welfare payment in all the rural counties (housing included) would be computed. This average figure would constitute the flat grant for all rural recipients. This efficient formula guaranteed economic misery for the mothers and their children. Welfare payments had not been raised since 1968 (four years of mild and not so mild inflation had passed by), and the level of payments, especially in rural counties where welfare recipients had never had a voice or influence, were inadequate. Below-subsistence payments were being used as the basis for determining the average rural benefit, which, in turn, would be the flat grant allowance.

OBRC's welfare rights organizing was now characterized by a new dynamic. Before, the organization had taken the initiative and organized around forcing the county welfare board to increase the housing allowance. Now, the issue was survival—welfare mothers were struggling in order to survive in the repressive national welfare climate. The proposed flat grant payment would allow Rice County welfare recipients $70 a month for housing. We were on the defensive. The goal now was to keep the benefit at $105.

Elgie Cloutier (now Elgie Cloutier Butterfield), one of the first active welfare mothers in Rice County, presided over a series of welfare rights meetings sponsored by OBRC. At the first meeting, several women volunteered to attend the state public hearing on the proposed flat grant system to be held March 5, 1973. They would gather more information about the flat grant program and report back to the group.

The public meeting in St. Paul was explosive. A large contingent of welfare mothers from Minneapolis and St. Paul came to the hearing to protest the new flat grant. They were angry about the reduced payments (urban recipients were also being cut) and articulate in expressing their grievances. They challenged state welfare officials to explain how families could live on the reduced flat grant budget. Several county welfare directors testified in support of the welfare mothers that the proposed flat grant payment was totally inadequate. The meeting ended with no firm commitment by the state to reevaluate the flat grant payments, but the pressure was building. The hearing had wide press and radio-television coverage, at least in the Twin Cities metropolitan area. Welfare mothers were in a position to enlist outside liberal support and take their case directly to the state legislature, where control had recently swung from the "conservatives" to the "liberals" (Minnesota has a "nonpartisan" legislature).

The OBRC representatives at the hearing did not speak up, but they were deeply impressed with the protest. They reported what they had learned at the next OBRC welfare rights meeting. The welfare mothers decided to take part in statewide protests against the flat grant system and to participate in a lobbying effort at the state legislature. Elgie Cloutier and several other mothers attended the protest demonstrations in St. Paul and met with Rice County state legislators. All of this was new to the OBRC people and they thoroughly enjoyed the political activity. As expected, the local legislators were generally unsympathetic, but the welfare mothers did receive strong and unequivocal support from a newly elected liberal legislator in Northfield. The problem with this activity was that it involved only a few OBRC members. Very few women had the time or were able to travel regularly to St. Paul. OBRC needed a local plan of action to involve more of the welfare mothers in this struggle.

Toward the end of March, at a welfare rights meeting attended by around thirty AFDC mothers, we decided on a local action. Elgie Cloutier was describing actions OBRC had taken to raise the flat grant payments. As she was summarizing the state public hearing, one mother interrupted to raise the question of why the director of the Rice County Welfare Department, Chester Pearson, had not attended the hearing to speak up for his clients, as several other welfare directors had done. He knew welfare mothers already received inadequate assistance, and after all, wasn't he supposed to be concerned about the welfare of his clients? Another woman expressed the opinion that Chester Pearson's protest would have clout; that it was one thing for OBRC members to oppose the flat grant; for the director of a county welfare department to speak up in support of welfare recipients would carry considerable weight.

The question was how to get the director to represent his "clients" on this crucial issue. Most of the welfare mothers had little faith in Chester Pearson. They felt he did not care about their problems; that he had been insensitive to their needs in the past. They were frightened of his power. Almost everyone was pessimistic about the chances of enlisting his support for OBRC's position. "What does he care?" "Why should he listen to us?" "What can we do to make him listen?" These were the kinds of remarks that characterized the discussion.

We got into a discussion of tactics. The organizers were instrumental in this discussion. We argued that OBRC people did not have to beg the welfare director to support the organization, that welfare mothers had the power to make him support the OBRC position whether he cared about the recipients or not. We devised a strategy that all the mothers were willing to give a try—though everyone had misgivings of one sort or another.

The strategy session took place Wednesday evening. On Thursday morning three AFDC recipients visited the welfare department office and requested Mr. Pearson to write a letter to the state Welfare Department opposing the proposed flat grant payments. Mr. Pearson said he would not send such a letter. On Friday six mothers went to Pearson with the same request. He again declined to send the letter and told the women he had made his position quite clear the day before. On Monday ten welfare mothers visited the welfare department with the same request. The director softened his position this time. He told the recipients he was sympathetic to their plight but it would be inappropriate for him to write a letter of protest. He told the women he hoped they would write their own letters of protest. The women said they would be back on Tuesday. On Tuesday fifteen mothers came to see Pearson. They were told he was out of town and could not be reached. They announced they would be back on Wednesday with some more welfare mothers. On Wednesday morning around twenty-five mothers and thirty-six children came to the Rice County courthouse. The visit was timed for 9:00 A.M. when the auditor, commissioners, judges, law clerks, and welfare caseworkers took their coffee break downstairs in the courthouse, where the welfare offices happened to be located. OBRC people took up all the tables while the small children played without adult supervision. The small courthouse was bedlam. The children were running around all over the place, and the noise level was unbearable. The commissioners, judges, welfare caseworkers, and other county officials could not believe their eyes. They were visibly shaken. Many of them congregated around Gordon Forbes, a minister from Northfield and the one "respectable" character in the OBRC delegation. They sought information and/or protection.

It was a perfect tactic. The welfare mothers were having a lot of fun watching the reactions of county officials to their protest. The officials were confused and frightened—mainly by the children. OBRC was exploiting their stereotypes of welfare families. They believed welfare children were uncouth and uncontrollable—well, they temporarily were out of control. The greater their obvious concern, the more the OBRC people enjoyed the demonstration. The OBRC "courthouse raid" might be old stuff in the city. Not in Rice County.

The director of the welfare department, who had said two days earlier he would no longer meet with any OBRC people, came out of his office and agreed to meet with the OBRC delegation. He requested that OBRC people leave the downstairs section of the courthouse and meet with him in regular chambers. The demonstration ended.

Artis Fleischfresser, a young welfare mother with four children, acted as spokesperson for the group. Before Pearson could say a word, she presented him with a letter written by welfare mothers to be signed by him and sent to the state commissioner of public welfare. Artis stated that since he did not seem to have the time the mothers decided to write a letter for him, that all he had to do was sign the letter. I was amazed by this tactic. It was not a planned action—at least by the organizers—and it required a lot of nerve.

She humiliated the director. Red in the face, he said he could write his own letter. Artis quickly responded that this was fine —that this was all the mothers had been asking for over the past week. *But* the letter would have to be written within a day and someone from the welfare department would have to bring a copy over to the OBRC office as proof. She was feeling her power, as were other welfare recipients. They were rubbing it in. Pearson, tense and even more humiliated by these additional demands, agreed to "cooperate."

The courthouse raid was the impetus for a strong welfare rights organization in Rice County. It was an enormous victory for welfare mothers. The tactics employed were out of all proportion to the demand; the mothers were asking the welfare director to write a letter. And it was in part a symbolic victory; there was no guarantee that such a letter would do any good. But welfare mothers had asserted themselves. They had successfully taken on the director of the Rice County Welfare Department, a man many of them feared. *As a group* they accomplished what none of them as individuals had ever accomplished. They had forced the welfare department to respond to their concerns.

There were several more statewide welfare demonstrations in Minneapolis and St. Paul. A few OBRC people attended these demonstrations. The protests received favorable press and radio-television coverage in the Twin Cities. Liberal constituency groups (church, labor, human rights) lobbied at the state legislature for higher flat grant payments. A liberal DF-L (Democratic Farm-Labor party) majority passed a fairer and more adequate rural-urban flat grant system. In Rice County, families would receive a $118 monthly housing allowance. This was a dramatic improvement over the proposed $70 allowance and a slight improvement over $105. Welfare mothers in OBRC had spent several months fighting for a higher flat grant. They were involved in successful state and local actions. In the process, they learned a great deal about the welfare system—the federal-state-county structure. Everyone felt it had been worth the effort.

In April (1973) OBRC became involved in what the local county daily called "the welfare war." It all started rather innocently. Kathy Leppert, aged twenty-three, mother of two small children, had written a letter in March to the *Faribault Daily* pleading the case that welfare recipients did not have adequate assistance and were treated unfairly in the community. She was especially upset with the proposed flat grant (in March the outcome was still in doubt). Ms. Leppert, fresh from the courthouse raid victory, hinted that welfare mothers might have to camp out in the county courthouse if they did not get fairer treatment. Her letter to the editor, in the form of a poem, went as follows:

> What would happen to the welfare man
> If in our position he would stand.

Trying to live on what we do
Finding there just wasn't enough to get him through,
Being put down by others who don't know
Our real circumstances, fights and woes.
Do they really think we want this life
Of having to battle, fight and strife?
Now they are thinking of giving us less,
Probably hoping we'll all die and be put to rest.
But little do they know
Without us they won't get any dough.
Maybe we should all find another way out,
Then it's be the welfare people who'd shout.
Only then would they really know
That we're not just trying to put on a show,
And all we're really asking of them
Is to understand our needs and be our friend.
If they'd show us where we could rent
For the amount they think should be spent,
We know not of any places such as these
But if so, we'd really be pleased.
Right now we don't know what we'll do.
But the courthouse would house quite a few.
If we are cut our amount
Then the offices might have to move out.

Kathy Leppert followed up her poem with another letter to the editor which was a response to the many anonymous, ugly phone calls and letters she had received:

I think we all know that welfare is from the taxpayers and we all know it is a load. I pay taxes. Okay! Do you as a taxpayer know where the money goes after it leaves you? Do you know that welfare is getting only 8.5% of your tax dollar in Rice County?

Everyone, especially the people on welfare, realize something has to be done. Do you think if we had another choice we'd live this way? Do you know how you're treated when people know you're on welfare?

Being on welfare makes your name no good. Since we didn't choose our circumstances and aren't left with enough money, what would you suggest we do?

"Go to work" is a No. 1 suggestion I've heard. Okay, where

are all the jobs to put all of us to work? And then, after paying babysitters and our transportation, how would we come out ahead? Is it fair for our children, who have already lost one parent, to lose the one security they have? Will the public take the responsibility to give this security to the children?

Many people say both husband and wife are working, so why shouldn't we? We don't because we can't, not because we don't want to.

And as far as taking my frustrations out on welfare, that is what welfare is there for—to help us, since there isn't any other choice. Is there? Does the taxpayer really know how welfare works? And, then, why is it some people get more from welfare than others? The taxpayer doesn't really know that the money is given to the people for whom it was intended.

Sure, the [estranged and divorced] fathers are getting by too easy, and everyone including welfare lets them. But we're the victims; don't blame us. Sure, this country has many problems, some relating to welfare. The way these problems are made is because of the divorce rate and morals in this country. Nowadays, instead of working out their problems, people run away from them, thus, leaving behind a family who must turn to welfare for help.

How else are we to survive?

OBRC's welfare rights organizing was by this time infamous in the county. Although Ms. Leppert had written the letters on her own and did not necessarily represent OBRC, the *Faribault Daily* felt compelled to set the record straight about welfare. In an editorial titled "The Welfare War," the paper attacked Kathy Leppert. The editorial started out, "Everyone seems to be criticizing the nation's welfare system these days, as indicated by today's People Column letter from reader Kathy Leppert, 1155 Willow St." After listing her name and address in the editorial column (a very unusual step), the *Daily* devoted a full editorial to rebutting Ms. Leppert for the readers in the community:

Ms. Leppert claims the system doesn't provide enough for recipients, particularly single-parent families. Taxpayers who don't receive welfare benefits feel recipients are getting too much.

Both sides have some valid arguments, although the proposed solutions leave a lot to be desired. The entire social services system needs a renewed look by the President and Congress, and the

goal should be a system which provides financial aid and job training for those who want to work, but refuses those who could
work but don't because they're temporarily better off under welfare.

In 1971, President Nixon remarked during the opening of the
White House Conference on Children:

"Today's welfare child is not so fortunate. His family may
have enough to get by on and, as a matter of fact, may have even
more in a material sense than many of us had in [the] Depression
years. But no matter how much pride and courage his parents
have, he knows they are poor and he can feel that soul-stifling,
patronizing attitude that follows the dole."

Ms. Leppert apparently agrees. She writes, in her letter: "Being
on welfare makes your name no good."

The statements by the President and Ms. Leppert are accurate,
we're certain. But most welfare recipients—for a number of reasons, not all of their own doing—prefer to accept social degradation and cling to the monthly welfare checks in lieu of working
for the same wage.

The factors which contribute to such an attitude must be reversed if the U.S. welfare system is to be shaped into an institution which truly serves society.

One of these factors is the idea that the government is responsible for adequately feeding, clothing and housing each of its
constituents—regardless of the constituent's willingness to work
for his own food, clothing and shelter. Ms. Leppert claims her
children will "lose the one security they have" if she were to get
a job. "Will the public take the responsibility to give this security
to the children?" she asks.

We submit that the responsibility for providing adequate food,
clothing and shelter—and thus security for one's children—lies with
the individual, not government. Any welfare system that provides
income for those who aren't willing to work destroys the free enterprise system and undermines the democratic principle. And we
think free enterprise and democracy, despite some weaknesses,
provide the best living conditions of all social systems man has
tried.

American government, we point out to Ms. Leppert, has already
done much to promote children's security by providing public education. Many single parents find this school is a double blessing:

it educates their children and it gives the parent an opportunity to hold a job without having to make special arrangements for day care.

But our argument isn't aimed entirely at the attitudes of welfare recipients. The government, by reforming the social services system, could do several things to stimulate people to get off the welfare rolls and into the job market.

First, it could provide day care funds for single parents with low-paying jobs—parents who otherwise would fare better on welfare than they would by working and paying a babysitter or nursery.

Second, it could provide job training for welfare recipients—training in jobs where the supply is low, so the welfare recipient would be able to get a job once his training is complete.

Third, it could require a welfare recipient to accept a job offer or get off welfare. This provision, we think, is of ultimate importance in making a reformed social services system work.

In any case, it's clear that most people on all sides of the welfare issue need to revise their thinking. Welfare can be a valuable resource by which society cares for those who can't work. But the present system won't accomplish that unless it's changed.

[*Faribault Daily News*, April 19, 1973]

Again, the organizing maxim that "the action is in the reaction" turned out to be true. OBRC people were furious over the way in which the *Faribault Daily* had tried to humiliate Kathy Leppert. The editor had indeed set off a "welfare war." A group of welfare mothers, working with the staff, wrote a blistering letter to the *Daily* representing OBRC's official position. The full text of the letter read as follows:

Your editorial "The Welfare War" of April 19 in response to the letter by Kathy Leppert is a mishmash of misinterpretation and misinformation and does little to advance the discussion of an appropriate public welfare program.

First, you imply that the letter is simply a plea for more money. That would be a very reasonable request as welfare benefits in Minnesota are still based on a 1969 standard of living and everyone knows that the prices have not remained the same, but that is not what Ms. Leppert asks. What she is clearly doing is protesting what society has done to her because she happens to be on welfare and showing the impossible demands that are made on her and her family. She wants understanding, not harassment.

Then you equate "security" with adequate food, clothing and shelter. What Ms. Leppert is talking about is something very different—the warmth and support human love and caring provide a child. She evidently feels that with the father gone the children need their mother that much more. We submit that no institution or organization could provide that security, and that you had better be very careful when you take it away by forcing the mother to work.

You are grossly misinformed, we are tempted to say you lie, when you state that "most welfare recipients . . . prefer to accept social degradation and cling to the monthly welfare checks in lieu of working for the same wage." We defy you to produce one shred of evidence, other than the street-corner comment that would prove that statement. The evidence goes quite the other way.

In this country there are now about 15 million people annually receiving some form of public assistance. Of these, 1 million represent families whose members are working full time but who do not earn enough to adequately support themselves. Another 1 million are blind or otherwise disabled. Two million are over 65. Eight million are children under 16, and 3 million are mothers. How many of these people do you suppose are going to be able to work?

As regards desire to work for those few who might be able to do so, studies have consistently shown an overwhelming willingness to hold jobs. The problem is with the jobs—they are not there. During the last several years there has been a work incentive program which has trained about 1.5 million people but found jobs for only 30,000. It sounds like a poor return on our tax dollars. Still, the average stay on AFDC in Minnesota is only two years.

Your editorial fails to address itself to the problems of welfare because of two basic reasons: One, you are trying to reform the individual and not dealing with the problems of society that have led to the individual's situation. Further, your image of the "welfare person" is a myth and bears no relation to reality. Two, and this stems from above, you have little understanding of the current welfare system. Consequently your solutions offer almost nothing. Let us discuss them briefly.

Day care is an obvious need and we agree that the government should help provide it, but the costs are considerable. Be prepared to pay those costs. You have noted, no doubt, that the Nixon administration is currently cutting day care funds in supposed "economy" moves.

Job training without jobs makes no sense. The low supply jobs you refer to are non-existent. Unemployment in Rice County is currently 6 per cent and has been for some time. Unless you are going to make the jobs, your suggestions are foolish.

Requiring recipients to accept work is already a part of welfare programs and is enforced in a variety of ways. What else did you have in mind?

The purpose of welfare, in your opinion, is to force people to work. In view of the fact that so few of the people receiving welfare can work, it seems appropriate for welfare to provide the needs of these people, not ignominiously keeping them in poverty and destitution. If you really want to reduce welfare rolls you are going to have to see that they are not forced so low they have no chance of recovering and getting on their own. That is what you seem to be proposing.

Your editorial is so full of unfounded myths and meaningless proposals it will serve to perpetuate misunderstanding about the welfare system, not do anything meaningful to change it. We feel it incumbent on you to either retract the editorial or to provide documentation of the statements you made. May we suggest that in the future you find out more about welfare than you evidently know now.

The letter was signed by Faribault residents Elgie Cloutier, 224 NE Second St.; Marge Jones, 832 SW Seventh St.; and Lee Lockwood, 704 NW Sixth St.; and by Kenyon residents Mary Rohloff, Route 2; and Therese Van Zuilen, Route 2, for Organization for a Better Rice County. The newspaper printed the letter and appended the following note:

Editors Note: The *Daily News* stands behind "The Welfare War" editorial as written. We point out that the sentence quoted from the editorial by the writers of this letter reads, in full: "But most welfare recipients—for a number of reasons, not all of their own doing—prefer to accept social degradation and cling to the monthly welfare checks in lieu of working for the same wage." [*Faribault Daily News*, April 24, 1973]

The most important thing about this "welfare war" was the solidarity it created among welfare mothers. They were united in their fight with the *Faribault Daily*. The paper had in fact unwittingly recognized them as a political force in the community by entering into the debate. Welfare mothers in Rice County were debating a conservative and powerful newspaper. They argued their case with anger and dignity. They were no longer ashamed or fearful.

In May, welfare mothers focused on child-support problems. For several months, women had raised the issue of child support at the regular welfare rights meetings. The organizing staff usually directed the discussion to other problems-issues. We were wary of child-support problems because the discussion inevitably brought out the bitter, personal feelings welfare mothers had toward their "ex." It was difficult to get the women to think politically about the problem. Moreover, we were not sure child-support payments could be developed into a successful organizing issue.

By May, welfare mothers in OBRC were too strong to let the organizers control the agenda-discussion. They resolved to take the initiative and raise the sensitive issue of child support before the Rice County community. The organizing strategy was chosen by AFDC recipients. This campaign would be by and for welfare mothers. The organizers' input was minimal.

The first step in their strategy was to make a videotape on child support to be shown on cable television throughout the state—including, of course, Rice County. The American Friends Service Committee in Minneapolis offered the equipment and technical assistance. Carleton students volunteered to help make the videotape. Welfare mothers had never put together their own presentation on child support. To our knowledge this would be the first such presentation anywhere in Minnesota. Welfare mothers felt the videotape was bound to get considerable exposure—to generate a great deal of publicity. The idea was that if the videotape received statewide publicity, the Rice County Welfare Board would feel considerable pressure to act on the grievances. Welfare recipients were not sure their own clout in the county would do the job; through the videotape they hoped to enlist support from a wider constituency outside the county. Hopefully, the videotape would give OBRC the needed leverage.

For two months OBRC people worked on this presentation.

Welfare mothers interviewed Rice County officials responsible for enforcing child-support laws, welfare mothers with child-support problems, and the general citizenry (random interviews with people on the street) concerning their attitudes about child-support payments. The interviews were complemented by carefully documented research on child-support costs in Rice County.

Initially, county officials were unwilling to be interviewed on videotape. The huge camera (operated by welfare mothers) was quite a weapon and very intimidating to local officials. OBRC took the position with officials that (1) the videotape would be shown throughout the state and (2) either they would consent to an interview or the organization would show blank chairs in the presentation and point out that Rice County officials were unwilling to discuss their responsibilities in handling child-support payments. This was a very sensitive issue, and the county attorney and welfare director, among others, could hardly afford to decline.

The videotape, representing several months of hard work, was shown on cable television and written up by newspapers in a number of communities throughout the state. An article appeared in the *Faribault Daily* (written by a young woman very favorable to OBRC who would shortly resign from the paper) summarizing the study, part of which read:

> One of the problems with AFDC as welfare mothers see it, is that many families would not need it if county authorities would find the children's fathers and force them to pay child support.
>
> Mrs. Smith's husband was ordered about four years ago to pay $75 a month child support. She hasn't received a penny. And Mrs. Jones stopped receiving $200 a month for her two children from her husband four years ago "when he learned how easy it was not to pay—he knows society will pay. . . ."
>
> Their statistics: About $466,000 of the Rice County Budget goes to AFDC payments. According to national averages, about half the fathers of these children should be able to make child support payments averaging $50 per child per month. Welfare officials say that statistics should hold true in Rice County. If so, the county should get $144,000 in child support payments annually. Last year they got $17,000. . . .
>
> What happens if a father doesn't pay child support? If the mother does not go to the welfare department, but decides to

work, she must contact a private attorney and pay court costs to take the father to court for non-support. If she goes to the welfare department for help, she fills out a form at the county attorney's office and he is responsible for finding and prosecuting the husband.

Mrs. Jones (anonymous name) took the first alternative. It cost her about $150 to take her husband to court after he hadn't paid any child support for two years. Just before they went into the courtroom he handed her a check and the case was dismissed. The check went toward paying the court costs and he didn't pay any child support for 15 months.

Mrs. Smith had a newborn baby at the time of her separation, so she went to the welfare department and the county attorney. She filled out the required form and never heard another word about her husband or child support, she said.

Both mothers say they feel frustrated and harasssed And Mrs. Smith noted problems with the Rice and Goodhue welfare departments, including suggestions that she live with a man rather than re-marry, have herself sterilized, or even have the children adopted.

The video presentation summarized, "There is another side to this question that has little to do with money, but which is also vitally important to us—our feelings, our pride and our sense of justice. Why is it that mothers have to bear the total responsibility of raising these children and the stigma of being on welfare? Why is it that the fathers seem to get off so easily? This does not mean we do not love our children, we do. It does mean that we think the fathers should also do their part." [*Faribault Daily News*, July 16, 1973]

The summary reflects the importance of the video presentation to welfare mothers in Rice County. They were taking their case to the community and attempting to change prevailing community stereotypes of welfare recipients and the stigma of being on welfare in a small-town, rural community. No longer were they on the defensive. OBRC welfare mothers were determined to have their dignity and rightful place in Rice County. In this sense, the video presentation was an important welfare rights issue.

The OBRC videotape called for the county welfare board to hire a "resource examiner" to find AFDC fathers and collect or prosecute on child-support payments. The pressure was on the welfare board. Welfare mothers had investigated the welfare department and county attorney's office, had found problems, and had exposed these problems in a widely publicized videotape study. There was some justice in this reversal of the usual roles—welfare mothers investigating the welfare department. But the proposal for a "resource examiner" took the welfare board off the hook. In seeking some measure of justice against their husbands and a fairer shake in the community, AFDC mothers had not considered the political problems with their proposal. It was one thing to put pressure on county officials to do something about child support to save the taxpayers money; it was quite another thing to control who would be the "resource examiner" or what his/her responsibilities would be. In the late spring and early summer months OBRC people were elated with the pressure they had brought to bear on Rice County officials with the videotape. In the fall, a "resource examiner" would be hired *without* their input and would be used by the welfare department as a fraud investigator, with OBRC members the main concern of his fraud investigations.

Overall, welfare rights organizing had over a nine-month period produced dramatic results. Welfare mothers, without any previous political experience, had won several major political fights. "Poor white trash" people, for years alone, despised, and powerless in the community, became a political force to be reckoned with. Strong welfare rights leaders emerged from this organizing campaign—women who viewed themselves as failures became effective welfare activists.

Elgie Cloutier Butterfield

Elgie Cloutier Butterfield was an active welfare rights leader during OBRC's first year. She became executive secretary and managed the OBRC office from January 1974 to May 1975. She recently remarried and moved with her new husband and youngest child to Minneapolis.

Elgie was one of the few people I know who could make the transition from being secretary to the Faribault Chamber of Commerce to being secretary to OBRC. She is a brilliant woman, and during her years with OBRC she was secretary, manager, organizer and friend to many OBRC people.

Can you tell me a little about your background?

I was born in Minneapolis at the university hospital, and I think it had something to do with the fact my folks didn't have enough money to have me born anywhere else. My father was on WPA, and we lived at that time in a house my father had built for $200. The outside was nothing but tar paper. I started out knowing what poverty was. We moved all around the country. My father worked in construction. I was in four schools in three states in the first grade. While we were in Idaho my younger sister got spinal meningitis. We were thirty-five miles from a doctor and had no transportation. She had a temperature of 108 degrees and it burned out her brain cells, and from that time on my parents spent all their money on doctor bills and trying to keep her alive. Our entire life was spent living from hand to mouth because all their money was spent on doctor bills and groceries. We moved back to Faribault when I was around ten so my sister could be put in the state school. I graduated from Faribault High in 1954 and then I got married and had four children. My youngest is fourteen now. We got divorced after ten years. We were living in Minneapolis at that time. I decided if I was going to raise children alone I'd come back to this area where I would be close to my parents. So I moved to Randolph and rented a farmhouse for about thirty-five dollars a month—it cost me about eighty dollars a month to heat it. I went to the welfare department in Goodhue County [county adjacent to

Rice] where I lived in Randolph and asked for medical assistance just to get the kids' teeth fixed because they were crying, their teeth hurt so bad. The welfare told me I couldn't because they had gone out and talked to all my neighbors and I was supposed to be having men there all the time because I was this divorcée from the big city. Automatically, when the gas man or farmer down the road came down and I'd have them in for a cup of coffee, well, I was apparently being a naughty girl and this of course was not the case. I just thought if that's what I gotta do, to go through, you know, to get on welfare, I don't want it. I moved to Faribault and got into a manpower training program which paid me enough money to go to vocational school. Then I got a real good job with the chamber of commerce—I stayed there for a few years as secretary to the manager. I liked the job because there was a lot of people contact and I learned a lot. Then I got married again and I quit work. The marriage wasn't good and didn't last long. So I went back to the chamber in a new position—publicity and public relations director. I handled all the radio-show and press releases and set up big meetings. Then the budget for the chamber was in the red and they had a different board of directors who didn't think my job was necessary—so I took another job at Crown, Cork and Seal Industries which turned out to be the best paying job I ever had—which is $450 a month. I worked there to 1972. I also worked bartending at night. Anyway, I was under tremendous stress working sixteen hours a day and taking care of the kids. The doctor made me quit. I was on welfare when I took the job with OBRC as secretary. Phyllis Hanson called me and said if I wouldn't take the job she was calling Elliot Sellner and tell him about me and the extra money I was making on the side. So that's how I was hired down at OBRC. But really it was not quite that way.

The initial contact I had with OBRC was that Dallas Culhane, a friend of mine, got a notice in the mail or a phone call or something telling her of a meeting. The purpose of the meeting was to discuss housing costs in Rice County and trying to raise, I think, the housing grant or something. She didn't want to go alone and I just felt this was an area which should be explored. So I went to the meeting and met Dudley Younkin [the community VISTA-OBRC staff worker]. Dallas brought up a problem she was having with the welfare department and they handled it right away. I thought this was great because she'd had this problem for so many years and nobody helped her. I wanted to work with this group and tackle some of these problems with the welfare department. We started working on the welfare department here on the flat grant. Another girl and I went in to talk to Mr. Pearson—we were the original ones to go in and see ole Chet. We went in to ask him to write a letter and he didn't like that. A few days later a few more girls went in with a letter and asked him to write it. He didn't want to write that letter so we started storming the courthouse, and we took mothers and kids and kids we were babysitting and went in and sat at all the tables in the coffee room so the welfare department didn't have any place to sit and have their morning coffee, and the kids were crying and screaming and running around and finally he agreed that day to write the letter. I think it united the mothers. You know, before OBRC got involved I think each welfare mother thought she was the only one who had a problem—it drew people together on a common basis. You could see in the girls: "Hey, we're going to finally break something"—you know, "We don't have to be treated like animals any more and we don't have to be looked down on just because we're in a situation we can't help." From this we went up to the Capitol and rallied for higher flat grant payments. That's when I got roped. From then on Dudley called me constantly, and I couldn't say no because I knew that there were things that had to be done.

When Phyllis and I came to work for OBRC in January 1974 everything was utter chaos. Sue Little (pseud.) who took Dudley's place as VISTA destroyed all the loyalty and respect he had built up for the organization; Sue led people by the hand to the point where they didn't have to do anything for themselves. She was going to be the miracle worker who was going to do everything for them. So we had this problem to overcome and still do to a lesser extent. There has been too great a drain on the staff because too many hours a day have been spent doing things for people that they could be doing and should be doing for themselves for their own good. But I think one of the biggest weaknesses we've had is internal problems, and I think this comes from the fact that we are an organization of people who have not had any leadership or working experience in the business world—you know, people who have never done anything in their life except exist. They have been born and got married and raised children. This is the first experience for many people in any organization or any type of leadership, and they don't know how to handle it. I am not talking about the general membership—they don't come forward enough—but the action council and staff—this is where the problem is. People have a little power and strength for the first time and they tend to go on an ego trip. Money is another weakness. We have many things to do, many things we are capable of doing, many things we have to do, and there is no money for it. The biggest problem is becoming self-sufficient, and I don't know the answer and I don't think anybody knows the answer. We are a poor people's organization and we don't have the money. Also, people are afraid of the welfare department. Many people are not proud of belonging to OBRC because it is so criticized in this town, and that is the trouble with the majority of the people. If you do nice things these people will come in, but if you keep causing fights these people will stay away. OBRC is definitely disliked in town—by the Establishment—because we are making them stand up and take notice. The majority of poor people are behind OBRC. We have gone knocking on doors, people have come into the office, some of the people have come through on the issues. Our influence in growing rapidly.

I look at the true members of OBRC as being radicals—but there are liberal radicals and conservative radicals. I am a conservative radical; you are a liberal radical. The difference is I want social change just as damn bad as you do but I want to be a nice girl about it, you know, and I don't think you can always be nice. I am not knocking it—sometimes the only way is to get up and scream and yell and alienate a different class of people. But I want somebody else to handle the screaming and yelling. For an organization like this to grow I think you have to have both. The organizers are only good for a year or two years at most. Anybody who has worked with OBRC will support it. Their feelings are with OBRC. The bonds between OBRC people are very strong. We feed each other. We give each other money for gas to get to work and we give each other clothes. We're a very close-knit family.

Why do you call OBRC a poor people's organization?

Because I would say the active, strong OBRC majority are either welfare recipients or handicapped or senior citizens or working poor. We'll keep trying to get power to make social change and continue to make social change until lower income people have as much dignity as the middle class. Get rid of that stigma and prejudice. We've got to get rid of that stigma and, you know, the longer I work with OBRC the more I'm sure we've gotta do it— we need membership and organization and power because alone these people can't do it. The most beautiful thing probably in my whole life outside being able to have children is the fact that I have seen people walk in that office absolutely in tears, torn apart, and feeling totally worthless—you know, like the point of committing suicide 'cause society thinks they're nothing— and getting some reassurance and gaining some confidence in themselves and coming back strong and standing on both of their feet and saying, "Boy, we're going to stick together and we're going to do this," and getting involved in OBRC and helping others pull themselves out of the same thing. You know, this is why I turned down other offers like twice my OBRC salary with the money and prestige. Because I feel self-satisfaction— my satisfaction comes from seeing other people have some self-confidence. It's hard to explain; it's an intangible. I can't tell you why I keep staying—okay, like a girl came in to us the other day—it's a long story which I won't go into for the reason she is in trouble with the Hennepin County Welfare Department. Okay, she comes to us broken down, an unwed mother who has got no reason to go on living. She came in and told us her problems, and we said we've got problems too—we've got a convention coming up and we need somebody to call people. From that day on there has been a bond—she comes to the office every day and working, full-time volunteer. Her mother babysits the child so she can work for OBRC. I mean, that's one example and I could give you twenty people who are doing the same. This is unique —where else can you get this kind of satisfaction? I feel I am a part of what made these people OBRC people—we're all part of a family and I feel as close to them as to my own blood family. I can't explain it any better than that, really—but everybody is helping everybody and nobody is standing alone. You know, when you've been a single parent and you've been alone against a good share of the town or, you know, society in general, and all of a sudden you belong and somebody cares, an $800 job or $1,000-a-month job doesn't mean a whole lot. I mean, I'm making enough [she made $433 a month gross pay] so that some way or another we'll make ends meet. Material things can't equal that feeling.

Francis Milligan

Seventy-year-old Francis Milligan lived alone in a trailer on Roberds Lake, near Faribault. He lived on $135 a month from social security and was an OBRC activist on welfare issues. In November 1974 he was elected at the annual convention to the fifteen-member action council. I was scheduled to interview Francis Milligan, but he tragically died on January 4, 1975. What follows is a brief OBRC testimonial written in *Hard Times*, the OBRC newspaper, and an interview with Francis Milligan carried in the *Minneapolis Tribune*, October 6, 1974 (this was part of a series of interviews in the *Tribune* with Minnesotans aged seventy and over).

> Francis Milligan left us on January 4, 1975. He told his story in the Tribune and in the local newspaper. In some ways, he was what one would call a shut-in.
>
> This morning, I received a call of sympathy from Washington, D.C.—Francis did not let the world shut him out. He gave hope to many people who are in the same situation—alone and living on a mere pittance of an income as he was and without family.
>
> One thing he did have was friends, all kinds from every walk of life. He was never afraid to speak out and voice his opinions and those of OBRC. He firmly believed in people standing up for their rights.
>
> OBRC has lost a senior councilman and community leader; however, he left us more determined to see that senior citizens have adequate housing and transportation in his home area.
>
> He also left us many new friends and made us aware of what self-determination can do, even in the most impossible situations —and, of course, left us with the memory of a wonderful friend who made the best hobo coffee in the country. [*Hard Times*, February 1975]

I was born in Faribault. My dad worked for 47 years in the

Rice County courthouse, as a custodian. He was always active in politics. Like he was on the board of the old soldiers home. I was the only one in the family. I had cousins but they're all gone now.

I went through high school selling wild ducks I'd shoot. I got 50 cents apiece. That was good money then. I had to have a class ring and I had to have one of those orange class sweaters. Kids now have cars before they graduate. I can't understand it.

I graduated in 1923, and the last two years in school I started working for the Rice County Highway Department. I worked there 18 years in all. Then I swung over to the State Highway Department, where I was for 20 years. I did some of everything. And I worked on construction for awhile and drove a semi for Hanson Oil Company for seven years. Oh, and I drove semi for a couple of years, hauling butter from the Dakotas.

I retired when I was 62. A lot of guys try to wait until they're 65 so they get more Social Security but I figure it isn't worth it. That little extra money a month doesn't mean so much if you drop over dead soon as you start getting it.

I get $135.90 a month from the federal government. Social Security. That's all my income. Period. No pension. That's pitiful. I get by because it's cheaper out here. I bought this trailer 14 years ago and lease the land for $50 a year, plus a dollar for use of the road. You can't live much cheaper than on $51 a year for housing can you? In the city, you couldn't do that. Some guys pay $15 a week in Faribault, for just a little room—hot and dirty and small. This trailer is luxury compared to that. I have a new rug I got for $3 off a friend, but I ain't going to put it down until winter.

I eat good. Look at all the canned goods I have piled up. Do you ever look at the pears and peaches at the store? The prices are going up already, so I'm buying that now. I store things up, like the chipmunks out here do.

But things are just like the welfare person said, "If you spend money, we'll give you more. If you had an apartment and all, we'd get more money for you." But I say, how the hell you going to spend it if you don't have it? I could have punched that welfare worker in the mush for saying something dumb like that.

I hit the sales and save money where I can. When there's a sale on Kleenex—five for a buck at Jupiter—you get them. I roll my own cigarettes, except I buy a pack when I go to town because I'm too busy to be rolling. But you can't save fuel oil. It was 18.3 when I moved out here and it was 32.9 last time.

I paid eight bucks—eight bucks!—for khaki pants the other day. That's plain old khaki. They're good pants though. When you're out hunting, you don't want bright colors or they'll see you coming.

The county pays for my telephone. The county welfare person said, "You should have a phone." I said, "Good, you pay for it." But there was a catch. I had to pay to have it installed. I had to put out $10.50, I think.

During the summer, I have friends stopping in. If you don't have friends you get lonely. There's Dr. Lee from Austin, Dr. A. J.

Lee. He's a professional man, a dentist. Nice to know guys like that. He's had a place here for 17 years.

All of Waterloo, Iowa stops in. Everybody who lives there has a cabin here. They're all here for two solid weeks when John Deere takes inventory. If it weren't for John Deere, there wouldn't be no state of Iowa.

Al Crossley is my neighbor, third door down. He flavors everything with wine. I say you might as well drink it and get drunk. I kid him about it. I said to him, "If you want bacon and eggs, you wouldn't know how to cook it without wine, by God." Him and his wife got dough, but they're nice people.

People like my hobo coffee. Boil water with grounds and let it settle. People say it's better than what they make with their $30 coffee makers.

By winter, everybody's gone. I watch television a lot at night during the winter. I'd watch wrestling every night if it was on. My machine went haywire last October so I bought a nice new one. I wouldn't have to worry for a while. I paid $180 for it and paid off $20 a month. It's paid now. If it weren't for the machine in winter and a snowmobile going by, it would be pretty quiet here. It is a good place to put on weight in the winter, when you're just cooking and watching TV and going to town. I'd say I weigh about 190 now. In the summer, this place looks swell but in the winter it's tough.

I was married. No children. Let's say my wife and me parted. That's enough to say. About five-six years ago, she went to

St. Paul or Minneapolis to see the bright lights. That's fine with me. I have some girl friends, but I won't talk much about them. I don't consider myself a ladies' man but I'm not crippled either.

I could get food stamps, but you need a lawyer practically to figure out all the forms. I'd have to pay $36 for $46 worth of groceries. It ain't worth it. The stuff you have to fill in, my God. They want your life history. I used to get food from the commodity program but they cut that out. I used to like peanut butter and canned meat and two pounds of butter. The butter would pull me through the month, if I was careful. It sure helped. I knew guys though who sold the food to bartenders. People misused it, and that was too bad for people like me.

I get real mad about the government. The only backing I had in the last three months is the OBRC (the Organization for a Better Rice County). Now the assessor is out to get me. I made a shed out of road signs that someone gave me, and they assessed it at $400, the same as my trailer's assessed. It's the principle of the thing. Farmers come in to see this little shed and they say, "No wonder why you're hollering."

I use the inside toilet in the summer, using a pail of water from the lake to flush it. I get drinking water from town, in big cans. I pump water from the lake for washing dishes, but by this time the water gets pretty green. It's soft though—better than Culligan's.

My health has got to be good, or when I'd hit that cold toilet seat in the winter I'd have a heart attack. Now that they're starting to charge for the big catalogues, you might as well buy rolls of paper.

Even if no fish are biting right now, it's a good life here. I can fish and I can speak my mind. That's one good thing about being poor—you can't be sued—so you might as well speak up. [*Minneapolis Tribune*, October 1974]

3

Beyond Welfare Rights

AFDC mothers were among the most abused citizens in Rice County. Their political problems were overwhelming. It was an emotional experience to sit in on some of the initial welfare rights meetings and listen to welfare mothers describe the manner in which they were treated by the welfare department. Our decision to concentrate on welfare rights organizing was based, in part, on anger and a sense of outrage about welfare policy in Rice County, not on any conscious strategy about how to build a strong, durable, political organization. The strong welfare rights orientation meant OBRC started out as a "bottom-up" organization comprised mainly of welfare recipients. From the beginning, welfare mothers were centrally involved in the community organizing.

The price paid for starting out this way was that OBRC became typed as a "welfare organization." The majority of poor people in Rice County were working poor, not welfare poor; and the majority of the county population were moderate-income residents, not the poor. If OBRC was to expand its power base, it would have to move beyond welfare rights. This was a very difficult task. OBRC was very controversial and many people did not like its welfare orientation.

Richard Nixon's "New American Revolution," more commonly known as general revenue sharing, provided the organizing handle to expand OBRC's service and social action beyond the core areas of housing and welfare.

The Nixon administration sold revenue sharing as an important step in reversing the trend of government centralization and putting "power back in the hands of the people." The experience of federal government support of local dissent through such citizen participation programs as community action programs and model cities was not to be repeated. The revenue-sharing concept outlined a minimal role for the federal government —to collect and distribute monies to local governments according to a predetermined allocation formula—and left local governments free to spend money on local priorities.

General revenue sharing was a real stab in the back for many local governments (especially big city governments). The Nixon administration dismantled numerous social programs, the net result being an overall reduction in the net flow of federal dollars coming into communities. Revenue-sharing monies did not replace these social programs, much less provide new assistance. Moreover, the balance of power in most local communities was such that what was in the "public interest" was surely not in the interest of poor people. We had no illusions about general revenue sharing; we hoped, however, to convert a conservative national program into a dynamic organizing campaign locally.

In April 1973 OBRC demanded public hearings be held in the county to determine how the $350,000 in revenue-sharing funds should be spent. The organization zeroed in on the importance of citizen participation and called upon the county board of commissioners and Faribault City Council to hold public hearings by June— *before* any decisions were made about local priorities.

Initially, the county board of commissioners opposed a public hearing as a "waste of time." Since the State and Local Fiscal Assistance Act of 1972 (general revenue sharing) had no citizen participation requirement, there was no legal handle to force the county board into a public hearing. But citizen participation was one of those nice ideas in the abstract that over time the county board found difficult to oppose. Once OBRC was joined by the Republican and Democratic parties, the chamber of commerce, and the League of Women Voters in the request for public hearings, the county commissioners acceded.

OBRC spent April and May contacting low- and moderate-income people about their concerns and working on several concrete proposals. It was a risky campaign. The Republicans and chambers of commerce were the ones with the clout. We did not want to involve people in months of work, only to experience failure at the end. The county commissioners and Faribault City Council had agreed to public hearings, and OBRC could claim some credit. But there was no guarantee that local officials would, in fact, respond to the concerns of OBRC people. They had never in the past been concerned about the needs of low- and moderate-income people. Furthermore, if numerous groups came to the public hearings with competing proposals, they would cancel each other out. Political officials could justifiably say there was no clear mandate. OBRC had to become a dominant force at the hearings.

The strategy was to align OBRC people and DF-L (Democratic Farm-Labor party) "liberals" in the county. A steering committee was formed to narrow down the liberal priorities. The final list included environmental concerns and OBRC "human rights" issues. The two major OBRC proposals were for a county housing rehabilitation fund and a county day care center.

The Rice County Revenue-Sharing Housing Rehabilitation Fund would be used to provide below-market-interest-rate loans for rehabilitation of low- and moderate-income residential properties. The interest rate was 3% and would cover the costs of administering the program. For the first five years, the county board was to put $50,000 annually into the fund. After five years, it would become a self-perpetuating trust fund.

The proposal did not have much of a chance. There was quite a market for housing rehabilitation loans, but the lenders adamantly opposed the program (though it would not compete with their regular business since they didn't make loans to low- and moderate-income citizens). OBRC was not able to organize in two months a strong consitituency of homeowners to push for the proposal. But we hoped the county board might find it easier to accept the day care proposal, secure in the knowledge they had firmly turned down another OBRC proposal. The housing rehabilitation proposal was defeated after the hearings.

OBRC's major priority was the day care proposal. Welfare recipients, working poor, and moderate-income people were behind this proposal. Families where both parents worked, often because of financial necessity, were in an impossible position. They experienced a great deal of strain and worry about the well-being of their children when they were left with a sitter.

The establishment of a child development center would take away this strain and worry. The program would serve working mothers, but a mother need not be working to enroll her child. The program was to be developmental and experimental, and nonworking mothers could also expose their children to the benefits of such a program. A mother could not be forced to work outside the home as a condition for participating in the program. The OBRC proposal read, "The emphasis is not on work training for adults; rather quality developmental care for children."

The center would provide free care for families with incomes below $4,000, small charges for those between $4,000 and $6,000, and a sliding scale for those above $6,000. A Child Development Council would supervise the operation of the day care center. Half of the members of the council would be parents of children participating in the program; at least one-third were to be poor people.

Day care was an important issue for OBRC. The steering committee was behind the proposal, which meant it had support from sympathetic liberals.[1] Welfare mothers were strongly in favor of a child development center in Faribault and were careful to write into the proposal the prohibition against using day care to force AFDC recipients into work. Most important, day care was relevant to the needs of many working-income families in the community.

The county commissioners held public hearings in early June. The largest and most vocal group at the hearings was the OBRC delegation speaking in behalf of the day care proposal. It was clear from the outset that the bulk of the money would go into various capital improvement expenditures—especially the new law enforcement center.

The OBRC delegation, which included a number of professionals, presented a strong case for developmental day care in Rice County. The commissioners were confronted with a difficult choice. They viewed OBRC as a militant, radical organization. They disliked social programs, were not sympathetic to poor people, and hated the organizers who they felt directed OBRC. On the other hand, to flatly turn down the proposal was to invite further conflict, and they were nervous about public controversy over the day care center. OBRC had a carefully documented case identifying the need for a day care program, and the commissioners were vulnerable to another attack on their "apathy and negligence." They took the easy way out and referred the matter to the welfare board.*

The director of the welfare department, under severe pressure from OBRC for several months, supported the day care request. The welfare board agreed to appoint a committee to (1) further refine and specify the nature of the child development program, (2) seek an acceptable facility for the program, and (3) propose a budget.

The committee was composed of two members of the welfare board, a nursery school teacher (who had worked closely with OBRC on the proposal), one social worker, and two OBRC members. Since the welfare board appointed two board members to sit on the committee, we were confident they intended to fund some kind of day care in the county. The issue was who would control the program and what would be the final scope and nature of the child development center. Moreover, finding a facility would be a real problem. Some of the county commissioners were confident the proposal would go no further for lack of a facility.

It took one month to find a location for the day care center. Negotiations with the churches in Faribault (the only real possibilities to house a day care center) proved to be disillusioning. The committee dragged its feet in searching out possible facilities, so it was left to OBRC people to take the initiative. Church after church with splendid physical plants turned down the request to house a day care center (at a reasonable rent). In one case, the minister did not want a day care center in his church. In several other cases, the church board turned down the request because the children might mess up the property. One minister said he was in favor of housing a day care center, but he could not support an OBRC proposal because the influential people on his board were adamantly opposed to OBRC. Finally, the Methodist church in town agreed to make the commitment. And even though the minister (unlike most of the other ministers in town) was unequivocal in his support, the decision was reached only after three very divisive church board meetings.

---

*It might be worthwhile to point out one more time that the welfare board consisted of the county commissioners plus two lay people appointed by the commissioners.

The Methodist church agreed to house the center provided there be no publicity about it. Most of the board members were socially concerned, decent people, but they were very wary of "this OBRC."

OBRC lost ground in the final negotiations concerning the day care center. The committee appointed an interim board of three which was later expanded to a permanent board of nine that included only one OBRC representative. He was a professor from Carleton and one of the few professionals in the organization. Unfortunately, he did not act as a representative. He made statements in the local papers but did not identify himself as an OBRC person. He negotiated on sensitive issues without consulting the membership. For example, he agreed the final day care board need not include an OBRC welfare mother. The welfare department was insistent about this. But OBRC people felt very strongly they should have this representation. He did not stay in touch with the OBRC membership about the day care board's decisions. In short, he did not identify strongly with OBRC and represented the people badly. The welfare board was to have the power to appoint six of the nine board members. At least one-third were to be lower-income, but no specific criteria for being lower-income was specified. OBRC had little input in shaping the final and important details of the proposal.

In September, the welfare board and the Rice County Board of Commissioners approved the day care center proposal. The *Faribault Daily News* carried this headline with its front-page story: "County Day Care Center to be Developmental, Educational." The article read, in part:

> The county day care center approved Monday by the Rice County Board of Commissioners is intended to be beneficial to families from all social and economic classes in the county by providing an educational environment for preschool children. . . .
>
> The county will provide $13,000 of the estimated total budget of $46,000 for the program's first year of operation. Assuming an enrollment of 30 children (for a start) about $10,200 would be generated by admitting 10 children whose tuition would be paid through Aid to Families With Dependent Children (AFDC). The federal government will pay 75 percent and the county will pay 25 percent of the monthly tuition of $85.00 for AFDC students. The program expects to raise about $15,300 from the tuition of

20 private students. The tuition paid directly by families will probably range from $42.50 to $85 per month. . . .

The proposal for a child development program was initially made at an open hearing on uses of revenue sharing funds June 12 by representatives of Organization For A Better Rice County (OBRC). The OBRC statement cited the need for the program.

"The 1970 census data show that there are 948 women in Rice county in the labor force with children under six years of age, and that there are an additional 1,560 women not in the labor force with children under six. We lack quality, developmental day care for children of working mothers, and without such a program other mothers are denied the opportunity to undertake full or part-time employment, training or education." [*Faribault Daily News*, September 15, 1973]

It was a significant victory for OBRC to get the proposal funded. Only one year in existence, the organization had pressured the county commissioners into funding an important social program. The organizing staff did a great deal of work, and not as many low- and moderate-income people were involved with the proposal as we had hoped for. This became a serious problem in the final negotiations on the proposal. But OBRC did move beyond welfare-rights concerns through the day care center organizing effort. The organization gained recognition in the county for its role in obtaining revenue-sharing funds for the day care center, and the organization recruited new members who were interested in day care.

Another organizing campaign connected with revenue sharing took place in the town of Faribault. In the spring of 1973 the Faribault City Council decided to end services of the Faribault Bus Lines except during school hours. This was an economy move that adversely affected many senior citizens. There would be no bus service during the summer when the public schools were closed, and during the school year the service would be restricted to a few morning and afternoon hours. Moreover, the city officials made it clear they were looking to the day when the Faribault Bus Lines would be curtailed altogether. They did not want to subsidize the private carrier any longer and had no intention of making the bus a public service.

The senior members in OBRC wanted to obtain revenue-sharing funds for some form of public transportation in town. OBRC took the position that in the absence of a clear alternative to the Faribault Bus Lines, the city council must raise the subsidy in order to make sure that elderly people would have some way of getting around town. The organization opposed the council's plan to sharply reduce and eventually discontinue the bus service. A few members came up with a proposal for reduced taxi fares whereby senior citizens would pay only half fare—with the city government using revenue-sharing money to provide the remaining subsidy to the taxi company.

OBRC launched a petition drive and obtained over 400 signatures to support its plan to use revenue-sharing funds for continued bus service or reduced cab fares. The city council delayed for several months, "studying" the transportation proposals. By August, OBRC was finally able to make the council consider its proposals and delay no further. The issue came to a head at an August city council meeting. The small meeting chamber was filled with a delegation of thirty OBRC senior citizens. It was a very hot and uncomfortable evening. The council proceeded with its formal agenda, with the OBRC proposals the last item of business. Although a number of older people were very tired and looked as though they might pass out, the council made no attempt to move the OBRC proposals up on the agenda. I thought their strategy of delay might work and, indeed, several senior citizens had to leave the meeting.

After several hours of waiting, OBRC people were invited to make their presentation. Senior citizens spoke about their need for public transportation and about the petition and the number of people supporting their request. They urged the council to use revenue-sharing money to continue the bus service or come up with some alternative form of public transportation that would respond to the needs of the elderly.

Mayor Robert Larson spoke for the city council. He reminded senior citizens and "you OBRC people" that the council was responsible to all the people of Faribault, not just senior citizens who wanted some form of public transportation. He then scolded them, "What you people are asking is for us, the government, to subsidize you. I don't believe the government should subsidize people. It is a bad principle." The mayor was lecturing to the people who had built the town on their backs. There were several bitter exchanges between the OBRC delegation and the mayor and other councilmen. The Faribault City Council was not about to spend any money on public transportation. They had their eye on other projects: airport improvements, police equipment, and a joint city-county law enforcement center.

The senior citizens did not have the clout to reorder the council's priorities. The OBRC delegation were poor people. Many senior citizens who owned their own cars and had money were not interested in the issue. Revenue-sharing monies for low-cost transportation was not a winning issue. We had made a calculated decision to work with senior citizens around this concern, in spite of the odds. OBRC became identified with senior-citizen issues. Several "seniors" with the time and ability became OBRC activists. The older people in town became aware of what they were up against. The Faribault City Council's insensitivity to their problems would become the basis for strong organizing efforts in the near future. Elderly people in the county were not very comfortable making requests to local government, much less demands. But after the encounter with the city council, OBRC's advice, "If senior people don't look out for themselves, nobody will," carried more weight.

In the middle of August, as the revenue-sharing campaigns waned, OBRC became involved in a major confrontation with the OEO Rice-Goodhue-Wabasha Citizens Action Council (CAC). The confrontation was inevitable. Many OBRC people had at one time or another been involved with or affected by the Citizens Action Council. Few of them ever had a positive experience. In the beginning, OBRC was essentially a group of people who were disillusioned and angry with the poverty program in Rice County. They had personal grievances with the agency and were anxious to shake it up. The organizing staff felt other poor people in the county, not necessarily members of OBRC, might be attracted to the organization if it could successfully challenge the CAC. We also felt a public confrontation with the CAC would generate widespread publicity for OBRC.

The timing was right in mid-August. Several staff people who worked for the CAC and were disillusioned with the agency approached us with documented proof of many procedural irregularities. The CAC had violated its own by-laws in several important respects. OBRC now had the necessary information to take on the local programs.

OBRC sent a letter to the regional OEO office in Chicago listing a number of grievances: (1) Poor people did not have adequate representation on the policy-making board. (2) Required
caucuses, where poor people could elect representatives, were
not held. (3) Vacancies on the policy-making board were not
filled. (4) The required committees to evaluate the progress of
the agency were not appointed. (5) The Headstart director was
hired without approval of the Parent Advisory Committee (PAC).
The organization demanded the regional office immediately rec-
tify these abuses or face a lawsuit. Copies of the letter were released to local county papers. The *Faribault Daily News* headline
read: "CAC Charged with Not Serving the Poor." The *Northfield News* headline read: "Group Questions Area Board." The
Red Wing Republican Eagle read: "CAC Excludes Poor, Group
Says." The local papers repeated the charges in the text of the
letter. The director of the agency and members of the board expressed shock at the OBRC charges and "reserved comment for
later."

We knew there would be a great deal of action and reaction in
this confrontation, and we were confident about the outcome.
We were absolutely sure of our information before taking on
the agency. Moreover, the Office of Economic Opportunity was
under tremendous pressure by the Nixon administration (for a
different set of reasons) and could not afford problems in Minnesota. Senators Mondale and Humphrey and U.S. Representative Albert Quie (from our district) were very influential on
OEO legislation. OBRC had contacted all of their offices. The
regional office could not ignore the OBRC letter.

Within a week, the Chicago office sent a representative to investigate the OBRC charges. The August 31 *Faribault Daily*
carried the following headline: "OEO Representative Hears about
Charges Leveled Against CAC." A small delegation of poor people and organizing staff pressed the representative, Margot
Machol, in a private meeting (private at her insistence) and added to the list of grievances. Several poor people accused the
agency of tokenism and related their experiences as outreach
aides—no training, no direction from the agency, and poverty
wages. The staff argued that the board of directors of the CAC
had never seen an audit and said that OBRC suspected graft.
The Headstart parents complained they did not have any say

over the approval of the new Headstart administrator. Other grievances included: good staff people who wanted to "serve the poor" were arbitrarily fired by the director, and personnel grievance procedures were not followed; rank-and-file CAC board members were never given any training; and the agency was run by the director and chairman of the board. We stressed to Ms. Machol that OBRC would not wait too long before taking legal action—that the problems were of too long standing.

As the conflict escalated, several newspapers carried editorials. The *Faribault Daily News* editorial began, "CAC on Firing Line":

> When charges of misconduct are leveled at a government agency, the news is rarely received with joy. But the current probe of the Goodhue, Rice-Wabasha Citizens' Action Council (CAC) may result in a more responsible public agency, even if charges by the Organization For A Better Rice County (OBRC) that the CAC is "not adequately serving low-income people" prove false.
>
> OBRC has asked the regional Office of Economic Opportunity (OEO) to investigate the CAC, claiming the tri-county agency has not been operating in accordance with its by-laws. OBRC charges that only three of 15 Rice County positions on the CAC board have been filled, and that the board has made decisions involving "half a million dollars of taxpayers' money" without the presence of a quorum.
>
> The regional Office of Economic Opportunity agency which oversees CAC funds, has not yet commented on the specific charges, but the OBRC says it will take the matter to court if nothing is done.
>
> If the charges are correct—and the regional OEO office admits they're "substantial"—changes should be made to insure the CAC functions according to its by-laws. Because it's a public agency, its by-laws have the force of law.
>
> But even if the charges prove false, we hope the CAC board takes a more "public" attitude in the future. In the past its meetings—which by law are public—have only rarely been publicized. Few people know that the CAC board meets the third Monday of every month, usually at Redeemer Lutheran Church in Zumbrota.
>
> Although its functions are much more specialized than those of most government units, the CAC board must remember that it is a public body, and the public has a right to sit in on its proceedings and scrutinize its decisions. [September 5, 1973]

The *Red Wing Republican Eagle* editorial, also of September 5, read as follows:

Open and Closed

Much sorting out of the facts obviously needs to be done in the case wherein the Goodhue-Rice-Wabasha Citizens Action Council is charged with not "serving poor people."

We hope citizens watch closely and objectively to see if the Organization For A Better Rice County is able to substantiate its claim that representatives of low-income families aren't given adequate representation on the council.

It was curious, however, that a major meeting on the charges was closed to the press. Apparently it's important to the Rice county group that the CAC does its business openly before low-income families and others, but the principle is given a good deal less weight when the shoe is on the other foot.*

The editorials were cautious. The *Faribault Daily*, while criticizing the CAC and giving some credit to OBRC, implied the OBRC "charges might prove false." The *Red Wing Republican Eagle* urged the citizens of Goodhue County to "watch closely" to see if OBRC could substantiate its "claim," and then unfairly criticized the organization for sponsoring a private meeting.

The controversy received statewide recognition when the *Minneapolis Tribune* carried the following feature article under the by-line of Warren Wolfe, staff writer.

Two-Fisted Group Fights for Poor Through Courts

Faribault, Minn.: A handful of people working with an organization to help the poor in southeastern Minnesota became discouraged with, as they saw it, "stodgy, ineffectual efforts to become advocates for the powerless."

So they formed a "two-fisted group that grapples with people's problems and gets things done," an organizer said.

And the grappling has raised a few hackles with some of the more staid agencies that have had to deal with the two VISTA workers and 30 unpaid volunteers who don't hesitate to take their disputes to court.

*Ms. Machol, the OEO representative, turned away reporters from the meeting, making it clear *she* wanted the meeting to be closed.

"You think of this kind of action in terms of the Twin Cities," said VISTA worker Dudley Younkin, 23. "I don't know of any other group like us in the state."

So far, the harmless-sounding Organization for a Better Rice County (OBRC) has:

Filed a formal complaint with the Chicago Office of Economic Opportunity (OEO) about alleged rule violations by the Goodhue, Rice, Wabasha Citizens Action Council. The council is the group that organizers broke away from last year.

Taken a township near Faribault to court over the township's refusal to turn over relief records. A judge signed an injunction and it was served on a township official before the township agreed to supply the records.

Protested to the Faribault School Board that lunch tickets given low-income school children unnecessarily identified them to fellow students. Other students paid for meals with cash. The board agreed and now all students eating school lunches are supplied with tickets.

Gone to court and to welfare-case referees in efforts to aid welfare recipients in dealings with the county welfare department.

Appeared before the city council urging that the city subsidize reduced bus and taxi fares for senior citizens.

Persuaded the county board to use revenue-sharing money to fund a day-care center, with costs based on ability to pay. The center, approved last week, could be in operation next month.

While all of these have rubbed some nerves raw, it was the complaint to Chicago OEO officials that drew the reaction.

Kenneth Tri, Red Wing, president of the Community Action Council board, was incensed that the group didn't first come to the council.

"Sure, we do have some problems getting representatives of the poor on the board. But what makes me so mad is that they didn't talk to us, they went off and complained to Chicago," he declared.

"When I'm wrong, you don't tell my wife; you tell me." he said Wednesday after spending the afternoon with an OEO field representative.

Tri said the action council board will meet Monday to decide how to respond to the complaint. "They raise some valid points and we accept responsibility," he said, "although I'd like to see this OBRC or whatever it is to do something positive instead of just complaining."

Another thing he wants to find out is just why the action council is acting as the sponsoring agency for the VISTA volunteers working for OBRC.

"What is that organization anyway? I don't know what they do or who's in it or anything. I'm trying to find out but I still don't know."

The VISTA workers, Younkin and Sue Little (pseud.), are not directly involved with the complaint, though they say they have received numerous complaints from the poor and from staff workers of several agencies dealing with the action council.

Younkin, son of missionaries in Thailand, was a student at Carleton College where he became involved in urban affairs studies in Rice County. He joined VISTA to continue the work.

Mrs. Little, 38, mother of five and wife of a retired Marine, lives in rural Kenyon. She joined VISTA after long involvement in the civil rights movement.

"I was one of those who kept getting beat on the head in the South," she said with a laugh.

Their reception in Faribault has been "somewhat cautious, I guess you could say," Younkin said. "After all, you aren't supposed to go around taking people to court; it just isn't done."

But people with problems are coming to trust them, Younkin said.

"People who have hassles with the welfare department or NSP or a landlord or whoever are learning that they can call us and we're willing to listen and stick our necks out, if necessary, to get some action. Nobody's ever done that for them before," he said.

Everyone doesn't believe that the group has been especially effective.

"They really haven't affected us that much," said Welfare Director Chet Pearson, whose department has been involved with five welfare appeals brought by the group. "They've been wrong sometimes and we've been wrong sometimes, but they haven't changed us."

Younkin disagrees.

"I think we've affected them plenty. I think they've become much more sensitive to problems of their recipients," he said.

Can the group survive the jostling and suspicion generated by its philosophy of dealing directly and firmly with problems of the poor and elderly?

"You bet we can," said Dr. Paul Wellstone, 28, whose Carleton students have conducted many of the studies in Rice County.

"We're building a coalition of welfare recipients, tenants and other people who traditionally have been powerless. We're here and people have to deal with us. But we're not here to attack, we're here to build—for a better Rice County."

The organization will hold an annual meeting and election September 27 in Faribault. [September 17, 1973]

The *Tribune* article was a very favorable treatment of OBRC. Most important, the fact that OBRC received statewide publicity enhanced the power of the organization. OBRC was a controversial and very visible organization. Its capacity to generate statewide publicity was a threat to local officials. The *Minneapolis Tribune* story set an important precedent. Later on, the organization would resort to this tactic in order to put local officials in the position of either supporting important social programs or risking bad publicity for their towns—a real threat to local boosterism.[2]

The publicity that surrounded the controversy raised the stakes for everyone involved. The credibility of OBRC was on the line in substantiating the charges, following through on the complaints, and getting some kind of substantive response from the midwest OEO office. We continued to correspond with the Chicago office and press for action. We threatened litigation and the escalation of the conflict if necessary—to include, for example, *public* charges of financial irregularities.

On September 21, the OEO midwest office issued a memo to the CAC which included the following directives: (1) An audit report must be shared with the board of directors each year. (2) The present Headstart director must have approval of the Headstart PAC. (3) There must be more training for board members, especially low-income board members. (4) Eleven open positions on the board from Rice County must be filled as soon as possible. (5) Vacancies from the other two counties should also be filled as soon as possible.

The memo substantiated the major OBRC charges. In addition, the CAC was instructed to "take the initiative with OBRC both to resolve their complaints if possible and to secure representation on the Board from OBRC." The CAC had no other choice but to meet with OBRC at the bargaining table and negotiate the problems.

The Citizens Action Council would make a formal response to the OBRC complaints at its regular board meeting September 22. Various county newspapers and the *Minneapolis Tribune* covered the meeting. The CAC publicly conceded to the OBRC demands. It was a tremendous victory for the organization.

The irony was that few OBRC people had any interest in attending the CAC meeting. The conflict with the OEO was not a participatory issue. A few organizers had done all the strategy work, had deliberately generated the publicity, had created the controversy. Many OBRC members were pleased to see the organization shove around the CAC, but few of them were directly involved in this fight. Given OBRC's criticisms of the CAC, this lack of rank-and-file member participation was somewhat ironic, and all too typical of manipulative organizing.

In fact, the organizers could not even get a delegation of people who were willing to travel the thirty miles to attend the meeting in Zumbrota. To put the finishing touch to this "hustle," we read a long OBRC statement which started out as follows:

> As staff members of OBRC we have been authorized by the President and Vice-President of the Organization, along with other interested members, to make the following statement. We hope that this written statement, as opposed to a shouting match between a large OBRC delegation and the Board, will focus on the essential issues which must be resolved by this Agency.

The CAC board, disoriented by the events of the preceding month, was grateful. The board made the concessions as mandated by the Chicago regional office. Manipulative organizing had triumphed.

On September 27, 1973, just five days after the CAC meeting, OBRC held its second annual convention. The organizing efforts around revenue sharing and the OEO confrontation had given OBRC a great deal of county publicity, both good and bad. Even the bad publicity was good. OBRC had real visibility, especially in Faribault, the county seat. The name of the organization had been kept "up front" throughout the summer months.

OBRC was identified with a broad range of issues and controversial fights in the community that were of *direct concern* to low- and moderate-income people. The organization was no longer viewed solely as "a welfare organization." This convention, attended by seventy-five people, marked the beginning of new constituency groups in the organization: senior citizens, homeowners, working poor, and moderate-income people. This coalition of constituency groups was crucial to expanding the power base of OBRC in Rice County.

The goal of moving beyond welfare rights was realized at the second convention. Welfare mothers still remained a strong force in the organization, holding five of the fifteen decision-making positions on the action council. But in addition to welfare mothers, senior citizens, working poor people, and moderate-income people elected their representatives to the board. Altogether, eleven of the fifteen positions were held by poor people.

The *Faribault Daily News* carried the following headline the next day, September 28: "OBRC Reflects on Past, Plans For Future." The article started out:

> Members of Organization For A Better Rice County (OBRC) jammed the Labor Temple Building Thursday night in spirited discussion of the organization's past and future actions.
>
> The occasion was OBRC's second annual convention, and nearly every member was heard from as the organization established formal by-laws, elected new officers, and passed resolutions taking aim at future projects.

It was an exciting citizens' convention. The people were proud of OBRC's accomplishments and determined to reverse the organization's defeats—public transportation in Faribault, for example. A broad range of issues was discussed, with the following ten resolutions passed unanimously by the membership:

1. Faribault is facing a transportation crisis, particularly for senior citizens. Busses are being cut back, taxi rates have gone up, the Jefferson Bus Depot has become virtually inaccessible in its new location.

   Resolved: OBRC should continue its efforts to develop a low-cost transportation system for Faribault and to see it is accepted by the City Council.

2. The pressing need for day care in Rice County will partially

be met by the new Rice County Day Care Program, suggested by OBRC and approved by the County Commissioners. *Resolved*: OBRC will continue to work to see that the Rice County Day Care Program is as good as possible.

3. Food Stamps will be coming into Rice County by June or July next year. Key to the success of the program is 1) how it is implemented and 2) the knowledge recipients have about the program.
   Resolved: OBRC should meet with the welfare department to provide input into the Rice County Food Stamp Program. It should also undertake an information program for recipients to make sure all rights are understood.

4. Housing is a basic human need and should be guaranteed to everyone.
   Resolved: OBRC will actively work to guarantee adequate housing to everyone. Specifically this shall include:
   a. Tenants Rights—advising tenants of their rights and responsibilities as tenants and working with them to see that the rights are not violated.
   b. FHA-235 Housing—seeing that contract provisions are lived up to by the contractor.
   c. Improving the supply of low cost housing in the county.

5. Everyone is a consumer. As such it is important that we know our rights and see that they are not denied.
   Resolved: OBRC shall conduct a campaign aimed at consumer education and clearly establishing the consumer as the most important part of business.

6. The Welfare System puts power in the hands of a few and takes it away from many. This is unjust and undemocratic.
   Resolved: OBRC will work in all possible ways to correct the balance of power, to establish as an unbreakable principle the dignity of all people in the Welfare System. This will include:
   a. Providing advocacy service and training.
   b. Developing recognized grievance procedures.
   c. Push the county to collect child support from fathers who should and can be contributing.

7. Adequate nutrition is basic to human growth and development. Programs exist to provide school breakfasts but have not been started in Rice County.

Resolved: OBRC should push for the establishment of School Breakfast programs in Rice County.

8. Medical costs cut into everyone's budget, taking more and more all the time. Many of the problems are beyond our immediate grasp, but some are not.

   Resolved: OBRC should work to reduce drug costs by:
   a. Comparing costs between drug stores.
   b. Urging the prescription of generic rather than brand name drugs.

9. The Goodhue-Rice-Wabasha Citizens Action Council (CAC) is a public body established to meet the needs of low income people in the three county area. Low income people are supposed to be represented on its board but this has not been the case recently.

   Resolved: OBRC will work to elect members to the CAC Board and see that all its operations represent the interests of those it is intended to serve.

10. Political parties are a basic part of American politics. To have real influence in political decisions it is often necessary to work within the parties.

    Resolved: OBRC will ask the Rice County Republican and Democratic Executive Committees to include a representative from OBRC.

The strategy of focusing on conflict issues to generate interest in OBRC had worked. The organization had matured greatly since the first convention. OBRC people, especially welfare mothers, who had given up hope that there was anything they could do to influence government and improve their lives, were now confident about themselves and the organization. OBRC people were politically much wiser, and the organization was stronger. Yet, the organizers had too large a role. The revenue-sharing and OEO organizing work was done by a few organizers. A large number of poor people were interested in OBRC. A few of them were strong and active organizers-leaders. But not nearly enough community people had emerged as leaders to take over the organization.

4

New COMMUNITY LEADERS

The staff of organizers played a critical role during the first year of OBRC's existence. They dominated the monthly meetings of the action council (the elected leadership of OBRC) and determined the entire organizing agenda—both the issues and the strategies.

The organizers were not highly trained. During the first summer, several students from Carleton College, Rick Kahn, Jim May, and Diane Smith, helped with the canvassing. Rick Kahn's housing expertise gave OBRC immediate leverage in determining housing policy in the county. Diane Smith worked very closely with several welfare mothers on the day care proposal. The students provided "technical assistance" to people and played a vital role in researching some of the issues.

Starting in the fall of 1972, the staff consisted of student volunteers, two VISTAs, and myself. The most important staff person was Dudley Younkin, a community VISTA, who managed the office and had the most direct contact with the people during the first year. He was a graduate of Carleton College. He worked on all the initial research in the county during the spring of 1972. In the summer, Dudley became a VISTA sponsored by the Rice-Goodhue-Wabasha CAC. After the OBRC-CAC conflict one year later, OBRC never had a VISTA again.

Dudley Younkin did almost all the individual advocacy work. He brought many people into OBRC because he was able to help them with their problems. He was knowledgeable about tenant, welfare, and consumer laws, and he was a kind and sensitive young man who gave each person his complete attention. He was especially important to some of the senior citizens. He was not always comfortable with conflict issues, and his style made OBRC, in part, a social service organization. But he came through for people who in the past had nowhere to turn, and they believed in Dudley Younkin and OBRC. When he contacted people about a meeting, they came.

After the second convention in the fall of 1973, Dudley Younkin left the area and moved to Wisconsin. His job was taken over by another VISTA, Sue Little (pseud.). Sue Little was in her late thirties, the mother of five children. She was a Headstart mother who lived in rural Goodhue County, about ten miles from Faribault. I knew her from my year with the OEO and felt she could become an excellent organizer.

Sue Little could not handle the job. Starting in October, just one month after the successful convention, OBRC began to skid. She did not come through for people on advocacy work. She was not accessible to people who came by the office. Her style was quite different from Dudley Younkin's. She told people what to do. She viewed them as her "clients" and herself as a lawyer. She was deeply resented by many people in OBRC, and in a critical two-month period OBRC came close to collapsing.

In November, OBRC attempted to meet the welfare board head-on over its decision to hire a "resource examiner." OBRC's videotape on child support had provided the impetus for this decision. But OBRC people feared the county welfare board was using the OBRC tape as a justification for hiring a fraud investigator to harass welfare mothers in the county. The title "resource examiner" was very ambiguous. The organizing issue was that OBRC demanded that welfare mothers in the organization have the right to interview candidates for the position and veto power over the choice. The welfare board would never grant OBRC veto power, but welfare mothers would settle for the right to interview candidates and make recommendations. This might give OBRC at least a handle for further conflict with the welfare board over the position.

Sue Little did the calling for the welfare strategy meetings, and it soon became apparent welfare mothers would not come if contacted by her. We could not get the mothers together and were unable to appear before the welfare board with large delegations. The county commissioners, angry over past OBRC criticism, legal action, and confrontations, drew the line. At the first board meeting in November, the commissioners voted unanimously to table the OBRC request on the resource examiner. Commissioner Martin Hachfield from rural Faribault who made the motion to table the request spoke for the board when he said, "You OBRC people have gotten to the point where you think you can run the welfare board. A lot of people in the county wonder whether we're doing our job any more. We intend to make our own decisions here, and that is all there is to it." The *Faribault Daily News* carried a front-page story on the meeting with the headline, "OBRC Request on Resource Examiner Interviews Tabled." We could not regroup before the December board meeting, where the commissioners flatly turned down the OBRC proposal. One commissioner argued that "letting welfare mothers help select the new examiner would be like hiring your own jailers" (a revealing analogy). The *Faribault Daily News* headline read: "Welfare Board Refuses OBRC Request on Resource Examiner." The paper carried the following editorial supporting the welfare board's position:

OBRC and Welfare Board

We're pleased that the Rice County Welfare Board refused to allow "open interviews" in selecting a resource examiner for the county welfare department.

The position of resource examiner was created last fall by the Rice County Board. The resource examiner would investigate alleged violations of court-ordered support payments—particularly those involving divorced males who refuse to pay alimony and child support.

"Open interviews" for the new job had been requested by the Organization For A Better Rice County (OBRC). OBRC said its members should have a voice in the selection of the resource examiner, but has not yet set forth any solid reason for such action.

We've always believed—and still do—that most government personnel matters should be "quasi-public": in other words, the press should be allowed to attend meetings about personnel matters, but the reporter attending needs to use discretion if a story is published.

OBRC claims that it has a right to help select the new resource examiner. We don't agree.

If a governmental unit were selecting a new county administrator, or a school superintendent, or a city manager, for example, the public ought to have a hand in the person's selection.

But establishing a public selection procedure for such rank-and-file jobs as resource examiner just isn't practical. If local government units had to go to a public committee every time they wanted to hire someone, they wouldn't have time to do anything else.

The public's elected governmental representatives—or their appointees—are the ones who are responsible for hiring and firing. Even in a new county administrator, a school superintendent or a city manager, the elected officials should have the last word.

If a person they choose doesn't perform his job, then the public has a right—in fact, a responsibility—to complain.

And that's the attitude that should be taken by OBRC: let the welfare board select a resource examiner; give that person a chance to acclimate himself to the job; and then complain loudly if the examiner isn't performing his duties. [Nov. 8, 1973]

The local paper made clear its strong support for the "resource examiner" position in another editorial six months later:

Stopping Welfare Fraud

We're pleased to learn that the new Rice County Welfare Department resource examiner has netted monetary results for Rice County taxpayers.

A Faribault woman pleaded guilty Friday to eight counts of wrongfully obtaining public welfare assistance, after an investigation by Resource Examiner Jim Nielsen. The woman was ordered to repay $1,970 to the county and was placed on two years' probation.

We take no great pleasure in seeing people punished. But we are pleased to see that Rice County at least is prepared to seek out and find welfare cheating that may cost Rice County taxpayers hundreds of thousands of dollars each year.

When the resource examiner post was authorized by the Rice County Board early this year, it was estimated that the position could save taxpayers as much as $50,000 annually. Friday's guilty plea marked the first courtroom results of the examiner's investigations, but it certainly won't be the last.

Nielsen says several other court cases are in the works. In addition, several out-of-court settlements have already been made, and the mere existence of a resource examiner apparently has prompted several welfare recipients to request that they be dropped from the rolls.

Such settlements, both in and out of court, mean that Rice County already is well on the way toward recovering enough fraudulent welfare money to cover the examiner's salary. And there's a good chance that the $50,000 figure will be reached.

If that proves true, the decision to hire a resource examiner will rank among the top county achievements of the year.

[June 18, 1974]

This editorial prompted the following letter to the editor from Phyllis Hanson, an OBRC activist:

Your editorial of June 18 on the subject of welfare fraud is a misrepresentation of several essential facts. It assumes that the majority of the estimated $50,000 to be saved by the resource examiner will be saved by finding AFDC mothers fraudulent. This is wrong. While it may be true that some fraud exists in the county, the majority of money to be saved will come from recovering child-support payments from delinquent fathers. We are aware of at least 45 cases of delinquency in the payment of child support to AFDC mothers.

In many cases, enforced payment would take mothers off assistance altogether. In other cases, public payments would be substantially reduced. In all cases the taxpayer would be saved unnecessary expense.

Editorials such as yours encourage the citizenry of this county to fix blame in the wrong place. In the five months since the resource examiner has operated, this is the first fraud case to be brought to public attention.

How about some publicity about the men who are delinquent in their support payments? That's where the real saving of taxpayer dollars will come, and that's where the resource examiner will prove his worth. How many men have begun payments in the last five months? How many non-support cases has Mr. Neilsen investigated? That's where we ought to be looking. How about examining the really big problems rather than misrepresenting the problems through irresponsible editorials.

The county daily reluctantly backed away from its original position with a second editorial in response to the OBRC letter:

> We agree with the contention of today's Peoples' Column writer: most of the tax savings resulting from investigations by the Rice County Welfare Department resource examiner probably will come from recovery of delinquent child-support payments.
>
> In fact, recovering such payments from delinquent fathers was the major reason the resource examiner post was established by the county board, and the *Daily News* supported that reason in an editorial early this year.
>
> We don't agree, however, that our editorial Tuesday misrepresented welfare problems. It stated: "We are pleased to see that Rice County at least is prepared to seek out and find welfare cheating."
>
> "Cheating" includes not only fraud by welfare recipients, but non-payment of support by fathers.
>
> Last week's plea of guilty by a Faribault woman to eight counts of wrongfully obtaining public welfare assistance was the first court conviction resulting from the new resource examiner's investigation. Because it was an important "first" for the Rice County Welfare Department, it merited an editorial.
>
> Future convictions resulting from the resource examiner's investigation—be they wrongfully obtaining welfare assistance or for delinquent child-support payments—will be reported by the *Daily News*. [June 21, 1974]

The debate on welfare fraud would go on throughout the coming months and gain in intensity as the county welfare department charged almost every active welfare mother in OBRC with fraud. In November–December 1973, the defeat over the resource examiner was a serious blow to the organization. The OBRC delegations that appeared before the welfare board were pitifully small in numbers. The welfare recipients who did come were discouraged at not having more support and were unable to act as powerful spokeswomen. A conservative county board was feeling pressure from powerful and conservative interests in the county, and the OBRC delegations could hardly counterbalance this pressure.

The organizing among senior citizens was also going badly. OBRC launched a campaign to reduce medical costs for senior citizens in the county. One of the resolutions passed at the second annual convention was aimed at reducing drug costs. Isabelle Goodwin, a retired nurse who was elected to the action council in September, conducted a systematic and comprehensive survey of the varying drug costs at different pharmacies in Faribault. This survey was complemented by a Carleton student study of comparative pricing throughout the county. In addition, Isabelle Goodwin had put together a consumer guide on generic drugs as an alternative to the more expensive brand-name drugs.

This organizing campaign had great potential. Medicare did not cover drug costs for senior citizens, and many of them spent 30% of their monthly income on drugs. The national strategy was to push for comprehensive Medicare coverage (comprehensive health-care coverage, for that matter), and OBRC could involve itself in national reform in a number of ways, especially in candidate forums. The local strategy was to provide a relevant service to senior citizens and all low- and moderate-income people—an OBRC shopper's guide to drug costs which presented information on where to go for the best price and on generic equivalents of the expensive brand-name drugs. Potentially, this relevant service, the shopper's guide, would lead to a major confrontation with the medical establishment in the county on OBRC terms. Doctors could be pressured to become more conscious of consumer costs (prescribing generic drugs whenever possible), and pharmacists could be challenged on the tremendous disparity in pricing. But OBRC did not have an organizer to coordinate this plan—to make it happen.

The most serious problem during the months of November and December was with the welfare rights group. It was falling apart. The VISTA, in the course of her advocacy work, developed a close working relationship with the welfare department. Welfare mothers did not like or trust her and were leaving the organization. Especially troublesome was the fact that she was providing the welfare department with information against a few welfare recipients in OBRC whom she viewed as undeserving. One of these women was Artis Fleischfresser.

Artis was a welfare rights leader in OBRC. She hated the welfare department and was not afraid to express her views publicly. She was the leader of the "courthouse raid." She was co-author of the day-care proposal, an elected officer of OBRC, a welfare activist. It was no secret the welfare department intensely disliked her. She was under close scrutiny and had no margin for error. When she made some serious personal mistakes, it left her open to the charge of being an "unsuitable mother."

In early December, Elliot Sellner, head social worker for the Rice County Welfare Department, appeared at Artis Fleishfresser's home with a court order and police escort to take her children into custody. The welfare department had given her no previous warning this might happen. Sellner secretly built up a case against her, with the help of the OBRC VISTA, and convinced a judge the situation was so serious the department needed to take the children away even before a judicial hearing.

When Sellner arrived with the police, Artis screamed at him, "What are you doing this for? You're not going to take my children from me!" He replied, "I knew you'd make trouble—that's why I brought the police along." The children (ages four and six) screamed as the police took them away.*

She phoned me, hysterical over what was happening. I was shocked. I knew she was going to have trouble with the welfare department and had warned her so. But I assumed the welfare department would notify her that they were pressing charges against her and there would be a court hearing to determine whether she was a suitable mother. In this way, she would have time to prepare the children. If the welfare department had the best interests of the children at heart, as they claimed, they would not have come to her home unannounced with the police and taken the children away. It was a brutal tactic that traumatized both the children and the mother.

When I arrived at Artis's home with a lawyer, Bill Johnson from Northfield, the police had already taken the children away. She was sobbing. Sellner stood some distance away watching her. When we walked into the house, he quickly approached Bill Johnson and said, "You can see the house isn't fit for animals to live in." Johnson asked Sellner not to say such things in front of a woman who obviously was very upset. Sellner, the social worker, responded by saying, "If you are worried about her sensitivity, don't—I doubt if she has any."

The welfare department held the children for a few days until the court hearing. The formal judicial hearing never actually took place. The assistant county attorney (attorney for the welfare board) announced shortly before the hearing that he would not prosecute because he did not think the welfare department

*Conversation with Artis Fleischfresser.

had sufficient evidence and was suspicious the charge might be a political vendetta. We waited in the courthouse for the foster parents to bring the children back to their mother. The welfare department had not informed them before the decision that they should be ready to bring the children back. They finally came, dressed in new snowmobile suits bought by their foster parents. As it turned out, they had quite a time—snowmobile rides on the country club golf course, new clothes, all kinds of gifts and benefits, all beyond the reach of their mother, all done in kindness.

The nightmare was over, but the action taken by the welfare department had its effect. We now understood the harsh sanctions the welfare department could invoke against activist mothers. Taking a woman's children away from her (or threatening to do so) is an effective way of keeping her in place. I saw Artis Fleischfresser, a militant welfare activist (among recipients in Rice County), on her knees begging Elliot Sellner (a man she deeply hated) for her children. She never forgot what happened to her. When I spoke to her in June 1975, a year and a half after this event, she said to me, "They did it to throw a scare in me. Looking back on it, I don't think they ever thought they would win in court. That's why I am not with them [OBRC] now. If OBRC called me and said, let's go down to the welfare department to stop them from treating these people so badly, I wouldn't go. I would be afraid. I don't want to face Sellner. I have no idea whether I have done anything wrong enough that he would take the kids to get even with me."

What happened to Artis Fleischfresser had a chilling effect on OBRC. The VISTA for OBRC had cooperated with the welfare department in taking action against an elected officer of the organization. Welfare mothers, in particular, were bitter and angry.

OBRC was close to collapsing. The organization had lost its momentum. It had not come through for people in the individual advocacy work. The organizing campaigns of November and December were failures. The organization was beset with internal strife. Most important, there were no effective citizen organizers to carry out the day-to-day political organizing.

This crisis forced the people who lived in the community and were committed to OBRC to take over the organization, and that is exactly what they did. The action council first dealt with the VISTA. Citing the VISTA manual, they made it clear: "The VISTA role will be to provide technical assistance and help leadership develop, *not to assume* leadership" (emphasis mine). Sue Little was told to work under the action council, the elected leadership of OBRC, or not work at all.

Several members of the action council volunteered to be citizen organizers. Phyllis Hanson, a welfare mother (stepfather grant)* and secretary of OBRC, volunteered to direct the organizing efforts. She came to the December action council meeting with a penciled-out proposal as to how OBRC might structure its organizing work. Included in this proposal were the job responsibilities for an executive secretary who would manage the office operations if OBRC was successful in obtaining outside grant money (at this time there was a pending $5,000 grant proposal with the Christian Sharing Fund, the social-action arm of the Catholic Church in Minnesota). After explaining her plan to other members of the action council, she disqualified herself from any funded position—thereby erasing any suspicion others might have about her motives for becoming active. This was a very shrewd and important move at a time when there was considerable internal turmoil. Phyllis Hanson had come to OBRC with a welfare problem. She was involved in some of the earlier welfare rights activities. She emerged from this meeting a leader in the organization. Within a few months, she would become a driving force in the organization. Therese Van Zuilen, Isabelle Goodwin, Elgie Cloutier, Joan Dietrich, and Patti Fritz joined Phyllis as citizen organizers.†

The first action taken by the volunteer staff was to oust the VISTA from the organization. They argued OBRC had outgrown the need for a VISTA, especially one who would not work for the organization. They pressed the issue by walking out of the office and refusing to do any organizing until the VISTA was removed. The tactic had (in retrospect) the unmistakable

---

*Although she remarried and was not eligible for Aid to Families with Dependent Children (AFDC), she received child-support payments through the welfare department.

†See in-depth interviews at the end of chaps. 1, 2, and 4. Joan Dietrich dropped out of the organization within a year due to internal strife (see next chapter on organizational problems) and is not an OBRC leader. Her name is included in recognition of her major contribution in welfare rights.

Phyllis Hanson stamp on it, and it worked. Confronted with this choice, the action council dropped the VISTA.

In the middle of December, OBRC received a $5,000 grant from the Christian Sharing Fund. OBRC was the first citizens' organization outside the metropolitan area to receive such funding. A major reason OBRC received the initial funding was that it was the only rural poor people's organization in the state; but of equal importance was the style of the people in the organization. When Christian Sharing Fund sent evaluators down to Rice County to talk with OBRC people, we set up a meeting out at Therese Van Zuilen's farm. From the time the evaluators arrived at the farm, we were sure the proposal would be funded. She had her own style of wining and dining. There was no wine or fancy food. But it was impossible to sit in her kitchen and not come away with a warm and positive feeling toward the OBRC president and the organization.

The $5,000 grant was a real shot in the arm. It was the first and perhaps most important grant the organization ever received. It enabled the action council to hire Elgie Cloutier as executive secretary and rent a small storefront office. It also gave OBRC people a new sense of confidence that their substantive accomplishments warranted this prestigious grant from the Church.* The Christian Sharing Fund grant also marked the beginning of an important relationship between OBRC and Bill Moore, an activist priest with a real understanding of community organizing, and Joe Schmidt, a lay member on the CSF board. These two men acted as liaison between the CSF and OBRC, and in this capacity provided OBRC people with counsel and support.[1]

In the middle of January the action council appointed me director of staff and chairman of the finance (fund-raising) committee. The idea was to give me a few months to work with the volunteer organizers and help build the organization during this transitional period. We were going to focus on a wide range of citizen concerns: food stamps, drug costs, welfare rights, consumer rights, housing and tenant rights, senior citizen transportation, and tax clinics. The tax clinics, modeled after the Movement for Economic Justice's (MEJ) work, would provide a relevant service—free tax assistance—to low- and moderate-in-

*The great majority of OBRC membership is of the Catholic faith.

come families. Welfare-consumer-tenant rights would involve a great deal of advocacy work. But the real emphasis would be on organizing.

Carleton College changed the scenario when I was fired in late January (it was called an early tenure decision). I still worked with OBRC, but the political fight at Carleton took a great deal of time. By necessity, Phyllis Hanson emerged as the catalyst and driving force behind OBRC's organizing activities. She was thirty-three years old, the mother of five children. Her father was a sharecropper, and most of her life she had known the meaning of rural poverty. She had a high-school education, unable to go to college because of lack of money and a serious epileptic condition.* She was married at seventeen, divorced at twenty-five and on her own with two small children. In 1968 she remarried, and she and her husband Rusty put their two families together (five children altogether). They had lived in Faribault for six years. Phyllis had been working full-time nights at a low-wage job until January 1974 when she hurt her back. She then spent her spare time battling the welfare department— trying to receive child-support payments (stepfather grant) and other forms of assistance. She first became involved with OBRC as a welfare mother trying to receive some help.

Her first organizing effort was around food stamps. The Department of Agriculture had announced it was abolishing the food commodities program and had proposed some new and very repressive regulations for food stamps. Rice County was to switch to stamps by July 1974.

OBRC publicized its opposition to the Nixon administration's "assault on poor people" and linked up with other citizen groups throughout the country in fighting the proposed changes. The grass-roots organizing in Rice County centered around the demand that the county commissioners hold a public hearing about the new food stamp program. There were significant problems with food stamps in terms of federal rules and regulations, but local implementation was also a key factor in determining whether people would be encouraged to participate in the program or not. The food stamp program would potentially affect close to 7,000 poor people in Rice County. Many of them were worried about it; they had only known commodities and had no infor-

*See interview with Phyllis Hanson.

mation about stamps. OBRC hoped to involve welfare mothers, senior citizens, and working poor people in a struggle to insure the best possible stamps program in the county.

In late January a delegation of OBRC members appeared before the county commissioners to formally request they hold a public hearing. The commissioners tabled the request. They argued that (1) there was not yet enough information about what the "Feds" had in mind and (2) there was no need for a hearing in any case; they were quite capable of running a fair program. Their opposition gave OBRC the opportunity to develop the issue—*low- and moderate-income people who are directly affected by the new food stamps program demand a public hearing in order to express their opinions about how to best handle food stamps in the county.*

OBRC sponsored an open meeting on food stamps the following week. Phyllis Hanson in just a few days did all the person-to-person contacting for the meeting. The small OBRC office was jammed with people who were concerned and wanted to do something about the food stamps program. The *Faribault Daily News* (Jan. 30, 1974) carried a front-page story on the OBRC meeting: "Food Stamp Program Explained." The article began, "About 60 people crowded into the Organization For A Better Rice County (OBRC) office at 607 Central Avenue Tuesday night to learn what to expect when the federal Food Stamp Program goes into effect in Rice county."

The article was not very accurate in capturing the mood of the meeting. In part, it was an informational meeting. Many people were worried about the stamps program and wanted information; food assistance for them was a survival issue. But the dynamic that underlay the meeting was not to tell people "what they could expect" but rather for OBRC people to tell the county commissioners what they expected of the program. A steering committee was elected to translate suggestions given at the OBRC meeting into specific proposals and demand once again that the county commissioners hold the public hearing.

The committee appeared before the county commissioners in the second week of February and demanded the hearing. They made the following specific demands: (1) the public hearing must be held in the evening so working people can attend; (2) the meeting must be held in the large courtroom auditorium to accommodate the large OBRC membership; (3) the welfare board must give one-month prior notice of the exact date and time; and (4) the welfare department must send out a notice to all recipients about the public hearing.

The county commissioners conceded to each of these demands. Their mistake had been in tabling the original request. Now that the public hearing had become a real issue, a point of controversy, they were not in a position to deny a public hearing. The commissioners knew from past experience they were vulnerable to charges of negligence and apathy. They also knew that more than a few "agitators" were now concerned about food stamps. They were not anxious to escalate the conflict any further.

OBRC's strategy was to make this public hearing a show of strength. Phyllis Hanson went to work preparing for the hearing. The first problem was how to systematically contact rural poor people. She wanted to go beyond OBRC's contacts with its core members, but the old food commodities list, swiped from the OEO, was no longer accurate. She therefore followed the time-honored OBRC tradition of swiping a new and updated list. An outreach worker with the agency was "an OBRC person." She swiped the 1974 commodities list from the agency's office, and seven OBRC volunteers worked the whole weekend copying the entire list. The new list was combined with OBRC's existing contacts.

Phyllis identified the vocal people from the OBRC meeting and asked them, along with a few OBRC activists, to choose names they knew from the lists and contact them before the public hearing. Therese Van Zuilen and Phyllis Hanson were joined by Francis Milligan, Patti Fritz, Gayle Aldrich, and Franie Dwyer in this effort.

The public hearing was held the evening of March 28. Close to 200 people attended (others came and left because there were no seats left). It was a major political event in Rice County. Rarely were 200 people ever assembled at a political meeting, not even at the Republican and DF-L county conventions. And these were poor people who had come together to express their concern that Rice County have a fair and well-run food stamps program. This was also an important show of strength for OBRC that proved organized poor people were a political force in the county to be reckoned with.

The public hearing itself got off to a poor start. The county commissioners were shrewd. They intended to control the agenda and use the hearing to inform people what kind of stamps program they would have. Accordingly, a panel of social-service professionals, including the state director of food stamp programs and a representative from the Department of Agriculture, began their lectures. We had to intervene. At first, Phyllis Hanson and myself were the major speakers, but other OBRC activists soon took over the meeting either by asking specific questions or by making specific demands.

The central OBRC demands were: (1) that food stamps be mailed to recipients or sold at community buildings, not banks; (2) that there be several food stamp centers throughout the county, all with a ground-floor location; (3) that four full-time outreach aides be hired immediately, aides who were low-income themselves and would have a good working relationship with food stamp recipients; (4) that the welfare department educate itself on the rules and regulations of the stamps program; and (6) that the program insure the privacy and dignity of each individual. A petition was circulated at the hearing to protest the proposed Department of Agriculture's food stamp rules and regulations.

It was disappointing that the organizers dominated the public hearing, especially at the beginning. Phyllis Hanson and other OBRC organizers had done a brilliant job in contacting people and motivating them to come to the hearing. But they had not carefully prepared for the hearing. They had not, for example, planned for the various scenarios that might be followed at the meeting. They had not caucused with groups of poor people who could have come to the hearing prepared to be powerful spokesmen. The organizers had become the leaders at the convention. On the other hand, almost all of them were community people who were food stamp recipients themselves.

The *Faribault Daily News* carried a descriptive story on the food stamp hearing along with the following editorial:

Food Stamps and OBRC

In a letter to the editor of the *Daily News* Wednesday, members of the Organization for a Better Rice County (OBRC) complained that local implementation of the federal food stamp program would be "repressive and insulting for all low-income Rice County citizens."

OBRC said proposed changes in the program would increase

red tape and decrease participation; would allow food stamp officials to cut off benefits arbitrarily: would force food stamp recipients into unsafe jobs; and would make strike breakers out of recipients.

We disagree.

Food stamps are a form of welfare, and welfare was never meant to provide people with lifetime assistance. It is meant to lend a temporary helping hand to people who are experiencing hard times, and, as such, naturally causes some inconvenience to recipients.

Strict welfare regulations are important for two reasons: first, the money for welfare comes from taxes, and the taxpayer must have assurances that his money isn't being squandered, and, second, welfare is somewhat alien to a free enterprise system, and it shouldn't become a way of life.

We disagree with most of OBRC's proposals:

—That the commodity program should be extended while the food stamp program is being launched (that would be a truly wasteful duplication of effort);

—That four aides should be hired by the county to help food stamp recipients (the county welfare department already has trained personnel who can do that);

—That recipients be allowed to receive food stamps through the mail (food stamps, like currency, are readily negotiable and thus cannot be mailed); and

—That food stamp distribution centers be open from 9 a.m. to 8 p.m. at least once a week (we don't see anything wrong with the present welfare department hours).

We do agree with OBRC on two points: that the welfare department must educate its staff on food stamp regulations (that's being done), and that the program should insure the greatest possible privacy and dignity for each recipient.

But we think OBRC could be much more valuable to the people of Rice County by helping the welfare department disseminate information about food stamps, rather than complaining about necessary food stamp regulations. [*Faribault Daily News*, March 29, 1974]

By this time we realized that the bad publicity was good publicity for OBRC. The county paper by devoting editorial time to the organization was, in essence, legitimizing the OBRC operation in Rice County.

The county commissioners conceded to some of the demands and rejected others. They agreed to mail out stamps to senior citizens and establish food stamp centers in community buildings with ground-floor locations. They refused to expand hours beyond 5:OO P.M. and denied the need to hire more than two outreach workers. The demands that welfare officials educate themselves about the program and that recipients be treated with dignity were of course not publicly rejected, though often violated in practice.

Phyllis Hanson had done a brilliant job in her first "action." Preparation for the meeting was sloppy, and she might have followed up the rejection of several pivotal OBRC demands with more conflict. But OBRC had forced the county commissioners into the public hearing. Phyllis and her volunteer staff had involved many poor people in this successful struggle. They took an important step in building the organization and establishing the new facts of life about the balance of power in Rice County.

In the first week of March, as a part of the food stamps organizing campaign, OBRC sponsored a meeting on "human rights." Whatever the term used, it was a welfare rights meeting. Phyllis Hanson wanted to bring welfare mothers back together again and spent considerable time preparing for the meeting. Around forty AFDC mothers crowded the small office for the meeting. It was a very heated meeting as welfare recipients laid out their grievances: personal harassment by caseworkers, unfair treatment of their children in school, discriminatory treatment by pharmacists, unfair denial of medical assistance by the welfare department, and inadequate flat-grant payments. The following poem, which reflected the mood of welfare recipients, was distributed at the meeting.

I was hungry—
And you formed a committee and discussed my hunger
Thank you

I was naked—
And in your mind you debated the morality of my appearance
Thank you

I was sick—
And you knelt and thanked God for your health
Thank you

I was homeless and lonely—
And you preached to me about that spiritual of the love of God
Thank you

You seem so holy, so close to God!
But still I am very hungry and very lonely and very cold.*

Phyllis Hanson translated these personal grievances into organizing actions. AFDC mothers would be trained as skilled advocates to help other recipients deal with the welfare department. The women would group together and march on Walgreen Drug Store to stop discrimination against AFDC recipients. OBRC would fight for higher payments and fairer welfare laws by gaining a foothold in the DF-L party. School problems would be tackled by electing representatives in the spring school board elections responsive to the concerns of poor people.

Welfare mothers once again became very active in OBRC. Working seventy hours as a volunteer organizer week after week, Phyllis Hanson inspired others with her confidence and enthusiasm. She was good at advocacy work but better at making people work for themselves. I was confused by her style. I kept looking for formal workshops, seminars, or something. She kept handing work out to people, forcing them to confront issues, meet face to face with officials, and succeed. She immediately trained a cadre of welfare mothers who became skilled advocates who helped other recipients in Rice and surrounding rural counties.

Within one week after the human rights meeting, welfare mothers took on Walgreen Drug Store. The drugstore had taken the position that people with medical assistance cards were not eligible for free delivery, as was everyone else, because they already were receiving free drugs. Ten mothers confronted the pharmacist, tape recorder in hand, and demanded that welfare recipients, like other people, receive free delivery of drugs. Another twenty shoppers joined the crowd out of curiosity. The pharmacist, taken by surprise by the confrontation and uneasy about adverse publicity, agreed to provide free delivery to welfare recipients.

AFDC recipients also organized against the welfare department. The issue was personal harassment by several caseworkers.

*Author unknown.

The mothers demanded a hearing with the director of the department. It was an interesting meeting in that it reflected how well the welfare department and OBRC understood one another. The recipients brought a reporter and myself with them to meet with Chester Pearson. He, in turn, invited everyone who worked for the department to the meeting. He did not wish to discuss grievances in front of a reporter or outside agitator, and the welfare mothers did not want to discuss their grievances in front of the entire department. A compromise was reached. All would leave except AFDC recipients and the director of the department. The women pressed their grievances, threatened litigation, and were promised a change of caseworker. After several months, the director was finally pressured to keep this promise.

OBRC began its effort to gain representation in the DF-L party in late February, when the party was to hold its local caucuses. One week before the caucuses, Phyllis Hanson had learned about the party structure; and though she and other OBRC people had never attended a party caucus, they were confident they could take over several of the caucus meetings in the "north end," the low-income neighborhoods in Faribault. The precinct caucuses took place on February 26, 1974. OBRC took over several of the precincts (there was the usual small turnout) and sent twenty-five representatives to the county convention.

This strong showing put OBRC in a good bargaining position. The problem was that Phyllis and other OBRC people were not sure what part they could play in the elaborate negotiations going on prior to the county convention, to be held March 16. They wanted a firm position in the party but didn't know how to best achieve this end. I suggested they contact Sy Schuster, a radical political activist and mathematics professor at Carleton. He was a brilliant political strategist who understood how to work with and not for people. OBRC people wanted to send a poor people's delegate to the state convention. The nominating committee, however, had already chosen its slate of delegates. Sy Schuster suggested OBRC people threaten to fight the slate of candidates at the county convention to see what kind of deal the nominating committee might offer them. The committee made the following deal—it would not put an OBRC person on its slate of delegates to attend the district convention but would give OBRC representation on the county DF-L central committee. Several members on the nominating committee were, in fact, sympathetic to OBRC and wanted the organization to have solid representation in the party. Phyllis consulted with Schuster, and they, along with the other OBRC people involved in this effort, decided that for long-term political effect representation on the central committee was more important. They bargained for four positions on the fifteen-member committee.

As it turned out, the nominating committee was challenged at the county convention. They had not included any farmers on the slate and were bitterly attacked from the floor. The farmers called for a system of proportional representation to be based on attendance at the county convention. They were successful in this challenge, and at this point various groups and factions started bargaining with one another to maximize their respective positions. Again, Phyllis Hanson turned to Sy Schuster. He persuaded her not to enter in coalition with the teachers, farmers, or union people but to try for a poor people's caucus. OBRC already had the representation on the county central committee. Now the organization had a chance because of this turn of events to send a poor people's delegate to the district-state convention. OBRC put together the required caucus and sent, for the first time in the history of the county DF-L, a poor people's delegate to the district convention.

The May school board elections in Faribault posed a difficult challenge for OBRC. Joan Schreiber, a strong liberal who had worked with OBRC on the day care proposal and was interested in the organization, was running for a third time for a school board seat. In fact, a woman had not been elected to the Faribault School Board since the 1940s. OBRC people knew Joan Schreiber would be responsive to their concerns and wanted to support her candidacy. But the organization could not depend on confrontation tactics which had always been its source of strength. Moreover, "low-income people" were the nonparticipants in local elections, and it remained to be seen whether OBRC could successfully organize people to register and vote in the election.

Phyllis Hanson went to work on the school board elections. Welfare mothers were concerned about their children's education and wanted to support a candidate responsive to their concerns. In addition, the election afforded OBRC the opportunity to involve a coalition of low- and moderate-income people in a collective effort to elect a candidate of their choice. The school board election would be a test of the organization's electoral clout.

Twenty precinct captains were appointed in lower-income neighborhoods. Residents were contacted by phone and in person. Transportation was provided for registration and voting. Overall, 250 people were contacted. OBRC delivered a bloc vote of 125–175 for Joan Schreiber. Though each voter could vote for his or her top three choices, OBRC voters "bullet-voted," disregarding any choice but Schreiber. There were three positions open in the at-large school board elections. Joan Schreiber was third in the voting. She received 700 votes, with a small 30-vote margin over the fourth place finisher. OBRC was the balance-of-power factor in the election. This was a great accomplishment for the organization. Phyllis Hanson, like any good organizer, made sure OBRC people were aware of their school board victory.

The other major organizing campaign that winter concerned senior citizen transportation. Isabelle Goodwin, a retired nurse receiving social security and disability payments (she suffered from degenerative osteoarthritis), spearheaded this effort.

OBRC took the initiative in early February by announcing its plan to form a nonprofit corporation to run a "dial-a-bus" in Faribault. Disgusted with the Faribault City Council, Isabelle Goodwin wanted to make an end run around the council and directly sponsor this vitally important service for the people of Faribault. Of particular concern to her were the senior citizens. The OBRC plan received a front-page write-up in the *Faribault Daily News*:

Local Mini-Bus Proposed

All-day, year-round public transportation in Faribault could become a reality again if a plan worked out by Organization for a Better Rice County (OBRC) is funded.

The plan calls for a mini-bus that would operate weekdays from 9 a.m. to 3 p.m. throughout the year on four routes within the city.

"It would be for people with more time than money," says OBRC transportation chairwoman Isabelle Goodwin.

She says the operation would be run by a co-op or non-profit corporation made up of people who used the service. Subscribers would pay an annual membership of about $10 per person, or possibly $20 per family. Advance tickets would be sold to members for about $5 for 10 rides.

The bus would cover each route every two hours, and people would be encouraged to call for a ride the day before, because the bus would pick them up or drop them off at their house. There would also be several downtown pick-up points where members could catch the bus home during the day. Any Faribault resident could become a member.

Ms. Goodwin is calling a meeting to get public response to the idea Friday night at 7:30 in the OBRC headquarters at 607 Central Ave.

She says the state Public Service Commission has reviewed the proposal and would okay a six-month trial period for the service.

The co-op could contract with Faribault Bus Lines for operating, maintaining, insurance, and radio dispatching of the bus, Ms. Goodwin said.

"I think the thing will work if it's managed properly," said Clarence Cornell at Faribault Bus Lines. Cornell says he would be willing to work closely with OBRC in setting up the service.

Funding, Ms. Goodwin said, is the next step. She says it would cost about $20,000 per year to operate the bus, or about $85 per day. She is looking for money on national, state or local government levels.

Once the operation was on its feet, she said, it could be largely self-sustaining through ticket sales and membership fees. [February 19, 1974]

The Friday evening meeting was crowded with senior citizens interested in the dial-a-bus. A full committee was appointed to continue work on the proposal. Isabelle announced that OBRC was sponsoring a meeting with the regional coordinator for the Governor's Aging Council to explore funding possibilities. Representatives from the Golden Agers, a social club of 700 that OBRC had its eye on, were invited to attend the meeting. The following month senior citizens met with Jerald Farrington at the OBRC office. The meeting received front-page coverage in the *Faribault Daily News*, and the paper took an editorial position on the OBRC proposal.

Dial-a-Bus Backers Encouraged but Cautioned
By Brian Roragen, *Daily News* Staff Writer

Senior citizens working to see a dial-a-bus operation in Faribault heard words of encouragement and caution from a spokesman for the Governor's Citizens Council on Aging Monday afternoon.

Jerald Farrington, regional coordinator for the Governor's Aging Council, said federal money for senior citizen transportation is available, but would require substantial local effort to secure.

Farrington explained his agency's funding requirements to a gathering of the Organization for a Better Rice County Transportation Committee, and representatives from the Faribault Golden Age Club, the Catholic Church and a regional level aging council.

First, he said, the need for such a service would have to be substantially documented, as well as the support it would receive from senior citizens. Then a proposal would have to be written that would convince the state council on aging to fund it.

Farrington, grey-haired and energetic, said that if the proposal was then approved, the Governor's Citizens Council on Aging would be able to carry 75 percent of the project's cost that was generated by senior citizen use.

As Farrington explained it, the percentage of local senior citizen use of a mini-bus service here would determine how much money the state aging council would put into it. The rest of the money, he said, would have to come from locally generated funds in the form of contributions, local government help, or bus fares.

He also suggested to the group that they write an application for funding jointly with a Northfield group that wants to build a senior citizens center there. Though the two projects are unrelated, he said both would have a much better chance of funding if their applications are written jointly.

Isabelle Goodwin, head of the OBRC's Transportation Committee, described how the dial-a-bus service would work.

It would be a non-profit corporation, she said, owned by the people who use it. It would cost a person about $10 per year, or $20 per couple, for membership. Advance ride tickets would cost about $5 for ten rides. Members would not be liable for any costs beyond membership fees and ticket fares.

For people over 60, Farrington said membership and possibly tickets would be paid for by the State Council on Aging, if the county funds the picking up and dropping off of members at their homes. They would be asked to call one day ahead for a ride to simplify routing. The mini-bus would make regular stops downtown to pick up and drop off members without appointments.

Faribault Bus Lines, she said, has agreed to handle driving, maintenance, dispatching, insurance, and the day-to-day cost of $70 to $80 a day, operating under contract with the member-rider corporation. A six-month trial clearance has also been granted from the state Public Service Commission if the project gets off the ground.

She added that it is extremely important for senior citizens and others who feel there is a need for such a service to call OBRC at 332-7451.

"We have to have an idea how many people would use it," she said. "Otherwise we may not get the grant to start with." [*Faribault Daily News*, March 26, 1974]

Mini-Bus Proposal

We were encouraged last week to learn that the Organization for a Better Rice County (OBRC) has proposed an all-day year-round public transit system in Faribault.

The plan calls for a mini-bus that would operate weekdays from 9 a.m. to 3 p.m. It would be managed by a co-op consisting of the people who used it. Subscribers would pay an annual membership of about $10 per person, or $20 per family and the mini-bus would pick subscribers up and drop them off at their homes.

But we're a little skeptical about OBRC Transportation Chairwoman Isabelle Goodwin's claim that the operation could be largely self-sustaining once it's on its feet. Faribault Bus Lines was forced to cut its city bus schedule drastically last year because not enough people were riding the bus, and the Faribault City Council didn't feel additional subsidies were warranted. (The bus line had been getting $5,000 annually in city subsidy before service was cut back).

City transit systems are going to have to be subsidized if they're to continue. The relatively few people who would ride a Faribault bus system certainly wouldn't be willing to pay the high fares necessary to operate such a service without subsidy.

And the current mass transit bill before the Minnesota Legislature is the best means of providing a subsidy, because Faribault

taxpayers won't be willing to foot a subsidy bill with local taxes, unless gasoline becomes next-to-impossible to get.
[March 26, 1974]

In mid-April OBRC issued a press release urging senior citizens to contact the organization if they were interested in the dial-a-bus. The press release pointed out that it was essential that OBRC document the need and interest for a dial-a-bus, if the program was to be funded. Within a week, over 300 senior citizens called. Isabelle Goodwin aggressively pushed the dial-a-bus among senior citizens and brought a large number of older people into the organization. OBRC had caught local officials by surprise with its transportation proposal, and subsequent meetings with state officials over the dial-a-bus generated a great deal of publicity for the organization; in addition, this was an issue around which OBRC could cement the allegiance of senior citizens.

Isabelle Goodwin was resolved that OBRC directly sponsor the dial-a-bus and have nothing to do with the Faribault City Council. She successfully raised the local money and support to qualify for state matching funds. Most important, she enlisted the support of the Golden Age Club for the OBRC proposal. The *Faribault Daily News* carried a short story on the progress of the dial-a-bus in late April.

Dial-a-Bus Back in Gear

Dial-A-Bus appears to be getting back into gear due to anonymous donations which the project's organizers feel are large enough to put state matching funds programs within reach.

The Dial-A-Bus committee, an outgrowth of Organization for a Better Rice County (OBRC) has received pledges of $1,000 from local sources. That, plus the pledged membership donations of the 200 or more people who have said they would subscribe to the service, is a solid enough base to apply for state transportation funding programs, according to the committee.

In the meantime, says committee chairperson Isabelle Goodwin, efforts are continuing to raise the rest of the needed funds. If enough can be raised locally, she says, state matching fund programs will provide the rest.

In the meantime a board of directors is being formed to oversee Dial-A-Bus operations. Bill Dittes, president of the Golden Age

Club, announced that he has named two of that organization's members with experience in accounting and business to serve on the Dial-A-Bus board.

"We're going to support the idea," says Dittes. He said that the Golden Age Club will try to inform its membership on details of the service and encourage them to support it.

"Some of them have needs to get to the clinic, some of them have needs to get to a store to do their shopping," he says. "This will certainly help them out in that respect."

"If we sit here and do nothing, nothing's going to happen," he concluded. [April 1974]

Isabelle Goodwin's determination that OBRC run a transportation program for Faribault citizens raised a very sensitive and important problem. Some of us felt it would be a serious mistake for OBRC to become directly responsible for administering the dial-a-bus program in Faribault. From an organizing point of view, it did not make good sense to absorb OBRC activists like Isabelle Goodwin in administering this or any other program. We did not have enough active people to both administer the dial-a-bus and move on to other organizing campaigns. Once OBRC activists like Isabelle Goodwin became involved in the day-to-day operation of the dial-a-bus (with legal and financial responsibility for the program), they would not have the time to work on other important issues—and this would be disasterous for OBRC. Moreover, the real principle was that the city council, which had the authority and resources, should represent and serve the people in the town, including senior citizens. It was their responsibility to write a dial-a-bus (or other transportation) proposal, contribute some of the funding, and operate the service. OBRC, given Isabelle Goodwin's strategy, was unwittingly letting the city council off the hook.

The Faribault City Council would of course balk at this commitment. The previous summer the mayor had lectured senior citizens that "government should not subsidize people." But OBRC had matured greatly since the setback one year ago. OBRC was a conflict organization, and we welcomed the chance to involve senior citizens in a successful confrontation with the council.

Phyllis Hanson talked with Isabelle Goodwin about a different organizing strategy. At first, she resisted the idea. But as she became bogged down in the complexities and red tape of raising matching funds for the co-op, not to mention the legal intricacies, she came to see the wisdom of the organizing principle that local government ought to provide this service for the people.

OBRC focused its organizing campaign on forcing the Faribault City Council to accept the OBRC dial-a-bus proposal, but with different conditions. OBRC took the position that it had done most of the work for the city council (writing a proposal, contacting state officials, locating funding sources) and that it was now up to the council as elected officials to serve the people by providing matching funds, applying for a state grant, and operating the service.

There were two meetings with the city council in late May and early June. Both times the dial-a-bus was tabled or "detoured." Local officials argued that lack of ridership would be a real problem as had been the case with Faribault Bus Lines. Confronted with OBRC evidence about senior citizen interest, they made the opposite argument, namely, that with heavy ridership the town would find itself involved in a public transportation program requiring too great a government subsidy. The arguments added up to one point—the town government had no intention of providing a dial-a-bus service for the people.

The *Faribault Daily News* carried a story summarizing the status of the dial-a-bus proposal in early June:

Dial-a-Bus Again Detoured

Dial-A-Bus was examined again by the Faribault City Council Tuesday night, but lack of solid information again tabled the transportation proposal.

Dial-A-Bus is a proposal to provide at least minimal public transportation at a reasonable cost within the city of Faribault. Isabelle Goodwin, who has spearheaded the project with Organization for a Better Rice County, describes it as aimed at "people with more time than money."

She envisions a mini-bus that would circulate over a two-hour route, picking up people at their doors. People would call for a ride a day in advance.

Tuesday night the City Council again expressed frustration over not being able to nail down precise cost figures on the proposal, though $13,000 per year in operating costs was mentioned several times.

Councilmen also referred to the fact that Faribault is going into its first summer without any public bus service. They expressed reservations about getting involved in a transportation project that could possibly involve costs approaching the $15,000 subsidy asked for last fall by Faribault Bus Lines, which the City Council refused to give.

City Engineer-Administrator Robert Cook reported that several government grant programs are available, but that all of them are temporary, lasting for six months to a year or two.

Though the council appeared to recognize that a need exists for transportation for the elderly, handicapped and poor, they foresaw two possible problems. Lack of ridership, they pointed out, led to the death of fulltime service by Faribault Bus Lines.

On the other hand, they felt, if ridership became heavy on the Dial-A-Bus, the city could find itself involved in an extensive public transit system that would be more expensive than the $15,000 annual subsidy Faribault Bus Lines had asked for.

With no solution in sight but with the question expanded to include Faribault's total public transportation situation, Dial-A-Bus was again tabled. [June 6, 1974]

In early July, controversy shifted from the dial-a-bus to "the Florence Hendricks case." It started out as a typical advocacy case. OBRC received a call from Florence Hendricks's neighbors asking someone to come out and help her. She was an old woman, aged sixty-nine, living alone in squalid conditions, in ill health, starving to death. When Phyllis Hanson and Patti Fritz saw her, they were horrified at her condition. Six months of poor people's organizing had made them aware of rural poverty conditions, but they were emotionally upset by her extreme condition. They were especially angry because the welfare department had sent two caseworkers to Florence Hendricks's house (in response to a complaint about her from the owner of a nearby snack bar), who had told her to clean herself up or else and had thrown such a scare into her that she had barricaded the front door of her house. When Phyllis and Patti returned from visiting Florence Hendricks, they told other people in the organization about her condition. OBRC people started calling local officials and friends to find food, medical attention, and better housing for her. It is ironic that Florence Hendricks became such an organizing issue because initially all the effort was toward getting her help. Most OBRC people were not organizers and were oriented (too oriented, from my perspective) toward advocacy work—helping people with problems. It was not unusual for the organization to focus all its attention on helping one person or family. No organizing ideology had ever changed (or will ever change) this basic orientation.

Two factors made "the Florence Hendricks case" a major political issue: local and state officials did not respond to the OBRC appeals for help, thus frustrating and angering many OBRC people who worked on this case; shortly after OBRC finally got her to a hospital for help, she died, and there ensued a heated argument about the cause of her death. OBRC charged official neglect and callousness; the welfare department charged OBRC had unnecessarily interfered with her "life style."

The OBRC people blasted everywhere in sight. There was extensive local and *statewide* radio, television, and newspaper coverage of the controversy. The *Minneapolis Tribune* carried a front-page lead story by Peg Meier, headlined "Passions Stirred in Faribault over Death of Recluse." The entire article is given below.

> Faribault, Minn.: Florence Hendricks lived alone in a tiny house on Faribault's Wilson Ave. She paid $35 a month rent for the house, which has no running water. There's a hand pump (broken since last winter and fixed by a neighbor only a few weeks ago), an outhouse in the backyard and a gas stove.
>
> A neighbor said Miss Hendricks "wasn't too clean for years." The litter was piled high; the stench so strong that people said they noticed it a dozen feet from the house, and the mice so unafraid of people that they scampered over human toes in broad daylight.
>
> But Miss Hendricks—69 years old and about 300 pounds—was content with her environment, her neighbors say. She didn't complain. She rarely talked with people, except for a few neighbors and merchants. She'd been alone since her sister died two years ago. Her only social activity was mass on Sunday mornings.
>
> A month ago, her situation began to grow worse.
>
> She became more and more confused. She didn't clean herself. She used a bucket inside the house as a toilet.
>
> And while a welfare-rights group and government officials bat-

tled over what should be done for her, she died, apparently of a heart attack.

Now some people in Faribault are smoldering.

"What happened to Florence Hendricks is wrong," said an outraged Phyllis Hanson of the welfare-rights organization Friday. "It's time to see what we're doing about this nation's poor. Every official we contacted was either out of town or said it wasn't his responsibility. It's come to the point where people are afraid of touching their neighbors because they might get sued. Everybody needs somebody else's approval."

Miss Hendricks's case drew attention when the manager of a snack bar called the county welfare department. He said his customers were complaining that she smelled bad when she came into the store. A case-worker and a county homemaker were sent to visit her June 5. They knew of her; she'd been on welfare for years.

About the same time, she was running short of food. The county had stopped its food commodity program in May and had switched to a food stamp program. To Miss Hendricks, this meant "the nice lady with the groceries" stopped coming once a month, neighbors say. She apparently never applied for food stamps. Neighbors were bringing in food.

One of the neighbors was getting more and more concerned. She called the Organization for a Better Rice County (OBRC), the welfare-rights group, and asked what could be done.

Mrs. Hanson and Patti Fritz, both of whom volunteer more than 40 hours a week to the OBRC, went to see Miss Hendricks. They found her trying to crawl into her house through a window because she'd forgotten where the door was. They calmed her and told her they'd be her friends.

Then they started telephoning officials to find medical attention and better housing for her. They contacted, or tried to contact, the mayor, city attorney, assistant city attorney, city councilmen, district court judge, probate judge, building inspector, county welfare officials, state welfare officials, health officials, public health nurse, Miss Hendricks's priest, the county chairman of the DFL.

We turned over every rock we could to find help for this woman," Mrs. Hanson said. "We got the royal runaround."

Many officials were out of town, she said, and most of the rest said there was nothing they could do.

The priest, the Rev. John T. Brown, meanwhile persuaded Miss Hendricks to let him drive her to a Faribault hospital. She was diabetic, trembling and covered with sores and filth. And while the battle raged in Faribault about her, she died Sunday night.

"At least she died between clean sheets," said Therese Van Zuilen, president of the OBRC.

Chester Pearson, director of the Rice County Welfare Department, said yesterday that he hadn't regarded Miss Hendricks's condition last week as an emergency and "it's still my opinion there was no emergency. I can't see the problem except that they (the OBRC people) are out for publicity."

The two welfare department employees who called on Miss Hendricks June 5 reported to him that she was lucid, reasonably healthy and "definitely not a problem," Pearson said.

The caseworker asked her if she'd like to be taken to a doctor, but she refused, Pearson said. He said that at no time did the OBRC people say she had a health problem. Rather, they talked of her seclusion and eccentricity.

(Mrs. Hanson disagreed. She said yesterday she repeatedly told welfare department officials that Miss Hendricks had no food or water and that her health was in danger.)

Pearson also said that after the OBRC had called his office several times, he arranged to have three people—the caseworker, an investigator and the public health nurse—see her last Friday. But when they got to her house, they learned from the neighbors that Father Brown had taken her to the hospital the night before.

Mayor Robert Larson said he thinks the OBRC was "trying to do the right thing" but was a "contributing factor to her getting awfully excited." Some people in Faribault have been saying that the OBRC's "interference" and "busy-bodyness" brought on Miss Hendricks's heart attack, but the mayor said he is "not necessarily" of that view.

The mayor's first reaction, when he heard of the Hendricks case, was that the rescue squad could take her to the hospital. But he learned that would be illegal unless she asked to be taken there or there was a court order, he said. The county attorney advised him the city had no legal right to take action.

Miss Hendricks's landlady, Mrs. Ted Dreissen of Faribault, said of the two Hendricks sisters, "They wanted to live that way. They wanted to be left alone. They didn't have much money. Rent was cheap. They had a pump and they had soap. There's no excuse for being dirty if they had soap and water. . . . We had nine kids in our family. We didn't have no bathtub or nothing and we were raised clean.''

To Mrs. Hanson and the OBRC, the case of Florence Hendricks is a prime example of how the welfare system fails.

"We're disgusted with the OEO programs and all the other programs," she said. "We the people are going to change things. We're not going to let the big shots on top write federal programs that don't help the people. And we're not going to let local officials pass the buck."

Miss Hendricks's kind of poverty is not uncommon in Rice County, Mrs. Hanson said. Rural poverty—less visible than its concentrated urban counterpart—is nonetheless the cruel reality in Rice County. More than 13 percent of all families have incomes of less the $4,500, the 1970 census showed. And 40 percent of all residents' incomes fall below the poverty line as defined by the Social Security Administration.

About a dozen people showed up for Miss Hendricks's wake Tuesday night. Mrs. Hanson put a rose in her hand.

"We figured it was time she had a flower." [*Minneapolis Tribune*, July 6, 1974]

The *Faribault Daily News* quickly came to the rescue of local government with the following editorial:

A Personal Choice

The death June 30 of Florence Hendricks was a tragic event, as all deaths are.

But we can't agree with those in Faribault who say local government officials should have stepped in to force Miss Hendricks to obtain medical assistance. Our laws don't—and shouldn't—allow such an obtuse invasion of privacy.

Miss Hendricks spent most of her life as a recluse, living alone for the last two years in a house on Wilson Avenue with a gas stove, a hand-operated water pump, an outdoor toilet and no bathtub or shower. But friends and neighbors say she apparently was content with her life-style.

It was her apparent contentment that frustrated members of Organization for a Better Rice County (OBRC) who tried to get local government to step in.

Local officials, in our opinion, did everything within their power to help. A caseworker from the Rice County Welfare Department visited Miss Hendricks last month, explaining to her that she was eligible for help in maintaining her home and for food stamps. But Miss Hendricks refused help.

Last week, Miss Hendricks's physical condition had deteriorated considerably. She was told that she was eligible for medical help, but again she refused. Father John Brown of Sacred Heart Church convinced Miss Hendricks to go with him to Rice County District One Hospital on June 27, where doctors found that she had large sores on her body and that she was extremely overweight. But still she refused medical aid.

She died June 30 of a heart attack, probably caused by diabetes and obesity.

Miss Hendricks's story is a plaintive, frustrating one. But her story is also one of self-determination, of a human being who was given a choice between life and death and chose the latter.

Miss Hendricks's friends and would-be helpers apparently are angry that someone didn't make the choice for her. But the laws governing commitment of a person to a hospital or institution wouldn't allow that. What's more, the law is right: a sane person ought to be allowed to decide for himself whether he should be institutionalized. [July 8, 1974]

Tuesday, July 9, the county paper carried a brief article:

Welfare Department Actions in Hendricks Case Backed

The Rice County Welfare Board supported the actions taken by the Welfare Department staff in the case of Florence Hendricks at its meeting Tuesday morning.

Miss Hendricks died June 30 of a cardiac arrest. Organization for a Better Rice County had charged that she was neglected by government agencies.

Martin Hachfelt, who was elected vice chairman of the board today, said, "The board concurs that the department acted correctly (in the case), that they didn't encroach on her individual rights while trying to meet her needs."

Chester Pearson, department director, commented, "Situations like this should be left to the professional people who have the legal responsibility to get involved."

What started out as an angry attack on local officials became

a major local and statewide controversy. OBRC put local officials—county commissioners, city councilmen, welfare heads,
judges, building inspectors, and doctors—under tremendous pressure. They did not like the widespread publicity and scrutiny.

At this point, Phyllis Hanson merged the Florence Hendricks
controversy with the dial-a-bus issue. OBRC wrote the following
letter to the *Faribault Daily News*, linking Florence Hendricks's
death with the need for senior citizen public transportation.

> It is unfortunate that the death, and the facts surrounding the
> death, of Mrs. Florence Hendricks has resulted in bickering over
> blame and defensive behavior on the part of Rice County officials
> involved.
>
> Organization for a Better Rice County (OBRC) expresses sin-
> cere hope that the case of Florence Hendricks will point us toward
> the improvement of social services for those in need of help in
> Rice County.
>
> A county in which over one-quarter of the senior citizens sub-
> sist on incomes below the government's poverty level is one which
> needs immediate attention. OBRC Action Council views the Flor-
> ence Hendricks tragedy as one which highlights county needs for:
> 1) adequate low-cost housing; 2) an extensive outreach program
> for food stamps, so that the Welfare Department can serve all cit-
> izens in need of food assistance; and 3) an improved medical-
> health program for all economically disadvantaged people. A trans-
> portation facility such as the Dial-A-Bus, which is currently pro-
> posed by OBRC, would be one step toward assisting senior
> citizens in their efforts to obtain medical aid when they are am-
> bulatory.

The Faribault City Council had twice rejected the OBRC dial-
a-bus proposal, and Isabelle Goodwin and Phyllis Hanson were
organizing people for one final confrontation before the August
deadline to apply for state funds expired. The *Minneapolis Tribune* again came down to Faribault to cover OBRC—to write
about the dial-a-bus campaign. Part of the reason for this extra-
ordinary publicity, I think, was that *Tribune* reporters who had
covered OBRC over the past year had become quite committed
to OBRC people. The following feature article appeared in the
Minneapolis Tribune:

Dial-a-Bus Program Is Issue in Faribault
By Warren Wolfe, Staff Writer

Faribault, Minn.: The Golden Agers and a human-rights group say a special bus system is needed in Faribault to help hundreds of elderly and infirm residents, especially now that the city bus is at least temporarily out of business.

The City Council says it's not so sure that all that many people really need it.

The result may be a packed house when the council meets next week.

"They won't believe us when we show them a list of names," said Patti Fritz, one of a dozen human-rights advocates in the Organization for a Better Rice County, "so we're going to let them see a few hundred bodies and see if the council still thinks they don't exist."

At issue is whether the city should provide about $5,000, to be matched by about $20,000 in federal or state funds, for a Dial-a-Bus program, in which a bus may be summoned to a subscriber's door for a ride to go shopping, see a doctor, visit a friend or whatever.

It isn't for themselves so much, officers of the Faribault Area Golden Age Club said last week as they interrupted discussion of this week's cruise on the St. Croix River and turned to plans for the specialized bus service.

"A lot of us have cars. We can get around pretty well," said President William H. Dittes, 79, a former school superintendent. "It's the older folks and the ones who aren't too well that we're thinking about."

The alliance between the Golden Agers, with 700 members, and the Organization for a Better Rice County, with about 1,000, started shortly after the first of the year when Edward E. Peterson, a Golden Agers board member, learned about a similar program in Mankato.

"There are quite a few towns around the state that offer bus programs for their senior citizens," he said. "So many people don't realize how important a problem transportation is for older people."

Even when the city-subsidized bus service was going last spring, Dittes said, it wasn't much help to the elderly.

"The bus operated when kids were going to school and when they were coming home," he said. "If you were going to the grocery store you could ride there or back, but not both ways. And you had to put up with a lot of yelling kids if you took the bus."

So more people have relied on friends, or paid several dollars for a taxi ride, or paid $1.50 for the taxi driver to ferry groceries from the store to their home, or walked.

"I really became convinced we needed a Dial-a-Bus last winter, when I saw an old couple walking to a store and stopping every four or five steps to rest," said Phyllis Hanson, another rights advocate.

The fight for a bus service, Dittes said, is "showing a few people that the Golden Agers don't just sit around playing cards. Sure, we do a lot with social activities, but that's not all."

The two groups have approached the City Council twice. Both times the council has been unimpressed. And the two groups aren't holding out much hope that the council will change direction this time.

But they do hold an ace and are putting it into play with one hand while the other hand tries to stir the council.

"We want the council to do its job," Mrs. Fritz said, "but if it doesn't we can get the bus service ourselves."

The two groups are forming a cooperative that, because it will include the Golden Agers, can apply directly to the Governor's Council on Aging and to the U.S. Department of Transportation. They've already talked to both agencies and have been encouraged to submit proposals.

"We've already got pledges for most of the $5,000 we'd need for the local share. If the council decides it doesn't want to help senior citizens the cooperative can pick up the ball," she said.

In fact, the five-member committee from both groups that is working on getting the bus service already has decided on a $10,000 bus and has about 200 people signed up for service.

Haggling with the city is a new experience for the Golden Agers, but the Organization for a Better Rice County has been tweaking official noses since it was formed two years ago.

It was started with two VISTA workers, but since they left last year, members say, it's become a stronger organization.

"We had somebody to lean on then," Mrs. Fritz said. "After they left we realized either we took responsibility and worked or we folded. Now we've gotten a lot more people involved."

Involved, in this case, means appealing county welfare decisions to state authorities, filing suits, badgering recalcitrant officials and, in general, "trying to keep government officials honest and responsive."

Sometimes the organization's advocates lead the battle over, for instance, the welfare department's reduction in a woman's benefit payments.

But they also try to train the people in trouble to fight their own battles.

"The greatest feeling in the world is the self-respect you gain when you fight like hell and you win," Mrs. Fritz said. "You realize you really do have some control, some power, over your own life. I know, because I'm a welfare mother and I've done it."

But battles over human rights often leave official feathers ruffled, and the organization has borne the brunt of criticism from officials and other residents who fear the group is too eager to join in battle.

"That's one reason I'm glad we're working with the Golden Agers on the bus issue," Mrs. Fritz said. "Some of them were a little wary of me because I'm a welfare advocate. But they have a better understanding of our problems now, and we have a better feeling for theirs."

Rolf Hammer, a member of both organizations, a former city treasurer and a member of the bus committee, agreed that the two groups understand each other better.

"Shoot, a few years ago I thought all the radicals were on college campuses," he said with a laugh. "Now I've discovered I've been one all these years and never knew it." [July 15, 1974]

I remember this occasion well for two reasons. After Warren Wolfe, who wrote the *Tribune* story, had spent the whole day interviewing, I got a call from Phyllis Hanson. She wanted to talk about his interviews with OBRC people. I asked her how the interviews turned out. She thought very well but was confused by a few questions Warren Wolfe asked. She wanted to know "if OBRC was an Alinsky organization." He had asked her this question, and she wanted to know what he meant. I told her about Saul Alinsky's work and mentioned a couple of his books. Phyllis said she wanted to read his books because Warren Wolfe said OBRC was an Alinsky organization and she wanted to find out more about Alinsky's ideas. She and Franie Dwyer subsequently read Alinsky and any other article-book they found on community organizing.

This personal story is significant in terms of what it says about the development of OBRC. OBRC activists, including Phyllis Hanson, the chief organizer, were not polished organizers. It was a bottom-up organization, and life experience had taught them about the need for people to band together, fight, and build power.

The second reason I remember this *Tribune* article is because of its impact on Patti Fritz. The newspaper reporter confused Patti Fritz and Phyllis Hanson in the pictures and quotes. Consequently, it was Patti Fritz who was quoted as saying, "The greatest feeling in the world is the self-respect you gain when you fight like hell and you win. You realize you really do have some control, some power, over your own life. I know, because I'm a welfare mother and I've done it." As a result of this article, Patti became mistakenly identified as a welfare mother in the community. Patti told me that up until this time she had always resented welfare recipients. She and her husband, both working full time, were barely able to get by and resented welfare payments. Once identified as a welfare mother, she got a real feel for what it was like being on welfare. This experience changed her views about welfare mothers and gave her a clearer understanding of their plight. It helped make her one of OBRC's most effective organizers.

The dial-a-bus battle continued until August. Throughout June and July the pressure was building. The town had received statewide publicity. OBRC followed up Florence Hendricks's death with a challenge to the city council to deliver for senior citizens. The organization hammered away at the theme of a town with no pity. The organization's activities and the summer-months publicity were a real threat to small-town boosterism.

The city council reacted to the pressure cautiously. They formed a subcommittee on the dial-a-bus, but they made no commitment to provide local funding for the program. They seemed determined not to give in to irresponsible OBRC pressure tactics. By late July, Isabelle Goodwin and Phyllis Hanson feared the subcommittee was going to sit on the proposal and not meet the state deadline for funding. With the help of Dave Knotts, a seasoned and talented political organizer who worked in Minneapolis and St. Paul but had a strong interest in OBRC, they developed a two-week strategy to force the city council to take positive action.[2]

OBRC demanded the city council put the dial-a-bus proposal on its agenda at the next July meeting. During the two weeks preceding the council meeting, OBRC delegations visited or called each member of the city council to urge approval of the proposal. Particular attention was paid to Harley Pettipiece, chairman of the dial-a-bus subcommittee. The delegations included OBRC people and Golden Agers. OBRC urged the councilmen in these private negotiations to vote for the dial-a-bus so there would be no more bad publicity for the town. Reminding councilmen the *Minneapolis Tribune* would be down to cover the meeting, OBRC people told them they, like the councilmen, wanted no more "outside publicity," especially bad publicity, but were determined to see a dial-a-bus for Faribault citizens. The leverage was OBRC's proven ability to generate widespread publicity, especially *Minneapolis Tribune* coverage, and the people used this leverage masterfully.

The negotiations were complemented by some interesting organizing tactics. OBRC passed out tickets in town for a drawing for a small toy bus to take place at City Hall the night of the council meeting. A senior-citizen rally was planned in front of City Hall, after which the drawing would be held.

A bad thunderstorm canceled the outdoor rally and discouraged attendance, but downstairs City Hall was crowded with senior citizens and other OBRC activists. As the councilmen came out of their caucus to go upstairs to the council chambers they had to walk through the large crowd. They were irate. For months, OBRC had put pressure on them for the dial-a-bus. Now the organization had sponsored a free drawing at City Hall and the building was jammed full of people; not respectable businessmen or professionals, but OBRC poor people. As Harley Pettipiece walked by Phyllis Hanson, she presented him with a toy dial-a-bus, painted bright red and especially made for the occasion. Everyone in the crowd started singing "For He's a Jolly Good Fellow" after Pettipiece was presented with the bus. Local officials were confused and disoriented by the bizarre tactics; OBRC people were having a wonderful time. They followed the city councilmen upstairs to the chambers.

The small meeting room was packed with people. The mayor opened the meeting, covered by the *Minneapolis Tribune* and local paper, with an uneasy statement about how pleased he and the council were to see such strong citizen interest. The council then proceeded to take up the dial-a-bus proposal. Harley Petti-piece rose to present his subcommittee's recommendation. Everyone knew his recommendation would be the council's decision, since they had all caucused (in violation of Minnesota's open-meeting law) several times before the meeting. Pettipiece stated that the town needed the dial-a-bus and recommended the city council grant the required matching funds and submit a proposal for state funding. The mayor and the other five councilmen voted unanimously for the dial-a-bus proposal. There was wild applause and shouting in the room. It was a tremendous victory for OBRC. One year ago, the Faribault council had shown no interest in a senior citizen's request to use revenue-sharing money for public transportation. In fact, the council had made old people wait almost three hours before they would even consider the question on their agenda and the mayor had concluded this affair by lecturing to them about expecting government subsidization. The balance of power had shifted in the past year.

The *Faribault Daily News* carried a story the next day on the council meeting, with the headline, "OBRC Actions Criticized: Dial-a-Bus Is Given Go-Ahead." The article read, in part:

> To citizens applause, Faribault city councilmen approved the first application for state funds to aid financing of a Dial-A-Bus program, but the applause died when the council made it clear they didn't approve of OBRC's actions in the affair. . . .
>
> Applause followed, but was halted with Mayor Robert Larson's chastising of OBRC. . . .
>
> "I ask you, in the future, not to make a farce of the city council meetings by passing out tickets for free drawings," Larson reprimanded. "It's totally disgraceful."
>
> Larson went on, "People of Faribault—you're being led by the nose by OBRC. You may think they're doing a great cause for you, but actually they're just seeking publicity and trying to make a name for themselves." [July 24, 1974]

The *Minneapolis Tribune* also carried a story on the council meeting, where Mayor Larson again expressed the feeling of the power structure in Rice County toward the Organization for a Better Rice County:

Faribault To Seek State Grant For Dial-a-Bus Project
By Warren Wolfe, Staff Writer

Faribault, Minn.: The Faribault City Council Tuesday night voted to seek state aid for a specialized city bus service that would serve largely the elderly and handicapped.

But the applause from about 50 supporters in the council chamber hardly had ended before the mayor and a councilman chastised one of the sponsoring groups and warned that the bus project could be jeopardized by further publicity activities.

The Organization for a Better Rice County (OBRC) is "trying to tweak your nose" by making believe it is supporting the bus issue for the good of Faribault people, said Mayor Robert C. Larson.

"Nothing could be further from the truth," he said. They're just "seeking publicity and getting a name for themselves."

The conflict goes much deeper than the bus issue, the mayor said yesterday: "They're on the backs of a lot of government agencies. If you go too fast they say you're cramming something down their throats: if you go too slow they say you're dragging your feet. I think they get frustrated by that and that's why they do some of the dumb things they do."

What piqued the mayor's anger Tuesday was that OBRC—an activist human rights group whose volunteers often champion persons in conflict with governmental groups—handed out tickets for a free drawing held that night at city hall. The prize was a replica of a bus that may haul the people in Faribault.

OBRC members said it was a way to publicize the Tuesday council meeting and inform people; the mayor said it was a disgrace and "made a public farce" of the meeting.

However, Councilman Harley J. Pettipiece, who has been critical of OBRC in the past, said yesterday that he disagreed wth the mayor's view that OBRC is not serious about the bus issue. He said he'll continue to work for the bus project.

A committee Pettipiece appointed about a month ago had been working on the bus proposal, he said, though he noted that the four members, including one from OBRC, had "communication problems" about what was accomplished.

"But it's the council's baby now," he said. "We've opened the door and we see that a significant number of people are interested. We'll see what we can do."

The council is seeking a state public-transit demonstration program grant of about $15,000, to be used with the city's $5,000, to set up a dial-a-bus project in which participants may call for the bus to take them to their destinations.

OBRC approached the council in January on the matter. After a number of appearances the group felt the council would not act. So OBRC joined forces with the Golden Age Club, formed a bus committee and was on the verge of applying for funds through other governmental sources when the council acted Tuesday.

That bus committee has secured more than 200 membership pledges and done preliminary work on bus routes, costs, and sources of funding.

Pettipiece said the city will consult with the committee to prove to state officials that there is a need for the bus service.
[July 25, 1974]

Now, with the council reversing itself and deciding to support public transportation to meet senior-citizen needs, the mayor was voicing his anger at the pressure OBRC had brought to bear on him and other city and county officials. More importantly, the mayor showed his frustration at not being able to change the new facts of life in Rice County, Minnesota. The balance of power had altered dramatically. New "community leaders" were emerging. And poor people were having a say about decisions that affected their lives.

Phyllis Hanson

I had this interview with Phyllis Hanson the morning of December 19, 1974. It took three weeks to finally nail down a time when we could talk. She was very tired and kind of discouraged at this time about OBRC. In the two months following the third convention, OBRC experienced serious internal strife and fared badly on a few issues. Although I was no longer active in OBRC, Phyllis knew I was, at this time, quite critical of her work. The interview was very tense.*

*There was a time gap here, which is a bit confusing. My interviews with OBRC people took place several months after the events chronicled in

I could have interviewed Phyllis again—we have worked very closely over the past two years—but I decided to let the interview stand. She always works overtime and has her moods of optimism and pessimism. This interview reflects the latter mood.

Preceding the interview is a brief statement she made to me in the summer of 1974, which summarizes her organizing philosophy.

> It takes time to gain knowledge from books and papers. The rolling wheels of poverty do not allow us this time. Knowledge is the only way to bring social change to the poor peacefully. If we split this learning time, and pass it one to another, we will have change. We will demand it once we know how to demand it. Our fear leaves us as we grow in knowledge and numbers. We are respected because we stand for a just cause, and we have regained our self-respect. [August 1974]

Jerry is pretty upset. They smashed the windows out of his car. He lives in the country. There is not much you can do to convince Jerry now.* I can't get my window fixed. Trying every place in town, I can't get anybody out to do it. I hope they're all busy—that that is what it is. I am getting pretty paranoid.†

Can you tell me a little bit about your background?

I was born in northern Minnesota, in Bagley, Minnesota. Mom and Dad moved from there when I was about four months old. They were broke, completely broke, destitute. At that time my father was farming on my great-grandfather's farm as a share-cropper. Mom and Dad were so broke at this time that they

---

this chapter. The next chapter deals with the above-mentioned problems.
*Jerry Kern, president of OBRC at the time of this writing, was formally charged with fraud by the welfare department a few days after the third annual convention and became an infamous-famous figure in Faribault.
†Phyllis often received threatening phone calls; after one such call a brick was thrown through the front window.

split up. When I was a baby, Mom went back to her folks. They had one baby after another—that was bad business. There were three of us then—twenty months between my oldest brother and sister and seventeen months between Florence and I. Then we moved to Springfield, Minnesota, on another farm. My dad farmed with horses. It was bad news. There was very little furniture in the house, and I remember it being cold. I remember having to bring in the wood, carrying in the water. But everyone was broke. Heck, I can remember being taken to school—all thirteen of us in the whole school—getting a ride on the horses. These were the years 1946 and 1947 when I was in first and second grade.

Dad wasn't making any money. That was sandy land down there. Dad was sharecropping on one-third and two-thirds. So we moved to Hector, Minnesota. Dad made a mistake; he made a verbal contract on a farm. In a year we were out of there. But we had electricity that year for the first time. I remember that. I was fascinated. I could not get over how you could turn on a light. Then we moved to my uncle's farm for about a year, and then my dad rented with cash there where I grew up. We were the same as our neighbors. I knew we were poor. Everybody else was, too. It didn't make any difference. You weren't different. You didn't stick out.

I got married young—very young. I was seventeen.

When I was fourteen I was in a car accident, and that was kind of bad news. I was smashed up pretty bad, and they did not know whether I would live or not. I was in and out of hospitals for that first year. It took them five years to put the pieces back together. I went back to school my sophomore year in a wheelchair—two or three months late. I have petit mal now but no more grand mals. They could not control it in high school. I was the type of person before the accident—and I am not saying this to brag—who did very well in school. I read by memory—never had to study. I had to go to a parochial school, and we had to do all this memory work. I was going to the Missouri Synod Lutheran. I remember reciting out of the Bible chapters. I can remember reciting Isaiah 53 and Isaiah 55. It was beautiful. It was good training. So when I got into high school it was nothing. Then I went back into my sophomore year after the accident, and I did not know what to do. I was stuck. I mean, I could not retain anything. I was shocked out. I tried to study and it was gone. It finally got so bad Dad and Mom and the minister tried to get me to quit school, and the teachers did, but I would not give up. It was so bad I was failing everything, dropping one subject after another until I was down to three. In speech I would carry around an object all day long, and I would get up and talk about that object. For social studies I would copy word for word in the chapter rather than reading it. I would write it out on paper, and that is how I started coming back. But I was in and out of the hospital and that bummed me out, and having seizures all the time. But I had some wonderful friends, and when I started going out they would haul me in to the doctor's office. Heck, it was the kids who hauled me in to the doctor's office because the teachers would panic and half-kill you, and my friends would help. My mom and dad thought I was crazy. They thought I was done. One of the reasons I got away from home was my mother told me I should be glad if someone would marry me so she and Dad would not have to take care of me for the rest of their lives because I was an invalid and never would be able to hold down a job. I would never be able to take care of myself. Then the doctors told me the same thing. I dropped out of school and left home.

I got married and went to St. Paul. I got a job. And that blew everybody's mind. It blew my husband's mind. I decided I wanted to start all over again and be alone. My parents tried to have me committed because I wanted a divorce. I could not get them to sign. So I went into the woodwork for six months and nobody could find me. I met a lot of interesting people then—sort of lived in the streets on and off. I was eighteen at the time. When the papers were drawn up to commit me, I went back to St. Paul with my husband. He enlisted in the service. We moved to Georgia. In Georgia I ended up in jail—for possession of a stolen car and stolen weapon. My husband was very perturbed at me. It wasn't very good. You can imagine, six months. He wouldn't give me any money and I was starving to death. The stubborn pride. Like hell I would go home after what they did to me. So I got a job. Had a boss you would not believe. Used his car and cleaned out the cash register. Went up through South Carolina and North Carolina. There were cops all over the place. I was doing fine until I loused up on the medication. I got panicking because I was going to have a seizure. I started taking the medication and then I said the hell with it and took the whole bottle. Evidently I went down screaming because I ended up being in an ambulance—then a hospital—then a jail. From there I had to talk my way out of that. I got my bail dropped from $10,000 to $1,000. I was in jail about a week. The day I was out on a $1,000 bail I packed my suitcase and hitched a ride to Atlanta and caught a plane for home. Paul was being transferred in the meantime to El Paso, Texas. Went to Texas for awhile, then in Germany for two years. Those were the good years of our marriage. It wasn't that fantastic, but it was the best years we had. Had my first baby in Germany. Had two children by my first marriage.

We got back to the states. I came back before he did. Stayed with friends in Rosemont [Minnesota]. Paul had a grand dream of great big fun and games, you know. I more or less put the screws to that. We bought a beautiful split-level house in Rosemont. Paul was in his social circle and I could not hack that— too many swingers. I got a legal separation and finally a divorce. All my relatives disowned me. I went to work for Control Data and started to put my life together. And when I was just about even keel along came Melanie and Rusty and the whole bunch. And after he met me he never went home. It was tragic. He asked me to marry him after he knew me for ten days. We lost everything. Rusty was in debt like you would not believe. And so we moved to Cannon Falls. We sunk financially. We were close to starving to death. The kids were nine, five, five, and three then. We got Paulie later. Rusty finally filed bankruptcy. We moved to Faribault to start all over again. He got a job at the dairy at two dollars an hour, and I went back to work. We moved to Faribault in 1969.

After child-support money stopped and we got Paulie—that is, when I went to the welfare department and got offered marriage counseling and this type of thing when I asked for assistance. This was in 1970. They would not give me anything and gave me a real bad time that you would not believe. Finally, they said I could have commodities, and that is where I met Therese and that is where I saw the forms for Headstart. I worked nights as a hospital aide and sent Paulie to Headstart for part of the day. I was elected secretary of Headstart; Therese was president. It was quite a gang. The parents rewrote the budget and shoved it down the CAC's throat.

Somewhere in that mess I went on to days. I went to psych-tech class at the vocational school. Took my test and finished. I met Gene McDermott there. He runs the school. He is still offering me a college education. I tell him he is just trying to get me out of the community.

At Headstart Therese is beginning to talk about this OBRC. And I am saying to Therese, "I have had enough of that stuff—I have got all I can do—just leave me alone." Therese says it is a good deal—"We can get together and hack some of these problems." I said, "When I finish work I'll look into it." I went to a few meetings on and off—welfare rights—I was still burned because they gave me such a rotten time when I went in. I became involved in the second convention. Dudley told me to nominate

Elgie, and of course she gets up and nominates me. All of a sudden, there we are. I went out to get a cigarette while she nominated me. We had met each other once before—when we made that film that summer—that's when I really came in—that's when I met you people.

I started December a year ago. I went on stepfather grant. I quit work. I went down for stepfather grant. I took an advocate with me—Marylis. I was determined to get welfare. I gave them a bad time. Mr. Pearson came out and said, "You have $77 coming the first of June." I said, "Like hell; I've got $242 coming right now and $121 the first of June." He turned white. He walked back in his office and yelled at the caseworker and she came out and said, "You are right." I said, "I'll take a $150 voucher right now," and went to Bonanza [discount grocery] and spent it.

It is a vendetta and I am not done yet. I went into welfare rights because there are some bastards there who are giving people a rough time and I don't like it. I don't like what they did to me, and I cannot see letting it happen to somebody else. When this one is straightened out, then there are other departments. They should be doing their job. But what they do is put screws to people when they are down and out. And I cannot see that. They feel like they are God. They think they are so goddamn good. I wonder where the money goes. There is a little hierarchy down there. They play God to other people.

Now it is a lot different, because I now believe in people. Now I believe the only way people can have a voice is if they get together—especially the little guy. In a town or community like this, you have certain power structure—the wealthy people who own the businesses and have people strung along who they are employing. These people are getting knocked down all the time. They barely earn a living wage with the wife working part time. There can't be any family life. Everybody is taking every hour of their time to just keep bread on the table.

How does OBRC help the family that is just getting by?

They can find out about food stamps, what's available; they can find out about medical aid. Like hell we don't help them. They don't know there is medical aid available to them. They just crash to the bottom and got nothing left. There's ways to get those medical bills paid, and there are ways to get food on the table. There is a way to help out those whose income is down. And, by God, if we take advantage of those programs there is going to be attention brought to the problems here. You can cover up things for so long, but if these people start taking advantage of the programs there is going to be some action. If all an industry's employees are on food stamps something is going to happen. It just stands to reason—I am not saying what or how, but you don't think 100 guys aren't going to get together and go and say, "Listen people, we are paying taxes to feed ourselves. Why don't you give us a raise?" This type of thing will happen, but in the meantime their kids don't have to go hungry and they don't have to lose everything they've got and be stigmatized.

Is it accurate to call OBRC a poor people's organization?

What do you call poor? If you call poor not having any power or any voice, we definitely are. If you call poor money-wise, we're not all poor—no. Our membership is in three different categories—senior citizens, welfare, working people.

What do you think are OBRC's main weaknesses?

Well, we've got some real bad ones right now, but that is going to change. First of all, I've been a fish out of water, put in a position I don't like. This position is a director of staff which I am giving back to the action council. I will be director of OBRC or organizer, whatever you want to call me, but I am going back to the people. I will not work out of the office any more. I can get to the people. That is one thing I can do—I can talk to people, and that is what I am going to do. I am going to start to organize. Others can call the shots; I'll find the people. I want to go to the people and talk to them. Organizing is an interlocking, building type of thing where people begin to depend upon one another and they become part—it is something I cannot put into words. In a way, it is selling. You've got a dream, an idea, a plan —you go to the people. I want to move out—we've lost contact with some of our people. Some of our welfare people—all the people I've missed—people who have shown spark and I haven't picked up on it—this is what is going through my mind: faces and people I remember and have got to get back to.

My idea is going out and talking to the people and not telling them a damn thing—I don't tell them, they tell me. And if they've got a problem it goes into the office and we do what we can for them. And then, you take when you come up with twenty problems that are alike and phase it into an issue you start working on. In a way you have to sell yourself when you are out talking to people. They have to like you—that is the selling point. But other than that, it is building confidence. It is saying, "Hell, if I can do it, you can do it. If I can stand up and have something to say, so can you." It is telling them you are a person, an individual; you've been kicked around long enough, the hell with this noise—they can't do that to you. I like you; let's have at them. Who the hell told you that? They don't give us any information —we don't have the right information, but we can get it down at that OBRC office.

We have got to bring different groups of people together. We probably never will get all that together. People will show up on their issues. This is why we have to have all different kinds of issues. We have to have one issue going for each group in the organization. We have to pick issues that interest the welfare mother, working man, and the senior citizen. Maybe in time you'll find one like tax clinics or food stamps that bring them all together. But that is not going to happen that often.

What would you say is OBRC's strength?

It has given back a lot of people their self-confidence. It has given a lot of people a lot of things. Even some who have turned and walked away from the organization angry have walked away a better person because, by God, they are standing up and speaking their piece, and to me that is an accomplishment.

What has OBRC done for you?

Put me $2,000 in debt. It has been a learning experience. I have learned a lot. I have made an awful lot of enemies and I have made an awful lot of friends. It is constantly changing and is never boring. I hate the internal conflict in this type of organization. It is very exhausting—but I think I have the answer now. My personal goal is to see where the core group is 300 people. We'll build to 2,000. Then in Mower County I want to build to a hard core of 50 people. I would also like to see organizing in Goodhue County so people don't get kicked so bad.

Patti Fritz

Patti Fritz was the resident cynic in/about OBRC. She often complained she did not know what she was doing in an organization like OBRC. She insisted she did not like most of the people in the organization. Yet Patti was a brilliant organizer. She knew how to talk with people, especially senior citizens. Most important, she was very careful about strategy. Patti gave real stability to the organization.

I am a troubleshooter; my role is always being the troubleshooter. And, you know, only Jim [her husband] and I realize this. I don't think anybody else really understands. You see, many times when we are talking about people's job descriptions, lots of times, I will get a look like, "What the hell do you really do?" And it is very hard to define. But that is exactly what I am. I am still the little middle-class lady, and that is the way the other staff view me. But I do have the respect of their knowing that they can go only so far with me and that I can become insane.

I have great respect for all them, too. I never liked any of them when I first started.

Way back at Greenvale I first got involved with OBRC. A welfare mother told me about this organization and something about rent credits. While I was living at Greenvale I think I was trying to start my own organization right there by myself because I felt discriminated against. I moved in and Jim was on the road trucking and I did not like the manager right off the bat. I view myself as the Joan of Arc of tenants rights. It started over there when he started telling me about all those "goddamn Catholic kids" and how rotten they were. Greenvale was built through the Archdiocese of St. Paul. I had to pay the full market-value rent to get in, but I was then poor and couldn't pay the money. I could have gotten the money, but it was the principle of the thing. All my married life I had been bailed out, and I just decided it was not too bad living over there and not having anything. Anyway, to make a long story short, I didn't pay my rent, so I was evicted by the sheriff. But I wouldn't move. I said I would live in the car with a three-month-old baby and three other small children. I was evicted twice while I was there but never moved anywhere except to my car. Finally, somebody on the board of directors of Greenvale intervened and came up to the apartment and told me I could stay. So a couple of months went by, and I did not pay any rent. Finally, I got my rent lowered because I was destitute. I did not have any money. We had large medical bills. I wrote a letter to the welfare department to apply for general relief. I had never had any contact with the welfare department, and all of a sudden I felt I should get somebody objective to talk to. I was very depressed. Of course, I was always raised on the idea you worked and you make your money work for you—that was my dad's idea. He did very well. I am the oldest kid. I suppose I was rotten. In Northfield I got in a lot of trouble when I was a teenager and had a pretty tough reputation. But now I have completely found myself. Having my own family makes a world of difference. Anyway, I finally graduated from high school in 1962. I went on to nursing school and got an LPN. Then I married eleven years ago.

I married what was supposed to be a rich boy in town but then drove him into bankruptcy. I take all the blame for that. So now I have all these mistakes I have made and the people I have hurt. And I suppose I am doing my penance with OBRC. I would love to take people and sit them down and tell them how they can save themselves a lot of grief.

I am saving that for my own kids. I am selfish—because I am very proud. The only thing I have done really well is to be a good mother. That is the most important thing to me right now.

When we filed bankruptcy, Jim lost his job as salesman for Gopher Shooters. One Friday afternoon at 3:00 P.M. he was called in and fired.

Now we live in Town's Edge which is moderate-income housing [a 236 project]. Our rent is up to full value out there now because of my working. See, you just can't win. But see, I have

learned from my experience with landlords that I have to negotiate with them, that I can't just say I am not paying—because
you get evicted that way.

I became active with OBRC after I moved out to Town's Edge.
The situation there was that there was no heat for about seven
weeks. And I started petitions. I really wanted to drag it out for
the impact because I had ideas of really blowing it out of proportion and getting my rent knocked down again. And I really
had my neighbors going. We joined together one night and had
a big meeting. We had the top rental manager from Rochester.
We aired our grievances. A few days before that I called Phyllis
from OBRC and she brought some kid from Carleton over, who
I passed off as a lawyer. See, all these people out there thought
he was a lawyer there and he was going to help us not pay our
rent. But he did not know what my intentions were, and as it
was we got the heat fixed and I got the rent reduced.* The people out there all love me and I love them—we got a good thing
going because we fight the management all the time.

After the meeting I really got into OBRC. I had been an acting council member, but I didn't think too much of OBRC. I
had come to the convention, and I think I always saw the reason
for the organization. And inch by inch I got into it, and I always used to say I was along for the ride and when I didn't like
it I would get off. And now I still feel I could get out.

I have my personal reasons for being with OBRC. This shit

*The "kid from Carleton" was Chuck Palmer, a brilliant young man with a
real competence in tenants' rights work. It would not have been difficult
to pass him off as a lawyer, except that he lacked the arrogance and pre-
tentiousness that all too often characterized most Rice County lawyers.

about putting the power back in the hands of the people—that is ridiculous—because they do have it. They have always had it. They have to be told they have it, to see it, and use it.

OBRC is bringing people together. I am seeing a lot of people. I mean, we all do have something in common. I mean, instead of going to work and then staying home and raising your family, I think we are getting together and seeing there is a way, that we should not let the Dean Purdees of the world [the owner of Gopher Shooters and member of the city council] have everything in the palm of their hands; that we too can do it. And the thing is to get the fear out of little people—I sometimes wonder whether that isn't impossible.

Why are you involved with OBRC?

OBRC is something for me to do. I like the power plays. I love meeting with and negotiating with councilmen. And always a little bit of me is saying this is fun and games, but a lot of me is saying and believing in what I am doing. And it may sound corny —but I suppose the reason I believe in what I am doing is because I believe I am doing the right thing—and helping myself and somebody. I am religious, you know. I don't like to come off as being religious. At the end of the day I always think at least I got that much closer to what God put me down here for. I am only here to get to God. God and I have always had a good working relationship. And he understands me.

I think what OBRC is doing is saying to the Dean Purdees, "You are sinful and you are wrong, you can't treat people like that, we are all equal. You are going to have to pay, if not in this life, then in some other life. So why don't you turn around right now and listen to these people—they have a say, they have just as much right over this town as anybody else." Why keep letting the hierarchy of the town rule it?

I really think OBRC has some clout now. I have a good feeling and bad feeling. I have always had a twofold feeling, and not just as a result of the problems of the past few days. I have always felt OBRC should do more for people. There is a neighbor of mine—she walks all over. She is in her seventies. The other day her purse was stolen—twenty-six dollars. She lives out at Town's Edge. She has no transportation, no money. Now why should she live like that? It is just not right. I would like to see OBRC do more for people like her—not to become a Salvation Army, but I think the public relations would be a lot better if they were to help out, if they were to give a handout now and then and do a little more for people, instead of asking them to give their five bucks for an organization that needs money to go out and organize. I know it takes money in these things. Does that sound Salvation Armyish though?

This town is ripe for organizing. Because your poor people are not your illiterate, ignorant, ghetto dweller (I don't really know if they are that ignorant out East). And poor people, working people, hate their bosses, absolutely hate their bosses. I am talking about generations of hate. If OBRC would generate that hate into something constructive, we would really have something.

I think times are really tough. Take people my age in their thirties. They have one good spurt left in them, and if we can channel that into something constructive they will break those chains that bind them to the power structure. There is much that can be done. People are hurting, including some of the small businessmen. I hoped OBRC would be the workingman's organization and show them, "Let's get together here and accomplish something."

A girl at work asked me last night where I like to work at best —OBRC or St. Lucas.* Definitely OBRC. It is so much more. It is exciting and life. I love it. If I did not have Jim and my family, I think I could really take off on it. But I always have to come back to Jim and my family, and my priorities are with my family first. I would really love to see OBRC grow and find my place in it—to be a back-up—to be there and have my fingers in all the pies, you know. This is my plan.

I am accused of being middle class. We are a real conglomeration of misfits. And because we are, we overlook a lot of eccentricities of each other and laugh about it. I do think we are close to each other. I try not to be close but I can't help it. I try to pad myself for when I might have to leave, to forget them, to erase them, to go back to my own life. I say that, but I know I could never do it.

Isabelle Goodwin

I interviewed Isabelle Goodwin in early December 1974. She is a remarkable woman. She spearheaded the entire dial-a-bus campaign and worked with senior citizens on a broad range of issues.

*A nursing home where Patti Fritz works as a nurse.

When she first became involved with OBRC, I was apprehensive. She openly disliked welfare mothers and was more conservative than most OBRC people. But over the year she became a key leader in OBRC. She gave the Faribault City Council all they could handle. In June 1975 she left Minnesota to go to Colorado in hope that the change in climate would help a very serious arthritic condition. OBRC people say she'll be back, that she won't be able to stay away, or that she'll cause so much trouble they'll kick her out.

When did you first become involved in OBRC?

It was in the fall of 1974 that I started with OBRC. I went to the annual convention, and I was correcting some of the parliamentary procedure when they looked at me and thought, "Who is this gray-haired lady anyway?" They kinda interested me. I was elected to the action council that night.

I was not in agreement with all their proposals—the welfare advocacy work. Like my standard argument with Phyllis when we go round and round is my parents had a small grocery store and we weren't on welfare. My dad took in like eight dollars a day, and he spent five dollars purchasing bread and milk and commodities to sell. The children across the street were on welfare. Once a month we'd go to the show and they had an extra ten cents for popcorn and we didn't—so welfare wasn't my bag. But I got involved in transportation and several other projects.

For our first meetings with the council on the dial-a-bus, they told us we didn't have enough concrete figures or to get out and get signatures and get more interest. So we did. Finally, we put on this final appeal. Time was running out and they weren't taking any action. So we had a lot of people there and we really

didn't do anything militant. When we presented Harley Pettipiece with the toy bus he took it in the wrong light—he had no
sense of humor. I think he had a mental and unresponsive feeling toward us. Occasionally we come on strong, but we first
make an attempt to come out with our coffee cups and our
soft-spoken voice and approach them, and if they brush us off
then we come on stronger, and if they still refuse to listen then
we come on stronger. It's the only way. I think some of the
people do come on a little strong because I'm basically conservative, but when they don't move you've got to put pressure
on them.

I feel that there has been a great deal of assistance for people
through OBRC. People who are basically told, "Get lost," have
found a place to come to. People listen to them, make contacts,
and because of this fact, the organization has grown in strength
and power and in ability to deal with issues. People are told
how to help themselves, and they are learning. They are not
told, "You are not worthwhile because you don't have the money and we don't have the time."

We have power by approaching people. We have the resources
to have knowledge about issues, and because we can find the
answers, this is the basis of power, and the fact there are people
willing to spend the time to contact lots of people. We now have
some additional financial aid where we can spend money on
phone calls to get help from the Twin Cities or wherever. There
has been a big change here because the people who have been
holding positions at city and county level have for so long failed

to listen to the needs of the people. They don't want to listen. This is changing.

Do you receive any money for your work with OBRC?

No, my financial situation has not improved since joining OBRC. I'm living off my assets and my disability check. This past year I got a seven-dollar and a nine-dollar check from OBRC to buy gas. These are the only two checks I got. Actually, my financial situation has gotten worse. I'm donating my car and gas. I like to see people pull themselves up. I do feel that some of these people who have been under the iron hand of the welfare have gained some of their self-respect back. And I like the work. I'm an Aquarian by nature. I have a great deal of energy and could not because of health reasons divert this energy. I needed something to activate my mind. OBRC was just what I needed. I feel the people have been more than close—because they have received me, and basically, you know, I'm considered an old lady by age standards, but they treat me like I'm their age whether it's social or working.

Can you tell me a little something about your background?

My family moved to Faribault when I was seven, and this has been my home. I'm interested in Faribault. I went through high school and went through nurses' training. I went into the service and got married in the service. My husband was always away from home so I raised the three children. We lived in Faribault. My husband and I were not close, and finally in 1960 we were divorced. I went back to work as an operating-room nurse. I worked full time through 1965, but the work caused a lot of pain in my back. I had degenerative osteoarthritis. So I went into nursing-home supervision and did this for several years. But I didn't get along with the administrators because they kept telling me not to worry about nursing care, just worry about how much it costs; and of course I'm a nurse first and if somebody needs care—well, they're not going to tell me, "You stay out of there and don't give them care; let 'em rot." The administrators would say, "How come you're spending so much time in that room?" I'd say, "Well, that patient needs care." Well, you know it happened once too often, so I had it. So I took a job as a school nurse one day a week—to build up my social security. I cannot work any longer because of what they call degenerative osteoarthritis. I've not been employed since 1971.

Before coming to OBRC, I was active in social organizations which did not demand much except attending a meeting or two a month. I've been an officer with the Disabled American Veterans, and I am a past president of the Eagles Club. But it got to be dealing with the same people all the time, and these same people will argue whether we should have well-done roast beef or rare roast beef, whether we should have roses or carnations— to me, it isn't all that important. Besides, you're not helping people; you're not directly involved. I get direct involvement through OBRC.

What are your personal goals for OBRC?

Well we've gone through the cycles of high and low—but hopefully it will stabilize. We are operating to serve people. We are using the people and personalities we've got and trying to spread the knowledge around. Like I've expressed to you before, if we complete the negotiations and get the dial-a-bus on the streets to serve the people's needs, I'm interested in seeing low-cost housing and congregate dining for senior citizens. I don't want to spread myself too thin, however. I can be involved, but only up to a point—I can't be overinvolved.

Rusty Hanson

One Sunday afternoon Rusty Hanson and I sat in the OBRC office talking about the organization. We never before had had the opportunity to spend several hours together in uninterrupted conversation.

I wanted to interview Rusty because he played a vital role in OBRC. He stayed in the background during public meetings with local officials—perhaps because he was Phyllis's husband—but as a member of the action council, Rusty was a strong leader.

What I am doing here is simply backing up Phyllis because I realize that if both of us were as involved as she is, there would be no personal life of any kind, so it wouldn't work. So I try to stay away from any of the nitty-gritty because that is a thing that has to be all-consuming—you think of nothing else. It is like that guy watching a football game on Sunday, nothing else matters and that is the way it has to be. So in the organization I am a council member, but Phyllis is the driving force—no, not me—I am a background person. I am actually a member in this town of what is the middle class. I have nothing to gain from OBRC immediately—in the future of course I see the real necessity for it, but by the same token, although I have nothing to gain immediately, I know tomorrow I may.

I mean—like, for instance, myself and my wife or Patti Fritz and her husband—he is being wise to the extent he stays out of the office as much as he can. He lets her do her thing and then they talk about it at home, as I am sure Phyllis and I do. But this type of person has to be very forceful, as Phyllis must be, and if you start arguing with her when she is sure of herself her immediate reaction is one to beat you down and get her idea across, which is beautiful, but it can't work of course in a personal relationship, especially if I happen to be feeling the same —then you are going to have bad news. We damn near hit that at first until I realized what the hell was going on. We talk about the organization, but I always back off when I feel myself too involved. Because when you get into strategy, for example, there may be four or five different ways of doing things, and out of the five three will work. So you could actually argue yourself to death over them, and I might be right, and then I go back and say, "See, I was right," so I don't let myself get carried away with it. I do believe that because Phyllis is in the position she is in she can't afford anything other than success. So from that standpoint I like to push and I do, but how it is done does not bother me in the least. Well, it does, but I am careful about it.

I sure do believe OBRC has been fantastic in how far it has come. Why do I consider it to be a success? I guess because actually if the staff can get together and get the council together it is almost unlimitless in what they can do, and in my opinion they have proved it. For instance, now take the Jerry Kerns thing.* A year or two years ago, if an OBRC member got in trouble he might get an hour with a local lawyer who would say, "Tough. Try plea bargaining." Well, now there is Doug Hall. Without OBRC there would not be Doug Hall. Because of Sy we had a better chance, but without the organization we would never have known Sy.† It all ties together. Take the dial-a-bus thing.

Now we may get some static on the thing because we pushed too hard too fast, but again if we hadn't pushed at all, then what? And the fact that we are able to push, and the power that these office people have is beyond belief, beyond what you even realize. For instance, a member is threatened with being turned in to the welfare department. It was a simple matter of calling the person and making a threat and making an offer he could not refuse, and he said, "Well, I will forget it." This shows organization.

I think OBRC is primarily a low and moderate-income organization. OBRC will improve lives; but to improve lives—that is a very slow thing. You can't, in a year and a half, you can't show one person whose life has been improved—that would be pretty hard to do. The government has been trying for so long. Take Jerry Kern—of course, because he belonged to OBRC is why he got into trouble. And how about all the welfare recipients? You are talking about a minority group, more or less, people who would not have any idea about how to protect themselves against the welfare department if not for OBRC.

*This interview took place in late December when the fraud charges against Jerry Kern were on everyone's mind.
†Rusty Hanson refers here to Sy Schuster.

The reaction of people I work with is a type of fear. It is almost like we are troublemakers—they stand back. I understand this attitude. They are not in trouble—they don't need us—so all's we can give them is trouble. It is like the guy with a million dollars. All's he wants is another million, he doesn't care about the guy under him. Outside of rocks through the windows and phone calls, we don't have too much trouble. First of all, Phyllis gets a call one night that she is as good as dead. Then two nights later we get a big rock through the front window. Well, she was not even home so, big deal, it didn't scare her. To me it was a sign of success. I thought, beautiful—we have got some reaction here, great. Of course I hate paying for the window. The kids are primarily unconcerned about the whole thing. Melanie can get pissed off about things she reads in the paper and might gripe to her mother, "Why don't you do something about that?" but otherwise there is no active way they could help. They don't get static from other children in school, I don't think. And none of our children are the type who would come crying to us anyway. Indirectly they might be affected—like detention which other children didn't get. Like I say, my oldest daughter is the type too where in social studies if a teacher comes up with something she thinks is wrong she will tell him so and they will go round and round. The guy says it is law; then she says, "Well, the law is wrong." Like I say, the pressure is a sign of success, and why are you going to let success bother you?

Phyllis worries a lot about it—too much, I think. I tell her to take a load off at home. But sometimes I am concerned. For instance, eight to four is a normal working day. You might have a couple of evenings when you work after supper—that is normal, too—but not night after night, day after day. That does at times get to me.

I see OBRC a lot like a kid who is six feet tall and weighs 130 pounds and is thirteen years old. Too much is expected because we have grown so fast. Like two years ago there was nothing here. Now suddenly they have an office and a staff of six. Sure, they can do wonders, but they cannot whip the world. You got to take one thing at a time. And there are times when they actually try to whip the world. Overall, I would say the biggest weakness is that the actual members are afraid to come forward unless it is something that bothers them personally. For instance, the welfare people will come forward when they have a problem. Two days later you call them up and say, "Well, we got to go to a meeting at the welfare department and raise a little hell—so-and-so is getting a bad time and I think we'll just go down and stage a demonstration." They say, "I cannot get a babysitter." I think that is normal, but the load on the staff is tremendous; they'll have to call 600 people to get the 100 and will be lucky if they get the 100. This goes on three days at a crack, so I can see there is not backing from the membership, but how to get it is another story. As long as you have problems you can solve, you are in business. But a person can't just back off after his problem is solved. Social conscience is just not there.

The most important accomplishment is just having survived and being here and having faced the establishment and having come off at least somewhat better off than before. We have done battle with the commissioners, the council, you name it, and we have never come off a loser, not always a winner either, but never a loser. To me this is fantastic. But people don't always know about this. And people have to see the signs of success before they will join in.

Can you tell me something about your own background?

I was born in Wabasha, Wabasha County—that is real hillbilly country down there. And my parents were raised in the same area. I got a lot of ideas from them. My father is a construction worker, and one of his favorite sayings is, "You can't beat city hall; you can shit on the steps but they are going to make you clean it up anyway." Of course, as a teenage kid, that infuriates you—you start thinking about what you can do about it. Anyways, I joined the service the day I was seventeen. I spent a couple of years in the service. I dropped out of high school in tenth grade. I was active for two years. Then I got out. Got married when I was twenty. Far too young, as it proved out—got a divorce after roughly ten years. I managed a turkey farm for six years. I worked in a gas station for a couple of years. I worked in a dry-cleaning shop for five years. Then I went to work for a bottle-making outfit in Rosemont. Then I come to Faribault— been with Land O Lakes for six years now.

I met Phyllis when I was in Rosemont. That was at the time of my divorce. We make quite a joke of this. My ex-wife decided to take off. So what am I going to do with these children? I have a choice—get a babysitter or get married. So I said, "Why screw around?" So I started looking. I met Phyllis. We actually told each other outright. She said, "I am looking for a man; I need a husband." I said, "I am looking for a wife; let's see what happens." My God, it worked out fine. I give her support for her work but it is not a matter of choice. It is just like your wife, she supports you in what you are doing. But it is not a matter of choice. Because you are good at it, you must do it. You have to do it. The same with Phyllis. She is good at it, she has to do it. It is very rewarding to her and to myself, because I can see her successes make her a better person.

OBRC is still typed as a welfare outfit, and that is bad news when you are trying to bring in the middle class. Communications is a big thing. The welfare people are used as a scapegoat thing. Everybody figures the welfare people are ripping everybody off. But you bring in this guy making $90 to $125 a week, struggling, and have him face this welfare person right here in this office; he is going to find out, she is another person just like myself and maybe she is right—there ain't no jobs for her. There is a communication problem. Take the food stamps thing. I have been through this with guys I work with. I know many of them are eligible but they won't apply because of pride. I use the term *pride*. I am not sure that is the right term. They don't want to bury their soul. I tell them, "Hell, you have been paying taxes all these years. You are just a big sucker." They say, "None of that welfare, I want nothing to do with that." You know, like Kennedy said, "Ask not what your country can do

for you but what you can do for your country." What a bunch
of bullshit! You know that was a real fakey deal in my opinion.
What the hell do you pay taxes for? In other words, we should
all kick in but nobody draws out. What are we kicking in for?
So we can go over to Vietnam and kill a bunch of people—what
the hell?

I see with OBRC a let-down first and then a restructuring. A
let-down because they have gone too far too fast. It is not a thing
you can do anything about. But we need to drop down and
look at it again. We have a new council and staff that have to
learn. The end result is we have to expand. OBRC cannot stand
alone. Actually, any organization that lasts for two years is fantastic. You go into a ghetto—you can find one thing in common
—all you got to do is find that one thing and you are in business.
Now you have worn that one thing out, then you start petering
out. Here there has never been that one big thing—other than of
course when we started out with the welfare. We don't have a
broad base, but we do have a base. I want to see OBRC grow
and interest the low and middle class. I would like to interest
everybody, but you have to start someplace and at the bottom
is the place we've started. Now we have to go up one step from
there—low income, low middle, and up the ladder. But we can't
fail; the word can't be in our vocabulary.

We're advocating for the people. And advocacy is always going to be the base. It doesn't matter whether you are advocating
for you as an individual or the Golden Agers as a group or labor
as a group. Hell, the whole damn thing is actually advocacy, no

matter how you look at it. Well, isn't that right? I mean, that is my opinion. You can call it organizing, call it anything you like. But when you go in to organize a group, you've got to advocate for them to start with. For instance, going down to Austin there, that could be a wingdinger—I am really enthusiastic about that— I got to hear more. We got some people here who could tear that damn welfare department apart. Pat Fritz could make them people stand on their head and bark for her. It is amazing the reaction—all I did was sort of stand back and watch the reactions of people down there. When they went in for that little demonstration, the shit hit the fan.* All's they were doing was passing out pamphlets and of course talking about injustice. And then the county attorney's door is wide open and he is standing there, so in they go. They collared him too. He was simply taken aback. Of course none of them were prepared for this. But the county attorney should know how to deal with this without getting all shook—which he did. Boy, was he shook! And what it did for the people—those poor people who went along; there is another Patti Fritz down there or Phyllis—with a little knowledge and a little boosting, she will really be something.

But OBRC is going to have one hell of a time going up the next rung of the ladder here—the lower-middle and middle class. We've got to hit the middle guy. They have the bucks. And then look at the clout we would have; first, the welfare people—what

---

*In mid-December, Phyllis Hanson and Patti Fritz organized a demonstration against the Mower County Welfare Department. Of particular concern to welfare mothers was the series of "midnight raids" which was part of the county's get-tough campaign against welfare fraud.

it amounts to is a coalition—welfare and the lower income and the middle income. See, the low income thinks the middle income is rich and don't like them as a group like I don't like the rich. It has to be a coalition group.

Phyllis, one night—she was sitting there. She starts looking a little blue and says, "You know, I really do use people, don't I?" And you know, that is what it is all about, isn't it? The welfare people will use the working poor to get what they want, the low income are going to use the welfare people, and they are going to use the next rung. They are all going to have to use one another—everybody has to be used and feel useful, though. That's my theory.

Franie Dwyer

Franie Dwyer is a welfare mother of four children. She lives in a small house in rural Faribault. She was introduced to OBRC through a phone call from Phyllis Hanson. "One Sunday afternoon a gal called me on the phone and started talking to me about how our economic situation was in this country and how bad our government was and, oh, just touched lightly on a lot of subjects. She hit a nerve because there I was. I agreed with her 100%. Why she called me I don't know—whether she called me at random or was trying to solicit new members or what, I don't recall now." She became more involved with OBRC because of her problems with the Rice County Welfare Department. "I went to see these people at OBRC. I knew where their office was and talked to Phyllis Hanson. I asked what could be done and how I could handle this situation. We decided that I was not the only one that was in this boat [harassment by a caseworker]. There were thirteen other girls that were in this boat, and she asked me if I would be willing to come and compile these names and complaints and look in the welfare book what the welfare department was doing fraudulent against these people." Since that time Franie Dwyer has become a brilliant welfare advocate and organizer for OBRC and in September 1975 began working full-time as an organizer in Rice County. This interview took place in July 1975. It was the last interview I conducted for this book.

AFDC or no AFDC, I have been working right along helping myself regardless. I think it is very important for people to do things for themselves and not to depend on others. I have to think this way—right? I would be a damn fool if I didn't. I told Phyllis I will work full-time as an organizer starting in September. I said to her I would try to stay with this until January or early spring before I decided to bail out. If I don't see I am making progress and I don't have more knowledge, I am going to call it quits. I don't think that is wrong, Paul, do you? If I see I am making some significant gains and that I have gained more knowledge and am really helping people, fine, I'll stay at it regardless of the money—because I can get along.

What is your prediction about OBRC for this next year?

Let me first go back a little and tell you what prompted my decision to take this job. I stopped in a place to get gasoline—this was about four weeks ago. It was very hot. And as I was sitting there with a gentleman I know, some other friends of his come over and sat down. I was talking to this guy who said, "You're from Faribault," and I said yes. He went on to tell me he was a social worker and did work for the Rice County Welfare Department at one time, and he told me of the graft and corruption and all the shady things that were going on within the welfare department and how he as an individual kind of tried to do something about it but he didn't want to take it too far because of his family living in that community. I don't know what that had to do with it—whether he was just afraid they would give his family a hassle or what, I don't know. This young man now works for the city of Bloomington; he no longer wants to be a social worker. Well, I don't know—it is an easy way to solve a problem—if it don't work, give up and walk away. I mean, it don't take anything—it takes more courage to say, "I am going to stay in there and try." Anybody can say "I quit" and drop out—you know this with your college students. That is the easy way out. So he was the one that kind of made me change my mind to decide to stay and fight the system. This is at the local level. My prognosis is that we do have good structure and if we can bring stronger individuals into our organization and do take the advice of some of these outside organizers, like forming the block clubs, we can make it work. Why can't we?

How will people respond to your organizing effort?

People will say, "Where have you been; we should have had something like this a long time ago." This is the response I have heard from people when I've talked with them. I don't really think it is going to be that difficult—if you have got an individual who is a good salesman. You have to be a good salesman in order to sell an organization.

Does OBRC have enough people to do the job?

Not at the present time, we don't. You know that as well as I do. We have a few Therese Van Zuilens and Phyllis Hansons, but we need more people who have that strong will and are going to make it work. We need do-or-die people. A lot of our people are fighting to stay alive themselves and this is why they can't be stronger. I think it takes people who have the time or want to really go into it and get paid and work as professionals at it or people who really see something that is really an injustice to them—that has really hit them in their own backyard—before they will get out and do anything. But the majority of the action council people are all working people and really don't have the time to do it.

How do you get the time?

How do I get the time? I take the time because it is something I want to do. And I am in a better position than some of those people. I am not saying this to be a smart aleck. I am saying I am getting along.

What are your reasons for trying out this organizing?

Like I told you, my parents had preached so long against welfare. And when I was a young woman and worked at nights and had small children and could only sleep a couple of hours a day, I really was against welfare. Now that I know all it does is put a roof over your head and a little bit of food in your mouth, I see it differently. I go out and work and they raise my food stamps. The little bit I've gained they take away from me somewhere else. They want to keep me right there and I think that is wrong. Or some of those shady deals like down in Mower County where I've worked. Some of those old people have been paying in social security all their lives and they don't have time to talk to them—and their checks should be higher.

Are you worried about the reaction of the welfare department to your work?

I am not really worried about their reaction to my work. I don't think the welfare department is going to bother me. I've showed them I have no fear of them and they treat me with a lot more respect. Since the time I organized recipients and we marched in to ask for a change of caseworker, they have left me alone, they haven't bothered me. And I have gone in with other people and they don't give me any hassle. And I am not worried about the welfare department at all. I am not doing anything illegal. I am not doing anything wrong. I am just fighting to see people get their fair share.

What do you think is the difference between organizing and the advocacy work you have been doing?

Well, there is a big difference. A majority of people can step in and open up a book and look up the law. The advocacy is learning the law—you then go in and fight hard for that person. Organizing is going out and selling a whole organization, selling an idea, selling a dream, getting people involved and interested, actually hitting them where it hurts worse in order to get them up on their feet and doing something about their problems. People have the attitude, "Well, there really isn't an awful lot I can do about it," and we are going to come along and tell them there is a lot of things they can do about it if they get together and work with some other folks and try—but as an individual they really can't do an awful lot. It is not until they get together and organize that they can get the job done. I can go up to City Hall or the county commissioners and say, "Hey, I want something in my neighborhood," and they are going to ignore me till hell freezes over, but if I brought everybody in my neighborhood they are going to have to listen to us. What choice do they have? If we keep coming back they are going to have to listen. So the difference between advocacy work and organizing is that in organizing you have to be able to deal with an awful lot of people and you have to be able to sell them on the idea that they have to organize to get the job done.

What is your prediction for yourself?

I will not accept money until I know I can do it. Organizing is very demanding. It's not a nine-to-five job you can go home and forget it. It's a lot of evening work, it's a lot of reading, writing, research, and phone calls. It's a real challenge. What I am saying is I will give it a good try and see if I can do it. I hope I can be part of an effort to make this organization go. If my name was never mentioned it would not make any difference to me one way or the other. Some people want a lot of recognition, but as long as I know I am doing a good job I could care less whether the rest of the world knew I was doing a job or not doing a job. Do you follow what I am talking about? As long as I am making the whole thing go—that is what counts.

5

ORGANIZATIONAL PROBLEMS

OBRC in two years had become a controversial and effective protest organization. Using a conflict strategy and engaging in tactics "outside the experience" of Rice County officials, OBRC was able to challenge and change public policy. Nowhere was this clearer than in the area of welfare policy. Legal advocacy work and militant protest activity forced the county welfare department to adhere to the law and treat "clients" with some dignity and respect.

The summer of 1974 saw OBRC make great strides in developing a broader financial base. In late July, Campaign for Human Development (CHD), the social action arm of the Catholic Church, awarded OBRC a $15,000 grant (to start in December) to expand its organizing activity in Rice and surrounding rural counties. The goal of expanding organizing efforts necessitated expenditures well beyond the internal fund-raising capacity of OBRC. The CHD grant gave the organization the needed money. People in the organization were especially proud that OBRC was among the 175 projects chosen for funding from 1,500 applications.

In late August, Heleny Cook from the Youth Project visited Rice County to evaluate Phyllis Hanson and OBRC. The Youth Project was committed to funding promising young people involved in community organizing. Heleny Cook, though only in her early twenties, had several years of organizing experience in the mountains of east Tennessee and was an astute judge of organizing work. She was very impressed with Phyllis Hanson and agreed to fund her, starting in September. This decision was important to OBRC. Phyllis had been working as a volunteer for nine months—seven days a week, fourteen hours a day. She had become OBRC's best organizer. But her own family was in a precarious financial position, and unless funding was forthcoming, she would have to leave OBRC for a paying job. The grant came just at the right time. Moreover, Heleny Cook provided Phyllis Hanson and other OBRC people with invaluable advice and technical assistance as a close working relationship developed between the Youth Project and OBRC.

The organizing victories and grants did not mean, however, that OBRC had become a strong and durable political organization. OBRC was not a cohesive organization. Its membership was put together around constantly changing and different issues. As a result, the organization had grown haphazardly. The challenge was to build a structure into the organization and to organize so that people could rise to leadership positions and act collectively on a broad range of issues.

OBRC approached the third annual convention, to be held in October 1974, as an important step in this direction. Too many people were on the periphery of OBRC. They were members in name only and did not really consider OBRC *their* organization. I often heard people say, *"They* are really trying to do something for senior citizens," or *"They* sure fixed the welfare department." Not *"We're* working with senior citizens," or *"We* sure fixed the welfare department." This was an important dynamic that could not be overlooked, especially after two years of organizing. Hopefully, the convention would bring more people together and directly involve them in the business of the organization.

OBRC was still a small family of fighters. The organization had grown immensely in the past year, but the action council did not reflect this growth.* It no longer represented all the constituency groups in the organization. The convention would give working poor people and working moderate-income people the opportunity to take leadership positions in the organization.

Finally, the convention would be a show of strength, a major political event in Rice County. If all the OBRC members gathered together, they would be more aware and confident of their numbers and power. Moreover, the convention would be an unsettling event for the local power structure.

*There were a little over 500 card-carrying members.

There were some misgivings about the convention. Phyllis Hanson argued that OBRC should have a number of mini-conventions in various small towns and villages throughout the county; that many people would not, or could not, travel all the way to Faribault; that an action council of fifteen elected at the convention would not, in any case, provide people with enough representation and opportunity for direct participation. She wanted to develop within OBRC a decentralized structure of decision making located in various local chapters in the county. Finally, she took the position that the convention would not reflect OBRC's strength and support among low- and moderate-income people. She was pessimistic about interesting various members, who were involved with specific issues, in the convention.

There ensued a debate over the priority that should be given to the convention. The staff of organizers and advocates argued they did not have the time to adequately prepare for a large convention; that people in the community had pressing problems that had to be taken care of; that there were crucial issues to work on. They were opposed to dropping this work and spending several months on a convention. While they believed OBRC should proceed with the annual convention in order to elect new leaders, they were not convinced it was a crucial event.

In late October the convention was held. It produced mixed results. The attendance was disappointing—around 130 people.* Included among the guests was a large delegation of social workers from the county welfare department. Their presence was testimony to their concern about OBRC and the impact made by the organization. Robert Snow, who was elected second vice-president, noted the welfare department presence and introduced a resolution calling for a "full investigation of the Rice County Welfare Department to make sure they live up to the law." There was wild applause as the resolution was unanimously passed. Jerry Kern, elected vice-president, gave a bitter personal account of his experiences with the welfare department in trying to purchase food stamps and urged that OBRC confront the department over its handling of the program. Isabelle Goodwin gave a

*Several days after the convention, OBRC received many calls from people who were disappointed because they had received notice of the convention one or two days after the event (this was especially a problem in rural areas). Even given this problem, however, OBRC should have done better.

fiery speech on the dial-a-bus, urging OBRC people to make sure the city government operated the service so it would benefit "the people."

The resolutions adopted at the convention reflected a broad range of issues. The emphasis was on welfare problems, the dial-a-bus, food and medical costs, employment, and housing. The floor discussion of issues was not sophisticated. People did not have clear documentation of the problems or a clear understanding of how to convert these problems into organizing issues. But they had a clear sense of what their problems were and of what should be the general priorities for OBRC. Participation by poor people characterized the floor proceedings. The agenda was determined not by the organizers but by various committees of OBRC people who had done the work on the issues prior to the convention. The organizers, in any case, were almost entirely volunteer and indigenous to the community.

A strong action council was elected that was broadly representative of the OBRC membership. Listed below are the officers and ten at-large representatives:

President: Pat Sargent, stepfather grant (AFDC), mother of two
Vice-president: Jerry Kern, food stamp recipient, LPN at Faribault State Hospital, father of four
Second vice-president: Bob Snow, seasonal manual laborer (tile layer), father of three
Treasurer: Frances Dwyer, AFDC recipient, mother of four
Gayle Aldrich, AFDC recipient, mother of four; Irene Wood, senior citizen, retired, volunteer; Gordon Forbes, United Church of Christ minister, father of three; Bernice Christensen, AFDC recipient, mother of four; Roger Tralle, auto mechanic and janitor, father of four; Francis Milligan, retired truck driver; Seymour Schuster, professor, father of two; Ruth Johnson, AFDC recipient, mother of four; Clarence Hanson, butter maker, father of five; James Fritz, fireman, father of four.

Several candidates running for local office came to the OBRC convention for support, the most important of whom was Dan Minnick, a small grocer, who was a candidate for the Rice County Board of Commissioners. Minnick was running against a two-term incumbent who was hostile to OBRC and poor people in

Rice County. OBRC people liked him as a grocer and felt he was a decent and fair person. They supported his candidacy for a seat on the county board.

Two weeks after the convention, OBRC delivered a bloc vote of 200 for Dan Minnick. As it turned out, he was elected by a two-to-one margin (1,600–800). OBRC had not delivered the crucial balance-of-power vote as it had done in the smaller school board elections, but Minnick had attended several OBRC social functions throughout the summer and fall culminating in his appearance and talk at the convention, and OBRC people considered his election a real victory.

Shortly after the election, the *Faribault Daily News* carried a feature story on Minnick, headlined, "Minnick: Human Aspect Important." The interview read, in part:

> Welfare is the biggest problem facing Rice County today, says Dan Minnick, fourth district county commissioner-elect. The county definitely needs its welfare program, and it will grow as unemployment increases. We're probably going to have more welfare than most other counties in the state, primarily because wages in Faribault are sub-standard. Some of the wages in town are pathetic. I think something should be done about them, but the county board probably can't do anything about it. I do think the town is under scale quite a bit.
>
> The county is going to be under pressure to keep its budget down. The big thing is, are we going to cut some programs for human need? Now is not the time to cut these programs. The human aspect is the big thing nowadays, instead of pushing them (people) back in the corner and forgetting about them.
>
> The county board must instill some confidence in the accountability of government. People don't care about their taxes so much unless they're way out of line. They just want to know their money is spent wisely.
>
> The welfare is misused is what you hear all the time. I can't believe its misused. One of the main problems is lack of communication between county government and the people. I think we should encourage the system (welfare) to go out and find people in need. [Nov. 12, 1974]

This was not the typical county commissioner talking. OBRC had not been without influence.

Before OBRC could build on the convention, the organization became involved in its most important legal case: the *State of Minnesota* vs. *Gerald Kern.** Jerry was a food stamp recipient. Due to the severe illness (acute rheumatoid arthritis) of his young child, he filed on October 21, 1974 (three days before the OBRC convention), for medical driving allowances which would have meant additional food stamps. At the convention, Kern had made a rather militant public speech about his troubles with the welfare department. Several people overheard some of the caseworkers saying, "We're going to get Kern." One week after the convention they did "get" Kern. His appeal for food stamps was heard and tape-recorded (illegally) by the welfare department on October 31, and on that very day Jerry was told by welfare officials that food stamps were being cut off and that fraud charges were going to be brought against him.

At first, OBRC thought the welfare department was simply trying to scare him, that this was an attempt to silence him. At one time or another over the past two years almost every member of the action council had been threatened with welfare fraud charges. It was a clear case of harassment, but this was nothing new to OBRC people, especially the core activists who were always under the close scrutiny of the welfare department.

Two days later things looked different. Kern received official termination notice of his food stamps. OBRC, recognizing the significance of this case, contacted Paul Onkka, a young attorney with Legal Assistance of Ramsey County (St. Paul). Paul Onkka had grown up in Faribault. Although he was extremely busy with legal assistance work in St. Paul, he was very committed to OBRC and handled important legal problems for the organization. Onkka represented Kern at a hearing before a state welfare officer on November 11.

Gradually, the case of Jerry Kern unfolded in this hearing. First, it was established by Onkka that the food stamps had been cut off illegally. This illegal action was repeated later in the month, and again the intervention of Onkka and Bill Johnson, a local attorney, was required to make the welfare department

---

*This account of the "Jerry Kern case" is largely taken from a brief article written by Sy Schuster for the OBRC newspaper, *Hard Times.* Sy Schuster, though not a lawyer by formal training, acted as counsel for Jerry Kern throughout his ordeal.

conform to the law. Second, it was determined at the hearing that the Rice County Welfare Department had been computing food stamp allowances improperly. Third, and most important, the welfare department announced its investigating officer (the "resource examiner") had turned over "evidence" against Kern to the county attorney and he would be charged with fraud.

It was a vicious affair. On November 14 the charges against Kern were filed by County Attorney James Korman. Korman wanted to send the county sheriff out to Kern's farm to formally arrest him and to make Kern pay bail (money he did not have). Sy Schuster intervened in behalf of Kern and persuaded the county judge to allow him to come in of his own volition and be released from jail on his own recognizance. Jerry Kern had, after all, lived in the county all his life. He was the father of four children, one of whom was very ill. His own father was dying of cancer. It was not likely he was going to "run out of town." The county attorney was well aware of these factors, but Kern had become a pawn in an ugly political fight between the welfare department-county attorney and OBRC.

Jerry Kern was vice-president of OBRC. The retaliatory action by the welfare department was felt throughout the organization. The welfare department had been successful in scaring some poor people away from OBRC. Caseworkers often threatened welfare mothers, telling them in no uncertain terms to stay away from OBRC. Now the OBRC vice-president was formally charged with fraud, a conviction that could possibly send him to prison. If Kern was convicted, it would strike a serious blow to poor people's organizing in Rice County. The future of OBRC was at stake in the Kern trial.

Kern did not have the money to hire his own lawyer. And neither he nor OBRC could take a chance with a court-appointed lawyer. The Rice County Bar Association was hostile to the organization, and there were few county lawyers who could be trusted. Paul Onkka, as a legal aid lawyer, was prohibited from handling criminal cases.* OBRC turned to the Legal Rights Center in Minneapolis. The Legal Rights Center had been set up in the late 1960s as an alternative to the Public Defender's Office. It came out of the Black and Indian communities. Its policy-making board was comprised of "minorities" and poor

*By statute, OEO Legal Services lawyers could handle only civil cases.

people in Minneapolis. Sensitive to the personal plight of Jerry Kern and to the further implications of the case, the board authorized Doug Hall and Jerry Peterson to defend Kern.

Doug Hall was the director of the Legal Rights Center. He was an experienced and highly competent radical lawyer, who had recently represented the American Indian Movement (AIM) along with William Kuntsler and Mark Lane in a trial that received considerable national publicity.

The news spread throughout OBRC that Doug Hall was defending Jerry Kern. When he came down to Rice County for the preliminary hearing and to meet Jerry Kern, the OBRC office was jammed with people. They had come to express their grievances against the welfare department, be in on the strategy, and support Kern. It was interesting to see how well Doug Hall worked with this large participatory delegation of OBRC people.

Doug Hall and Jerry Peterson presented the alternatives to Kern. They told him the welfare department did not have much of a case and they could probably get the charges dropped through private negotiations; that he would not have to wait months for a trial with the charges hanging over his head or take the risks involved with a jury trial; that he would find the legal process frustrating and would not be able to present much of what he and other OBRC people considered evidence against the welfare department.

Everyone waited for Kern's reply. Kern wanted to go to trial. He made a strong, emotional statement that the trial would give OBRC the opportunity to destroy the welfare department-county attorney's credibility; that he wanted, once and for all, to put a stop to the welfare department's harassment of and retaliation against OBRC people, so that no one would have to go through what he had experienced.

The organizers were very pleased. Over the past year, the welfare department had threatened numerous welfare mothers (all OBRC activists) with fraud charges. An OBRC welfare advocate would get on the case, and the charges were always dropped. In half the cases, the AFDC mother became even more committed to the organization. After all, when the welfare department threatened her, OBRC backed her all the way. But the other 50% dropped out of the organization. They felt it was too close a call and they did not want to be under the constant scrutiny of the welfare department. Not only did the welfare department's tactics scare welfare mothers away from the organization but the case-by-case advocacy absorbed a tremendous amount of time and energy. The Kern case would give OBRC the organizing handle to turn the tables on the welfare department and put it on the defensive.

The county attorney had not counted on Jerry Kern obtaining this kind of legal counsel. As the case was proceeding toward a trial date, the defense lawyers attempted to obtain copies of the evidence against their client. Although their request was ruled "proper" by the county judge, the county attorney refused to supply the evidence, meanwhile turning over prosecution of the case to his assistant. Then, on the very day of the hearing on the defense's right to see the evidence, March 3, 1975, all the charges against Kern were dropped.

This was what OBRC feared would happen. The welfare department and county attorney's office wisely backed down from a legal confrontation. They were afraid to deal with Doug Hall in the court, and they feared OBRC would successfully define this as a political trial. The front-page article carried in the *Faribault Daily News* (March 4, 1975) is somewhat revealing:

Welfare Fraud Charges Against OBRC Official Are Dismissed
By David Hest, *Daily News* Staff Writer

Welfare fraud charges against a rural Faribault man who is vice president of a local poor people's rights organization were dismissed Monday amidst accusations the charges were politically motivated.

Four counts of obtaining food stamps illegally were dismissed against Gerald Kern, Rt. 3, by Gary Peterson, assistant county attorney, after he met with Jerod Peterson, Kern's attorney. Kern is vice president of Organization for a Better Rice County (OBRC).

"This is just plain clear-cut harassment," Phyllis Hanson, executive director of OBRC, said Monday after she and several other members learned of the dismissal while waiting for a hearing on the matter in the courthouse.

The charges were politically motivated, she said. "A conviction would have been a killing blow to a grass roots organization," Seymour Schuster, another member, added. Members of the organization and other poor people would have been afraid to apply for welfare for fear welfare fraud charges would have been brought against them, he said.

Assistant County Attorney Peterson and Welfare Director Chester Pearson later denied the political harassment charges.

"I know now what they can do to you," Kern said. "I wouldn't have done what they've done to me. I'm more decent than that. I wouldn't have the guts. I'm not that low."

Kern said the charges were brought against him over a mixup in allowable medical expenses. He said he had been commuting to a Rochester hospital daily to visit a sick child on doctor's orders. "They (welfare department) didn't recognize that I had a sick child," he said.

"They are there to serve the people," he said. "They aren't doing their job. Or they don't have the staff to do it."

Peterson later told a reporter the charges had been dismissed because the state may not have been able to prove its case. "I think there are some serious questions here that the state could prove Gerald Kern guilty beyond a reasonable doubt," he said.

"As far as I'm concerned, there were not political overtones at all," Peterson said. "In my estimation, this is not a political trial. We're not looking beyond a person to his political affiliations. It is unfortunate from anybody's standpoint, when he's brought through the court system."

County Attorney James Korman originally brought the charges, all misdemeanors, against Kern in November. Korman turned the case over to Peterson after his appointment in January to the assistant county attorney's post.

When asked why charges were dropped before the trial, which was scheduled for March 17, Peterson said, "I'm sure the charges were brought in good faith." He said new evidence or other matters may have led to his decision.

"The accusation is totally untrue," Peterson said. "We have no membership list (of OBRC). We don't know who members are."

Bringing welfare fraud charges against anyone is totally up to the county attorney, he said. Only one person has been convicted of welfare fraud in Rice County in the past year, he said.

The outcome was very frustrating for Jerry Kern and many other OBRC people. From late October until early March, Kern lived with the threat of a jail sentence and fine. Newspaper accounts of the charges had damaged his good name. His family, already burdened with medical and financial problems, was under tremendous pressure. He would receive no compensation. There would be no apologies. A lawsuit for libel or harassment would be too difficult and costly. The welfare board-county commissioners-county attorney had not been able to get the conviction which might have been a death blow to OBRC as a grass-roots poor people's organization. But it had been a defensive fight all the way. OBRC never got the chance to organize around the Kern trial. The Kern fight had dominated the OBRC agenda for four months and it had drained people's energies. Very little organization building took place during these months.

Serious internal problems also plagued OBRC for several months after the convention. The Youth Project and Campaign for Human Development funding brought about some unexpected consequences.[1] Real tension surrounded the decision of who among the volunteers was to get funding. The OBRC concept was that the organizers should come from within the community. Thus, OBRC people, the great majority of whom were low-income, were competing for a few paid organizing positions. The case of Phyllis Hanson points to the kinds of problems this created for the organization.

Phyllis received a salary of around $6,000 a year from the Youth Project. I had written the initial letter to the Youth Project about her work. She understood organizing by instinct and was my choice for Youth Project funding. I had worked closely with Phyllis and felt she was the best organizer in OBRC. I was phasing myself out of OBRC and felt she was the logical choice to become chief organizer and director of staff. She was a community person who had come up through the organization, and hopefully she would bring up many other people in the organization as organizers. The idea was that the action council *and the organizing staff* were to be community people.

The concept of organizers coming from within the community was something I pushed very hard in OBRC before leaving in October 1975. But it was a concept that was really fully supported by the OBRC membership. The choice of Phyllis Hanson to direct the staff was supported by the action council but generated real dissension. Other volunteer organizers, some of whom had been with OBRC longer than Phyllis Hanson, were resentful they had not received the funding. A good many of them were AFDC recipients who longed to get out from under the control of the welfare department and were keenly disappointed with the decision.

Phyllis Hanson had been on welfare herself. She had a bottom-up perspective and understood poverty in Rice County. This gave her important advantages over an outside organizer. But it also made her vulnerable to various charges. Some people felt she was out to "rip off" money, gain social status, and build a personal power base. A serious internal split developed which was very exhausting to all involved. Several welfare mothers who had been with OBRC from the start opposed her and took their case to other members. The organization was bogged down in internal fighting. Ultimately, several key OBRC people resigned in protest against her appointment as director. Others stayed on but were suspicious of her.

The Campaign for Human Development funding generated slightly different problems. OBRC used this money to pay several more staff people (there were now two more paid staff in addition to Phyllis Hanson and Elgie Cloutier). As OBRC relied more on paid staff, the organization lost many of its volunteers. OBRC people became less active and depended on the staff to carry on the work of the organization. Before, there had never been any distinction between staff and rank-and-file membership. Now, a rigid distinction developed. Some people made the argument openly, "They get paid for the work, so why should we do it?" Others wanted to actively contribute but were intimidated by the idea of a paid, full-time staff. Moreover, there was suspicion about the staff's preliminary work in other rural counties. Part of OBRC's funding from CHD was to expand organizing efforts into surrounding counties and Phyllis Hanson was pushing hard in this direction. Many people felt she was ignoring Rice County and did not understand what "she and her staff were doing running around other counties." The Youth Project and CHD funding was essential to sustain OBRC and enable the organization to expand its organizing efforts, but it did have the unfortunate effect of causing conflict and limiting participation among OBRC people.

The internal fighting pointed to a fundamental problem—OBRC

was an organization without any clearly defined ideology. Those of us who founded OBRC and did a great deal of the initial organizing had a basic ideology: OBRC, in contrast to the OEO program, would be a conflict organization which would challenge the balance of power in Rice County. It would "take on" town and county government, which was dominated by large farmer and chamber of commerce interests.* It would be a bottom-up organization through which poor people would gain power and make local government responsive to *their needs.* When we left, we made every effort to insure that Phyllis Hanson and other OBRC activists who understood this organizing ideology had a strong position in the organization. But during the first two years, we never made a serious effort to develop and articulate a clear sense of purpose for OBRC that would be understood by the membership. We assumed most people would develop a solid understanding about organizing from their personal experiences with the organization. It did not work out this way. Much of the resentment toward Phyllis Hanson was (is) because many OBRC people, including some of the most dedicated and active members, do not understand the history of the organization, how or why it was conceived, or what its goals are. This important problem underlies much of the internal strife within the organization.

A very sensitive issue concerned the difference between advocacy and organizing. The OBRC office sign reads, "OBRC—People Helping People to Help Themselves." Most of the membership puts the emphasis on the word *help.* Before OBRC, poor people had nowhere to turn. As OBRC gained visibility in the county, more and more poor people came to the organization with their political, legal, and personal problems. OBRC activists, of marginal income themselves, wanted to respond. But this individual advocacy work required enormous investments of time and detracted from the task of building a strong and dur-

---

*The majority of county commissioners were prosperous farmers—American Farm Bureau members, solidly Republican, very conservative in ideology, and especially opposed to welfare. The towns were dominated by chamber of commerce interests. For example, when the Faribault City Council held public hearings on revenue sharing, citizens were invited to make suggestions to the councilmen *and* a representative from the chamber of commerce.

able organization that could change some of the institutions which created so many of the individual problems in the first place. By "building for power," OBRC could change the way the welfare department, schools, the housing authority, the employment office, the police and lawyers, and other county and city officials dealt with poor people. Without a change in the balance of power, poor people would have individual problems forever.

A split developed in the organization between those who argued the emphasis must be on institutional change and those who argued the major priority must be "in helping people." The majority of OBRC people supported the advocacy approach. They felt that when someone called with a welfare or tenant problem or came to the OBRC office hungry, not knowing where the next meal was coming from, the organization had to respond. They felt that a family or individual that came for immediate help could not wait for the future. They argued that if OBRC did not come through for people on individual problems, the organization would lose them.

The advocacy and organizing approaches were not mutually exclusive. Important points were made by those on both sides of the question. To be a good organizer, you had to come through for people. To help someone was certainly not a crime in organizing. Good advocates, by solving problems for individuals, were building support for OBRC. The problem was that most OBRC members understood only the advocacy approach. Helping people, no matter how low their income or social status, was to them what OBRC was all about. Many volunteer advocates could not understand why they did not receive funding for the organizing positions. They felt their advocacy work was organizing and were disappointed and angry when other people got the jobs.

A failure to understand the important role of "constructive conflict" also became a critical problem, especially as OBRC gained recognition in Rice County. Many members were (are) proud of this recognition and justifiably so. The problem arises because, as they see local governments deal with OBRC, they like and want to hold on to this newly found "respectability." OBRC, after two years of existence, became an established interest group in Rice County. OBRC people now had political status and respectability. Local officials knew them on a first-name basis. And for some OBRC people, respectability became the main goal. They felt the political conflict of the past was no longer necessary. They preferred to quietly negotiate with the councilmen and commissioners and cooperate whenever possible. Local officials invited them to become an integral part of the political process, which of course precluded agitational confrontation politics, and they felt OBRC should accept the offer.

The dial-a-bus negotiations dragged on through the late fall and early winter months. OBRC had pressured the council to apply for state funds, but important details relating to fare structure and local administration of the service had to be worked out. Patti and Isabelle acted, alone, as OBRC representatives in these final negotiations. All the people who had fought so long and hard for the dial-a-bus were cut out. At no time did OBRC actively involve its membership in the final stages of the dial-a-bus campaign.

In mid-December the Faribault City Council held its final meeting on the dial-a-bus. Patti, Isabelle, and Phyllis were there.* The organizers had not notified OBRC people about the meeting. They had not even kept the membership up to date on the status of negotiations about the final (and important) details. They had not made an attempt to gauge membership opinion on the crucial issues such as the fare structure.

Phyllis recognized this secret negotiation-cooperative strategy as disastrous for OBRC. She came to the council meeting confident she had persuaded Patti and Isabelle to oppose a fifty-cent one-way fare as being too expensive for low- and moderate-income people (the OBRC constituency). They did not oppose the fare, for fear that any conflict at this point would jeopardize the whole proposal. When the mayor reminded them that OBRC had an obligation after all of its trouble making to get ridership for the program and make it a success, they readily agreed. The meeting ended on this note of cooperation.

The dial-a-bus campaign which started out as a brilliant organizing success ended as a dismal failure. Patti and Isabelle were

*Phyllis insisted on attending the meeting, over Patti and Isabelle's initial opposition. I came as an observer when Phyllis notified me about the meeting and was surprised to see Isabelle and Patti angry over my appearance—they were intensely dedicated to cooperation with the council.

the real leaders-organizers of this campaign, but they should not have become self-appointed OBRC representatives. They should never have conceded to local officials' demands that OBRC people be kept away from council meetings. They should have opposed the prohibitively high fare structure. They should not have acceded to the mayor's position that the burden of proof was on OBRC to provide ridership and make the program work.

OBRC was a grass-roots poor people's organization. It flourished when masses of people were acting (successfully) on issues that directly affected them. OBRC's conflict tactics—the polarization and controversy created by these tactics—were the most important reason the organization had involved so many poor people in its organizing efforts, including the dial-a-bus campaign. OBRC was a citizens' organization, not a local government. It was open and accessible and consulted with its members before making decisions; at least, this was the idea behind the organization. It did not have the resources to become responsible for recruitment or the administration of the dial-a-bus program. It was the job of local government to administer the program and provide the service for the people. It was the job of OBRC to fight for programs responsive to the needs of low- and moderate-income people, without becoming responsible for the administration of these programs.

Isabelle Goodwin and Patti Fritz did not understand these issues. Their confusion and ambivalence about organizing, especially about conflict, made them vulnerable to the threats of local officials. OBRC people were to read in the local paper or hear from friends about the final dial-a-bus program, a transportation service too expensive for poor people. There was a sense of betrayal as people asked whether this was the dial-a-bus they worked so hard for and how it was they were not told about the final city council meeting. Quiet negotiation with the Faribault City Council was disastrous for the organization.

By the end of December, when I conducted most of the interviews for this book, OBRC was on the decline. The dial-a-bus campaign ended badly. Internal fighting absorbed a great deal of time and energy. The Kern case (which was not resolved in late December) created tremendous tension within the organization and dominated the agenda. The advocacy work went on, but this would not build an organization. OBRC, along with Migrants in Action, an organization in the Twin Cities concerned with the rights of migrant farm workers in Minnesota, filed a lawsuit against the director of the Minnesota Department of Welfare and was a plaintiff in a national lawsuit against the Department of Agriculture—in both cases the issue was the lack of funding for an adequate outreach program to notify the rural poor about the food stamps program. But the legal actions received scant local publicity, dragged on indefinitely, and involved only a few people. In short, very little organization building had taken place since the convention.

The late George Wiley had an organizing maxim that he applied to his work: "You make a winning plan, and you make it happen." OBRC was no longer making careful plans. Issues were missed, or several half-baked issues were brought up over and over again but never followed through. The failure to develop issues gave the organization an unclear image, and active membership dropped off.

In December, OBRC began publishing a newspaper called *Hard Times* to provide an alternative viewpoint to local news reporting. Franie Dwyer, a welfare mother and key OBRC activist, sold close to $250 worth of ads to get the paper started. The eight-page paper, complete with news stories, pictures, features, and editorials, was published monthly.

Many OBRC members worked hard to make the paper a success, along with their children, who delivered the 8,000 copies throughout the county. Communication within OBRC was a real problem; no money and long distances made it difficult for poor people to stay in touch with one another. The paper was an attempt to meet this problem.

Communicating as an organization within the Rice County community was also a major problem. The *Faribault Daily News* (the only county daily) became increasingly hostile to OBRC as the organization became a threat in the community. A host of promising young reporters came and went as the editor frustrated their efforts to provide fair or even any coverage. Editorials and news coverage became decidedly anti-OBRC, but bad publicity was better than no publicity. The conscious effort to "black out" the organization from news coverage was a much more serious concern. The local paper often would not carry OBRC press releases, notices of OBRC meetings, OBRC letters to the editor, or news concerning important OBRC activities. When Father McNamara from Campaign for Human Development came to Faribault in December to make the formal announcement that OBRC had received a $15,000 CHD grant, the St. Paul-Minneapolis Archdiocese requested that the local papers cover the event. The *Faribault Daily News* refused to send a reporter to the presentation. When Congressman Albert Quie met with various groups and organizations in Rice County, his meeting with OBRC was not covered by the paper. These are but a few examples of the attempt to shut off OBRC from news coverage.[2]

Hard Times was a response to this problem. The paper was a major undertaking, however, and at a time when OBRC had lost its organizing momentum the priority on the paper was misplaced. Soliciting ads, writing the paper, and getting it out took up much valuable organizational time and money. The paper created an intolerable burden for OBRC activists who were already overworked and who needed additional time for organizational building. After four months, the paper folded.

OBRC sponsored free tax clinics starting in February 1975. The clinics, for low- and moderate-income families earning below $7,500, should have been a tremendous success. Movement for Economic Justice provided OBRC with invaluable technical assistance on how to make tax clinics a relevant service. Many working and moderate-income families in Rice County were, in essence, paying a "tax on a tax" by taking their forms to various tax-return businesses. By providing this free service, OBRC hoped to pull more people into the organization. OBRC activists would not become absorbed in this service program, as they had with the newspaper. Students from Carleton had been trained by the Internal Revenue Service under OBRC sponsorship and were ready to help staff the clinics.

OBRC did not follow through on the tax clinics. The organization did not go to the unions, churches, and senior citizen groups. There was very little publicity. Communication within the organization was sloppy. As a result, the tax clinics never got off the ground.

The welfare rights group fell apart as the organization failed to build on welfare rights issues. The implementation of food stamps was still an important concern, with long delays in eligibility because of inadequate and inefficient staffing by the welfare department. OBRC did not act on this concern. Caseworker harassment continued, though to a lesser extent. The day care center, originally an OBRC proposal, was operated at hours more convenient to the providers than the recipients and did not reflect the realities of split-shift work. Local realtors and landlords discriminated against welfare mothers. Welfare payments were still very inadequate. OBRC did not take up any of these issues.

OBRC had successfully involved its membership in the previous school board elections (May 1974), but there was no follow-up on school board matters. In March (1975), some parents who were members of OBRC asked the organization to help them put a stop to the physical punishment meted out to their children at one of the "low-income" elementary schools in town. The elementary school was located in an OBRC neighborhood, but the organizing work was never done. Rural people had been talking about getting a school breakfast program started, but there was no follow-up on their proposal.

Senior citizen support fell off. The fare for the dial-a-bus was too high. OBRC pushed for congregate dining but did not bring senior citizens together to force the county board of commissioners to fund this badly needed service. The Faribault Housing Authority proposed a senior citizen housing complex at the edge of town; OBRC people were angry because the housing authority had never held public hearings on the location and wanted a change in site. OBRC did not act on the issue. There were a range of services that should and could be provided for senior citizens and other OBRC members: consumer booklets on the comparative pricing of drugs in the county and generic-brand-name cost differences, drug discounts and reduced doctors' fees for OBRC senior membership, a food co-op, and mechanical assistance for home repairs, to name but a few. OBRC never developed such a program.

Small farmers and homeowners wanted to fight the recent property tax reassessment (fall-winter 1975) in the county. The county board of commissioners hired an outside consulting firm to do the reassessment, and there was a great deal of suspicion about the firm's work. Small farmers felt the firm did not understand farm property, and moderate-income homeowners felt their property had been overassessed relative to the property of people who lived in the more affluent neighborhoods. OBRC could not find the time to thoroughly research and organize around these grievances.

Finance was a critical problem. There were (are) two major obstacles to self-sufficiency. The social change activities of OBRC made it difficult to tap local funding sources. United Appeals, service organizations, and private donors were not willing to give readily to OBRC. The OBRC membership were mainly poor people who could not afford to pay a high membership fee.

The Campaign for Human Development, Youth Project, and Christian Sharing Fund money could never be raised locally. OBRC could not expect to be financially self-sufficient, but no serious effort was made to move in this direction. During the third year, there were some bake sales, dances, pancake breakfasts, and other benefits to raise money locally, but very little planning went into these events and they were not particularly successful. Most important, the organization still did not have a solid, dues-paying membership.

The internal structure of OBRC was weak and discouraged participation. Phyllis Hanson recognized this at the time of the convention. She advocated a decentralized decision-making structure by developing local chapters in the small towns and villages throughout the county. The fifteen-member action council involved too few people in the decision-making process, and a Faribault-centered operation did not reflect the concerns of all OBRC people, many of whom lived in other parts of the county. Strong people in the organization not on the action council were blocked from decision-making positions. Less active members were discouraged from becoming more active.

It had been a very difficult third year. Yet, OBRC did survive. And sometimes the organization flourished. In late November (1974), a small group of welfare mothers from Austin, Minnesota, a large town of 25,000 in Mower County about sixty miles south of Faribault, came to OBRC to ask for help. The Mower County Welfare Department had instituted a highly publicized campaign against welfare fraud. The department set up its own investigatory procedures, which included "midnight raids." Welfare investigators, in violation of the mothers' constitutional rights, raided their homes late at night to see if there was a man there. Presumably, the welfare department was trying to prove that a woman with a man in the house had a source of support and did not need welfare assistance. Aside from the illegality of this action, it terrified welfare mothers in Mower County. OBRC had gained notoriety in surrounding rural counties and often received calls for help, in particular from welfare mothers. The organization had represented welfare mothers in Steele, Waseca, Wabasha, Goodhue, and Le Sueur counties. It was difficult for OBRC people to turn down requests for help. The advocacy work created a terrible financial and staff drain on the organization. Advocates often traveled more than 100 miles to handle one appeal. The appeal from the Austin women was handled differently. Phyllis told the women they could petition for OBRC support-affiliation. She told them they had to raise the funds to cover one-half of the expense of a staff person (to be supplied by OBRC initially) plus phone and office expenses; that if they could show there was interest and support for community organizing in Mower County, OBRC would help them. The idea was to pass on OBRC experience and knowledge in other counties so poor people could handle their own problems and issues. If successful, OBRC could expand its financial and political base in other parts of southern Minnesota.

The delegation of welfare mothers from Austin met Phyllis Hanson's conditions, and OBRC moved into Mower County dramatically. Phyllis, Patti Fritz, and Franie Dwyer organized a "raid" on the Mower County welfare office. A small delegation of welfare mothers (eight, plus three OBRC organizers) walked into the welfare office unannounced, distributed welfare rights booklets to caseworkers, and demanded a meeting with the welfare director and county attorney. They barged into the office of the county attorney and notified him that the welfare department and county attorney's office were in violation of the law and warned him to stop the degrading and unlawful investigative policies.

It was a dramatic and highly successful action. The welfare officials were shocked by the demonstration. The confrontation caught them completely by surprise. Their fear and confusion did not escape the notice of the welfare recipients, who had mustered up considerable courage to participate in this demonstration. This was the first time in the history of Mower County that welfare recipients had publicly protested against the welfare department. The *Austin Daily Herald* carried a front-page story the next day headlined, "Protestors Decry Policies Degrading Welfare People." The protest also received local radio and television coverage.

The demonstration was followed by extensive organizing. A welfare rights group was formed with several mothers trained as welfare advocates. Franie Dwyer spent several days a week in Austin walking through low-income neighborhoods and meeting with small groups of people. After several months of canvassing, she put together an organization in Mower County—Organization for a Better Mower County (OBMC)—made up of a good cross-section of welfare recipients, senior citizens, and working poor people.

In Rice County, OBRC also had a major organizing success. Starting in January, the organization launched a strong organizing drive around the Housing and Community Development Act (CDA). The town of Faribault, classified as rural by the federal Department of Housing and Urban Development (HUD), was eligible to compete for a portion of CDA money ($4.5 million) that had been allotted for rural communities in Minnesota. The CDA was based on the revenue-sharing concept. It consolidated many of the categorical programs previously funded by HUD and gave local governments considerable discretion in determining priorities. Faribault officials applied for funds to finance "capital improvement" projects—tennis courts, softball fields, and other park improvements.

The city council held two "public" meetings in early January to discuss their CDA plans. The first meeting was never announced, and the second was sprung on local residents before they had an opportunity to grasp various CDA alternatives open to the town. At the second "public" meeting, the council reaffirmed its intention to apply for CDA monies for park improvements and a well-pumping control system.

OBRC had been actively involved in housing concerns for several years, working with tenants and small homeowners. Adequate housing was a major priority of the membership. OBRC people had no idea what the CDA was all about but wondered whether CDA funds could be used directly for housing. The Center for Community Change and the Youth Project provided

OBRC with the important research and documentation that had so often been lacking in other recent issue campaigns.[3] Armed with a wealth of information about the CDA, OBRC took on the Faribault town government.

An OBRC delegation came to the January 17 "public meeting." They attacked the Faribault council for keeping Faribault citizens in the dark about the CDA and labeled the public meeting a farce. OBRC announced it would hold a public hearing on the CDA January 22 to give people a chance to talk more about it and about their needs and concerns and the impact the council's current decisions would have on the town. Phyllis Hanson stated the OBRC position, which was quoted in the *Faribault Daily News* the next day: "It's a matter of priorities. In these times, do the citizens of Faribault really want their tax dollars going to pay for tennis courts and picnic tables?"

The OBRC hearing was held in the storefront office and attended by senior citizens, tenants, landlords, homeowners, low- and moderate-income people. Eugene Wieneke, the city administrator, was there to represent the city government. It was an agitational meeting as people zeroed in on their housing concerns and demanded to know why other local officials were not at the meeting. The *Faribault Daily News* ran a front-page story on the OBRC meeting headlined, "City Residents Express Concern about Housing." The article started out,

> Housing was the top priority for approximately 30 persons who met Wednesday night with City Administrator Eugene Wieneke. They expressed concern that improved housing be made a part of Faribault's community development plan. The meeting, sponsored by Organization For A Better Rice County (OBRC), was called to give residents the chance to ask questions about the housing situation in Faribault and to request that housing rehabilitation be made a priority item by the city council. [January 23, 1975]

Phyllis Hanson had solid information about the CDA and knew inadequate housing was a major improvement priority. She and other OBRC speakers pressed Wieneke publicly as to how Faribault expected to get funding for a proposal which did not have a priority on housing. OBRC argued Faribault was throwing away a chance to receive CDA monies to improve housing in the community. The argument carried weight as even

the *Faribault Daily News* took a favorable editorial position on
the OBRC housing request. Privately, OBRC threatened to go to
the area HUD office if necessary. People in the organization had
become skilled in the use of leverage, and this threat carried
weight. OBRC was widely known in the state and in a position
to protest the existing town proposal to the point where HUD
would not touch it.

The public protests and private negotiations were successful.
A strong delegation of OBRC people brought their proposal for
housing rehabilitation (CDA monies could not be used for construction of new housing) to the January 29 council meeting.
The city council, just twelve days after the OBRC hearing, re-
ordered its priorities for the CDA grant. The *Faribault Daily
News* on January 30 carried a front-page article on the council
meeting: "Council Approves Housing Request." The first para-
graph of the article read: "In an apparent response to citizen
demands, the Faribault city council Tuesday night approved the
inclusion of a $130,500 request for housing rehabilitation in the
city's preliminary application for federal Community Development Funds." It was a tremendous victory for OBRC.

Overall, OBRC's third year produced mixed results. Given the
enormous problems of the organization, it is significant that
OBRC survived and even pulled off some important victories.
OBRC people were recognized by the power structure in Rice
County. Local officials and public agencies were more responsive
to poor people. OBRC people could influence policy and local
elections. In this sense, OBRC was a force to be reckoned with,
an established interest group of poor people for poor people in
Rice County.

OBRC had not, however, established itself as a strong and durable political organization. In this respect, the third year was a
keen disappointment. From the beginning, OBRC was conceived
as a grass-roots organization. Community people were to fill
leadership and organizing positions as soon as possible. OBRC
organizers would be low- and moderate-income people who lived
in the community. They would not be "hired guns" brought in
from training institutes to "organize the people." OBRC organizers (paid and volunteer staff) would come from the rank-and-
file membership. They would act on the *membership's agenda*.
The price paid in efficiency would be compensated by participa-

tion and the assurance that a genuine grass-roots people's organization would be developed.

The vision was (is) important. Faith in the ability of organized poor people to make their own decisions makes this kind of organizing attractive. OBRC has consistently operated on this premise. But several conditions have to be met to make this vision come true. If community people are to run the organization, from leadership to organizing positions, there should be a pool of leaders and organizers ready to take command. Those of us who founded OBRC were not sensitive enough to this problem.

I had worked closely with Phyllis Hanson. I felt she could handle the job as chief organizer for OBRC. She turned out to be an effective organizer, mainly because of her own instincts and by learning from experience. Since I knew many remarkable OBRC people who knew poverty first-hand, understood the importance of dignity and self-respect, and were not afraid to take on "important people," even at great risk to themselves, I was confident there was a core of OBRC activists to help her with the business of building for power. But the citizen activists did not understand clearly what organizing was about. The challenge was to change the pattern of power and this meant organization building. Too few OBRC people recognized this challenge or knew how to meet it.

OBRC had been sustained only by enormous investments of organizing effort. Poor people were dispersed throughout rural Rice County, and it was an arduous task to group low-income people around new and varied issues. It was not like organizing at a factory where everyone came to work in one place. And it was much more difficult in terms of time than walking through urban neighborhoods where large numbers of people lived in close proximity to one another. Phyllis Hanson missed numerous issues during the past year and found it increasingly difficult to keep OBRC going. Even with additional skilled organizers, it would be very difficult to build a countywide organization by organizing effort alone. Only with a new structure and a serious effort to develop local leadership and organizing initiative could OBRC achieve this goal.

Participation is important to political organizations like OBRC because it is linked closely to the goal of developing strong leaders. The annual convention and monthly action council meetings did not provide enough opportunities for participation. OBRC had to develop neighborhood chapters in Faribault, its major base of operation, and village and town chapters throughout the county. Action committees in the neighborhoods and towns-villages could start work on *their* issues, and most importantly, local leaders and organizers would emerge to fill the vacuum in the organization. An efficient, smoothly functioning, decentralized political structure was an unmet and necessary condition for OBRC's growth and survival.

At the final writing of this book (fall 1975), OBRC was beginning an intense organizing drive to build local chapters throughout the county, starting with neighborhood chapters in the town of Faribault. The goal was to build a cohesive membership of 4,000–5,000 low- and moderate-income people who could act collectively on a political agenda. It remained to be seen whether this drive would be successful. Several OBRC people committed to the drive would first have to be trained. The work would be very difficult for OBRC organizers, all of whom have families and would feel the strain of the seven-day-week schedule.

In Faribault, several neighborhood chapters in the "north end," the low-income section of town, did come together around the dial-a-bus issue in mid-July 1975. They successfully organized to bring the dial-a-bus fare down from fifty to twenty-five cents. The leaders in this action were all new people to the organization, and it was a promising first step toward building a solid OBRC structure in Faribault.

In early August, a new organization called ARISE was to be born. ARISE—Against Rural Injustice, for Social Equality—represented the culmination of OBRC organizing efforts in surrounding rural counties. Strong contingents of low- and moderate-income people were organized in Mower, Waseca, Steele, and Dakota counties and were ready to join OBRC in a southern Minnesota organization spanning five counties. Campaign for Human Development had renewed the OBRC grant up to $21,000 to provide the funding for this expansion.

After three years of accomplishments, OBRC chose to launch a major organizing drive to develop a new internal structure, stronger leadership, and to build poor people's organization in surrounding rural counties. A citizen organization played a vital role in the lives of rural poor people in Rice County, Minnesota.

Whatever their mistakes, their accomplishments were their own. Active participation nurtured political consciousness among the "new community leaders." These OBRC activists were determined to build a stronger OBRC.

6

BREAD AND ROSES

Why did people come together in OBRC? How did the organizers seek to maintain their interest and commitment? What consequences did this have for the organization? James Q. Wilson,
in his important work, *Political Organizations*, offers the theoretical perspective that

> the behavior of persons occupying organizational roles (leader,
> spokesman, executive, representative) is principally, though not
> uniquely, determined by the requirements of organizational main-
> tenance and enhancement and that this maintenance, in turn,
> chiefly involves supplying tangible and intangible incentives to in-
> dividuals in order that they will become, or remain, members and
> will perform certain tasks. . . . It is with respect to voluntary asso-
> ciations that the effects of incentive systems are most clearly vis-
> ible, for by definition members cannot be coerced into joining
> (except, perhaps, in the case of labor unions) and most members
> (professional staff excepted) do not earn their livelihood by their
> participation.[1]

He distinguishes four general kinds of incentives. *Material incentives*: "These are tangible rewards: money, or things and services
readily priced in monetary terms." *Specific solidary incentives*:
"These are intangible rewards arising out of the act of associating that can be given to, or withheld from, specific individuals."
Collective solidary incentives: "These are intangible rewards created by the act of associating that must be enjoyed by a group
if they are to be enjoyed by anyone." *Purposive incentives*:
"These are intangible rewards that derive from the sense of satis-

faction of having contributed to the attainment of a worthwhile cause."[2]

The OBRC organization model relied heavily on tangible, material inducements. The organizing campaigns—improved food commodities, expanded food stamp program, higher welfare payments, a county day care program, the dial-a-bus, and CDA money for housing rehabilitation—all dealt with pressing economic needs of poor people. The welfare, tenant, and consumer advocacy programs can be considered in the same light. These incentives had built-in limitations for several reasons. First, they could only be delivered once. Poor people came together in OBRC to fight for a dial-a-bus or an expanded food stamp program, but once the organization delivered the benefit (an organizing victory), there was no reason for them to stay active in the organization. They had gotten what they wanted-needed. Many people came to OBRC with individual problems (landlord-tenant, welfare, consumer). After receiving the concrete benefit (legal and/or political assistance), they did not actively contribute to the organization. Their problem was taken care of, and the incentive to associate was no longer there.

The short-range nature of material incentives was compounded by the "free-rider problem." Once OBRC obtained its objectives, the nonmember received the benefit(s) equally with the members.[3] The dial-a-bus and expanded food stamp program, for example, benefited members and nonmembers alike. The organization was hardly in a position to demand these programs be provided by the city or county government for OBRC members only. Why join OBRC and make yourself vulnerable (a realistic fear grounded in the experience of OBRC activists), if you will benefit from the service or program whether you are a member or not?

Phyllis Hanson and her staff recognized the "free-rider problem" and talked about making some changes. For example, they discussed package programs such as tenant-welfare-consumer-tax assistance, a food co-op, and shopping discounts for members only. Many OBRC people were reluctant to accept what seemed to them to be a callous policy, feeling the organization should help anyone in need. The issue was never resolved.

Packaged benefits might be a response to organizational maintenance needs, but the organization had to focus on political-conflict issues to *expand* its membership and power.[4] This was a more serious problem—the need to always come up with something new. It required enormous investments of organizing effort. Poor people were dispersed throughout Rice County, and it was almost impossible to sustain an organizing effort of grouping low-income people around new and varied issues. Phyllis Hanson missed numerous issues during the third year and found it increasingly difficult to maintain momentum.

The organizers, lay leaders, and rank-and-file members were not motivated solely by material inducements. If this had been the case, the organization would have folded, because it was impossible to tie the organization's activities consistently to personal gains. Many OBRC people responded to collective solidary incentives. OBRC provided tremendous social support for poor people. Many close friendships developed within the organization. Previous to joining the organization, many poor people were isolated and lonely; the association with OBRC made an important difference to them.

OBRC people who responded to collective solidary incentives were dedicated to the organization (some of the activists interviewed in this book respond primarily to collective solidary incentives). They were not, however, interested in a political agenda. They did not think in terms of a maldistribution of influence and power in society (their community) as the cause of poor people's problems and were not committed to "building for power."[5]

The organizers, not "outside organizers" but "community people," were motivated primarily by purposive incentives. They were committed to building a strong poor people's organization in Rice and surrounding rural counties. Their activities toward this end became divergent from the activities of other strong OBRC people who responded to collective solidary incentives. A split emerged not only between the activists and the more passive rank-and-file membership but among the activists themselves. There was internal fighting over whether OBRC should emphasize grass-roots organizing rather than advocacy work, engage in political conflict, and expand into other counties. The choice of Phyllis Hanson as chief organizer was, in the first place, a source of controversy.

The Campaign for Human Development and Youth Project

funding accentuated the problem, and not just in terms of who would be hired as staff. These grants were the organization's financial lifeline. Even if the organizers had not been motivated by purposive incentives, the outside funding dictated goals for OBRC, directions the organization had to move in. CHD's priority was for OBRC to expand its efforts into surrounding rural counties. The emphasis was on "institutional change." While no one really knew what this meant, it was clear, from the terms of the CHD contract, that OBRC would have to operate on a strong political agenda if it hoped to get further funding. The Youth Project, Phyllis Hanson's employer, stressed the same priorities. Thus, the requirements of organizational maintenance and enhancement dictated that the organizers "build for power" throughout southeastern Minnesota.

I wrote the CHD and Youth Project proposals. The OBRC action council knew I was trying to raise money but did not have any input. Moreover, I made no real effort to make sure they would understand Campaign for Human Development and Youth Project priorities and the terms of OBRC funding. Phyllis Hanson and her staff were left to deal with the problems created by this serious mistake. Under extreme pressure to produce for the funders, they exacerbated the problems. They moved rapidly (and dramatically) into other counties, building ARISE, but in the process made little effort to work closely with the OBRC membership, thus creating further suspicion and distrust among the people in the organization who responded to different incentive systems.

The second major issue raised by OBRC's failure to firmly establish itself concerns the role of the organizer(s). This issue is closely interrelated with organizational maintenance-enhancement needs. Again, it is a question of incentives. "Poor people's" organizations or "low- and moderate-income people's" organizations can deliver material incentives for just so long. It is virtually impossible to sustain this incentive system for the individual member. Solidary incentives are not sufficient, especially if the organization wants and/or needs to act on a political agenda. Lay leaders and rank-and-file members must be motivated by a sense of purpose to sustain their *political* participation.

A problem arises because many organizing models overlook the promise of citizen participation as a means to the full development of individual capacities.[6] When one strips away the rhetoric, the typical organizing strategy for working with poor people is: (1) Poor people will only respond to tangible, material inducements. (2) The organizer must offer concrete benefits to enlist their participation. (3) It is very difficult to motivate the people, and demands on the membership should be minimal. (4) The organizer will have to make the crucial decisions about goals and tactics.[7]

This model, which may be critical to early success, in the long run creates serious organizational maintenance-enhancement problems. Organizers become locked into this model, and not just in the early stages of their work. They presuppose that poor people will not respond to purposive incentives and do not make an effort to develop broadly based organizations which involve as many poor people as possible in significant ways. It becomes a self-fulfilling prophecy. The people in the organization do not understand organizing goals and tactics and they do not respond to purposive incentives. Since other incentive systems, alone, cannot sustain political participation over a long period of time, community organizations are often unable to institutionalize themselves.[8]

Saul Alinsky had a name for the student radicals in the 1960s. He called them political astronauts. He was impatient with their inability to effectively communicate and work with people. It was part of Alinsky's genius to make a very simple and basic point: People draw from their own experience about what the world is like and they learn it is not a world you can change that easily. They are not fools about taking principled stands that will mean the end of their livelihood.

This important insight was a badly needed corrective to some of the "movement organizing." Alinsky's emphasis on economic self-interest was well founded. The problem is that many organizers are so oriented toward economic self-interest in the building of organizations that they miss out on many important opportunities to bring people together, vitalize, and move them. Narrow-based economic organizing overlooks the fact that people have large desires which go well beyond concrete economic gains.

While I organized with OBRC and in the course of writing this book, I puzzled over the question of why poor people joined

OBRC and made the commitment *to get organized.* Few of them had been politically active before joining the organization. Most lost income from their involvement with OBRC. The transportation and babysitting costs were not an insignificant expenditure for poor people. Many OBRC people caught hell from neighbors and co-workers and spent endless hours defending their participation in the organization. Many were threatened with loss of job, bank loan, apartment, and/or welfare assistance. In some cases, these sanctions were invoked.

The conclusion I have reached is that successful organizing is built not on "economic rationality" but rather on dignity and a sense of purpose. Poor people dedicated themselves to OBRC out of a sense of purpose. Once they realized their voice could make a difference (the crucial importance of organizing victories), they viewed themselves in a different light—as strong and independent people not afraid to speak up for their rights. This important change in self-concept was combined with two other factors to sustain participation: (1) the people had a role to play in the organization—they had responsibilities which had to be met if OBRC was to be successful; and (2) the people had a goal they believed in—that through their efforts they could improve the community (country) and bring about more fairness and justice and a better life for low- and moderate-income people. These are the factors that sustained participation.

I am currently engaged in a comparative study of poor people and low- and moderate-income people's organizations throughout the country. The project is by no means near completion, and there are many organizations yet to visit and study, but I have again been impressed with the fact that successful organizing has so little to do with our usual understanding of rationality and self-interest. There are many interviews and observations I could draw on, but it would be beyond the scope of this book. I would like, however, to draw on an interview I conducted with Wade Rathke, chief organizer of Arkansas Community Organizations for Reform Now, better known as ACORN. ACORN is widely known as perhaps the most successful example of community organizing in the country.[9] Rathke is in fact now directing similar organizing campaigns in South Dakota, Texas, and Tennessee. He is a brilliant organizer, and in my week with ACORN I found a great deal of empirical evidence for many of his organizing concepts.

I asked him what he thought, on the basis of his experience, was the key to organizational maintenance-enhancement needs. He emphasized (1) the structure of ACORN—that local groups were able to stay involved on a wide range of issues, and that since ACORN was a statewide organization with regional offices throughout the state, local groups were able to link up on city-wide, countywide, regional, or statewide issues; (2) a fundamental maintenance structure which provided daily benefits such as discount prices, a food co-op service, and a newspaper to members; and (3) the "process of organizing." He was especially interested in talking about the process of organizing.

> There has been in my mind an historic confusion in community organizing over the difference between self-interest as a tactic and as a strategy in and of itself. In my view, organizations are built on expectations, not on interests. People have to get something, but what they get for the most part is defined along the lines of changes and expectations about themselves, neighbors, class, community, state, whatever. People always look at the contradiction in terms of the mythology of this business and say, "Well, isn't it amazing that x leader is working so hard on this issue and stands to gain nothing. This is a guy who deserves a pat on the back." Bullshit. Almost all leadership is never involved on the basis of self-interest. In fact their activities are against any clear definition of what we understand as self-interest. It has to do with a radical change in the expectation they have of themselves, the status they gain as leaders, and a whole lot of other things. When 225 ACORN members ran for the Quorum Court a year and a half ago here in Pulaski County, it was against every one of their interests. They stood to lose status in the community, to be red-baited, seen as radicals, take hell at work, home, and almost everywhere else. Yet, they ran because their expectations of themselves were changing very radically from being, you know, a $3 an hour blue-collar lift-truck driver on a warehouse dock to sitting on a $9 million budget. What says they should do that? Nothing says they should do that except an organizing process that x's the ante in terms of what we have as residual strength in terms of large membership and what that can potentially accomplish because of the value of those individuals meted together.
> That's a big problem. Most organizations, or a lot of organiza-

tions, view their membership as troops, and I am not trying to bait those organizations. I understand the analogy and all that. The fact is if you are going to stabilize a membership you have to have a lot more. And in my view the risks are always too high to organize for everybody. That it is ridiculous for organizers to say that membership is involved in the organization for any different reasons than they are. One of the first things we do is to ask our organizers to evaluate their own past experience with organizations and what they did; if they were just 1 of 100 Boy Scouts in a troop or were they more active. If they were active, why was that; and if not, why was that? If they didn't feel they had any role in it, any job to do, any opportunities to lead, they didn't stay active in the organization. Our membership operates exactly the same way as our organizing staff. The problem with organizing structures in many organizations is that it assumes a fundamental difference between the organizers and the membership. We don't do that. If you organize based on schizophrenia, the organization will reflect that schizophrenia. You will have all those staff-leadership splits that plagued our work, for example, in welfare rights.

ACORN's membership and leadership is more outrageous in their goals than the majority of the staff that has to deal with the details of the work. The leadership has some fairly outrageous views about what this organization could or should do. My job is to encourage the increase of these expectations.

There are many organizers who work long and hard days for little money. They are dedicated political activists who act out of a sense of vision. Successful organizing is based on the recognition that people *get organized* because they too have this vision.

Myles Horton, founder of the Highlander Folk School and a man with years of rich experience as an educator and organizer, shared with me some of his wisdom concerning the role of self-interest in organizing. He is worth quoting at some length:

The first thing you have to do is to disassociate material self-interest from other self-interest. It is in the people's self-interest to get certain respect. It is in their self-interest to feel good about doing something good for somebody. It is in their self-interest to be told they helped somebody grow up. It is to their self-interest to go to bed at night and feel good. That is self-interest. Not material self-interest. So if you use that concept of self-interest first and lump it with the material, then I would say self-interest is key. But not material self-interest. Some people get the impression that that is the only self-interest there is. Alinsky was very sad about what happened in the Back of the Yards in terms of their racial prejudice. Because the goal of racial equality was very important to him. I just don't want people to think that the material is all Alinsky meant about self-interest.

If the only thing you organize around is self-interest (economic), then that's what you are going to get. The people say, "What's in it for us materially?" and you've got to deliver. They do a bookkeeping job and say, "What have I got out of it?" So you've got to deliver whatever you promised. Then it is a question whether a benevolent dictator could deliver better—probably. If that is all you are doing, you better examine whether that's the best way of delivering material benefits. I think organizations have to have some material bases to have a broad base. But they have to have more than that to have a broad base and a sustained base. When I was organizing textile workers, and they were a very low-paid group of people—that was in the depression of thirty-seven—people used to laugh at me because I talked about brotherhood, international problems; I talked about people having a say in their lives; I talked a lot about people not being pushed around by the boss. Some organizers would say, "These people are hungry; they are not interested in that." *They were wrong.* These people were interested. They loved to be reminded that they could do things for themselves and they loved to be told that this union was more than bread and butter. This didn't distract from organizing. *I would say that there is no group of people that is so poor that they don't want Bread and Roses—there is none and anybody that misses that is selling people short, is selling them short. They have missed one of the best bets to organize.*

OBRC was born locally in response to an OEO agency which could offer poor people only patronizing social services. These services were of no help to people who had pressing economic needs and wanted some dignity and justice. OBRC filled this vacuum and played a vital role in the lives of poor people. If I had to pick out the most significant thing that has happened since OBRC's inception, it would be the dramatic change in political consciousness among the poor. Poor people have become an effective political force. This is what makes the OBRC story so important.

The glaring deficiency in the OBRC experience is the failure to rigorously apply an organizing model emphasizing leadership development. To motivate people to begin and continue a long struggle for social and economic justice requires that they have a clear understanding of this distant goal and, most important, how to reach it. OBRC remains a weak organization in this respect. But community organizing in the streets of Faribault and back roads of Rice County has been at least a partial success. With this success has come a little more bread and justice for the rural poor.

Postscript

I finished writing this book in the fall of 1975. One year later, OBRC collapsed. Now, a group of OBRC activists is forming a new organization which they hope will be broader in membership and stronger than OBRC.

If we are to be successful, we must learn from our experience. In the last chapter, I wrote, "The glaring deficiency in the OBRC experience is the failure to rigorously apply an organizing model emphasizing leadership development." It was this failure that ultimately caused OBRC's downfall. We did not fully understand the *process* organizers must go through in order to develop a strong and broad-based leadership in community organizations. With the benefit of hindsight and an additional two years of research into grass-roots organizing, I now have a much clearer sense of what's involved in this process.

A Working Definition

The words *leaders* and *organizers* mean different things to different people. *Leadership* is usually defined as people who speak for and act for a group. A sharp distinction is drawn between the organizers and leaders: the organizers do the work and bring people into the organization; the leaders speak at meetings while organizers stay in the background. Discussions about leadership development get bogged down on the question of whether staff should speak or pass notes at public meetings: "You can't let the meeting go down the tube," but "You musn't show you don't have a people's organization."

I reject this rigid orientation which clearly separates the functions of organizers from those of leadership. Many good leaders are good organizers, though they must never be from outside the relevant community, be it geographical, cultural, or a particular constituency group. More importantly, the work of building a strong, durable people's organization has to be shared among a large number of people, of whom the organizer is one person. As many people as possible must intermesh to do a variety of things, involving many different kinds of skills.

Leadership development also means something more than raising a few people to a higher stage of development. It has nothing to do with teaching people junior-chamber-of-commerce skills. It is not "media star" organizing where one or two people who are folksy and articulate and militant are picked to speak before the media and attend all the conferences.

This kind of organizing sows the seeds of its own destruction. The leaders become split off from the membership. Their role is not the leadership of the people. They do not even have the time to listen to the concerns of the rank-and-file. Their role is a special relationship with the organizers, outside people, and the media. The organizers are viewed as management, granting favors to those members who are the most cooperative, those the organizers like the best. The people are alienated from both the organizers and "the leadership."

Si Kahn summarizes the importance of collective leadership very well:

> We have been conditioned by one-person leadership—that one person is to have all the skills. There is, in fact, a tremendous cross-section of skills that you need to have an organization: bring people together, work with people on an individual basis, strategy development, legal-paralegal skills, research and analysis, use of the media (leaflets, films, newsletters, theater, music), politics and government, and economic tactics, to name a few. All are part of organizing-leadership skills. There are few cases where one person can have all these skills. You must have a *leadership group* where there is a sharing of skills and needed backup.*

*Si Kahn is a highly skilled organizer with a tremendous amount of experience in rural, small-town communities. He is currently working with textile workers in Roanoke Rapids, North Carolina. I interviewed him in April 1976.

In other words, it is not true that only certain people have talents. What is true is that only certain people have certain talents. If leadership skills are defined broadly (as they should be), and if the emphasis is not on "what can people do" but rather "what can people working with people do," there will be plenty of opportunities for members to take leadership positions.

Leadership development viewed as developing a few individual leaders is a counterproductive goal. It contradicts the idea that in numbers there is power. A strong organization that wields power must have among its ranks *many* dedicated, skillful activists. As an ideal, when those in the power structure ask the question, "Who are your leaders that we should speak to?" the answer should be, "Anybody!"

"Leaders are found by organizing, and leaders are developed through organization." Nicholas von Hoffman warns us against "the great hunt" for the "natural leader": "He does not exist. If he were there—that wondrous all-purpose leader that every organizer dreams about in his moments of exasperation with and anger at his would-be constituency—you would not be necessary."

Von Hoffman insists that we not divorce the goal of developing leadership from the organizing process or lose sight of the paramount objective—to build an organization that wields power. This is a particularly important point, because it is too easy to get caught up in the dramatic impact your organizing is having on an individual's life. What happens to people personally is important, but the focus has to be on indigenous leadership serving indigenous leadership, on people working together in an organized way, not people going off and working as enriched individuals. Most of what low- and moderate-income people come up against is organized, and that is why they must organize and build their own organizations. Dave Knotts put it very well:

> I agree that individual growth is a very desirable thing, and I would emphasize the building of strong people. But that's not enough. *The problem is, the way you get things done is through organization.* It would be nice if the NAM [National Association of Manufacturers] had the attitude that organization is not as important as the individual *but they don't.**

*Interview, June 1976.

The emphasis on building an organization, then, is not mis-placed, as long as organizers understand that the strength of community organizations is dependent upon the strength of the people in the organizations. This statement would seem to be self-evident, but apparently it is not, given the number of or-ganizations which are essentially staff operations run by the organizers. There are a number of important factors to look at in analyzing this problem, and let me hasten to add that in many cases organizations end up being staff-run, in spite of the best intentions of organizers.

The Mystique of the Organizer

There is a whole set of unrealistic notions about the role of the organizer, unfortunately held by some organizers, which parallel von Hoffman's description of the hunt for the great leader. In this case, it is the belief in the great organizer. He builds the or-ganization. He builds the power. He cannot afford the luxury of time to develop leadership. He cannot restrain and restrict him-self by some fuzzy ideal that does not work. He is highly trained in the secret techniques of organizing; he holds the secret knowl-edge how to win. Especially in the early stages of organizing, he must think, act, and decide for all.

I call this the "mystique of the organizer," because, while I believe professionalism is important in the sense that organizers should be rigorous and live up to high standards, I cannot for the life of me think of any new or complicated techniques or tactics that people haven't known about for a long time. Some organizers are not unlike so many other professionals—they in-sist that people cannot do without them. This viewpoint is de-structive. The best organizers are people who organize themselves —they are the leaders. They have a much better sense of their situation than the outside organizer, however well versed he might be in basic principles of organizing. What they do need to know is that they have this knowledge. Of course, organizers are competent in analyzing political and economic structures, figur-ing out various access routes to the people in decision-making positions, and planning effective strategy. But the really skillful organizer "has a sense of what is possible and combines this with the knowledge, ability, and skills that people have in the situation" (Si Kahn).

The Development Process

The failure to develop a strong and diversified leadership in community organizations is more often caused by organizers' failure to understand what's really involved in the leadership development process. Myles Horton talked with me about the importance of the process.

> Developing leadership is hard work—people often don't take the time. One of the reasons organizers don't put in the hard work and spend the time is that they have from my point of view an incorrect analysis of how you go about it. They seem to think you have a good idea and go out and share it with people and that people will immediately show an in with their idea on the basis of its popularity or, to them, sensibility or rationality or on the basis of peoples' need that this is supposed to respond to. I say "supposed to," because if I had to figure out what your need is I am guessing.
>
> What I consider the appropriate way to deal with a problem is to say that people have to be moved from where they are to where you would like to see them in terms of organization. There is a process at work that enables people to take their knowledge and experience they have and expand it and extend it until it will encompass a stage beyond that in terms of cooperation and working together and understanding. You don't skip the process, because if you skip the process you are moving people faster than they have any understanding, and when the crunch comes and they are supposed to put out or work or be loyal then you have a gap in their development and they don't have the stamina or understanding. In other words, you have to have a process that enables people to internalize—to learn how to use in their own way the things that combine for group and collective action. They have to get that through the process of growth.
>
> Most people see a beautiful rose and they say, "Let's get a rose," and they take a knife and cut off the rose and say, "I am going to take this and have a rose bush." What I am saying is you got to know the root system and you got to know that rose is go-

ing to be stinking in a week, so you might as well not transfer that rose. What you got to do is to get the roots, start over again, attend it, nurse it, pet it, get it growing—then you have flowers forever. It is that kind of process, rather than achieve the goal in one step. I think organizers get impatient. They don't think you have to go through this process—when the people are not responding they don't think they are making any progress. They don't see the rose, but they don't understand that stages of growth are necessary—so that they don't get any satisfaction or encouragement out of the stages of development. Therefore, they lose interest because they don't see anything happening—it hadn't bloomed yet. That's why I say it's your analysis, your way of analyzing, that enables you to stay with things long enough to lay the groundwork. You are getting the groundwork done—you attend it very carefully at the start. But once it gets going, it spreads like yeast. A lot of very good people are not willing to put the time in because they don't understand the process—that things are happening underneath the surface that you can't brag about, take credit for, see, or measure—but that's the way you organize.

Much of the community organizing I have observed over the past few years, including my organizing with OBRC, short-circuits this process. Organizers start from the premise that victories are critical to the building of people's self-confidence and to the building of the organization. This is a sound principle. The trouble begins as organizers attempt to move from one quick victory to another in order to build momentum. Since the organizers have the more immediate skills to manipulate situations, they do the bulk of the work rather than waiting for people in the organization to take over part of the work. The people are not given the chance to use their knowledge and skills, and as a result they are left behind. The organizations become "staff operations" or fall apart.

In the early stages of organizing, organizers ought to have given more thought than rank-and-file members about what is required to build a strong organization. Otherwise, they ought not to be organizing. I do not wish to minimize the role of organizers. They have a major responsibility to develop and assist local people. The longer the haul, the tougher the fight, the broader the leadership an organization will need.

To work with people who are poor and powerless or moderate-income and powerless and help develop their skills to get power takes a long time because you are dealing with people who have been put down over a long period of years. In this sense, we are talking about very basic changes in people. These changes do not take place in a matter of a few months.

Si Kahn summarizes what's involved in this process:

> What happens in the process of building an organization is really critical because you are developing leaders with the skills to meet issues and problems under any circumstances whether they move away or the organization goes away. You go about this task very slowly. Really, you can't talk about giving skills to people—that is the wrong way to put it. People learn mostly through experience. . . . People learn things by doing things, and that is the most effective way of organizing people and helping people grow; and that also is a very slow way of organizing because it means you have to create these kinds of situations where people are a part of the situations and a lot of things experts could do more quickly and more efficiently. You have to wait while people catch up. And you have to break through a tremendous lack of self-confidence that has been hammered into people. What you often hear is, "We just can't do that." It's sort of like, "If you're so smart, why aren't you rich?" The poor and working people have bought the myth—"It is obvious low-income and working-income people cannot lead themselves or they wouldn't be poor and working-income." This has been sold to people so hard and so long there is always this element of self-doubt.

The problem is that organizers are under strong pressure to ignore this development process. In part, the pressure may be ego-related. The organizer feels a real need to have something she or he can point to as a concrete victory. Unrelated to ego problems, there is a compelling need to keep the morale of the people up by having early successes. Finally, organizers are responsible to other people besides the people they organize. There are the outside funders: church groups, foundations, liberal contributors, and the canvassing operations. They are not impressed if the organizer emphasizes the importance of process and explains that she has spent the twelve months laying the groundwork—getting to know people and encouraging people to decide what kind of structure they want and what they want to do. The outside funders look for a formal organization, officers, by-laws, plenty of media actions, plenty of press coverage, and the mass convention attended by hundreds of people. This is what the organizer has to sell to them, or, in the case of canvassers, what they need to sell to others.

Organizers are forced to take the short-run payoff. Myles Horton describes what often happens:

> If the timetable is set by getting money or publicity, you can't do a sound organization job—because your tempo is set by something having nothing to do with the people you are dealing with. You've got to go through these processes, however slowly or long they take. And it all depends on the situation. In a crisis situation people might learn in a week what normally might take a year. Or it might take six months or a year. If you aren't free to spend the time necessary, then people are not allowed to learn. You have to say, "Look, I'll tell you what to do. I'll first explain it to you." People say, "Yes, we'll vote on it." People will vote on anything. People are just generous. But they don't understand or learn anything. What they've learned is they don't have a say in the learning process. That you've manipulated them, that's what they learn. From then on—"What is the use of us learning because he is going to tell us what to do anyway?" *You've killed the whole process right there.*
>
> Now if the goodie that you offer is appealing enough or they think they are going to get something out of it, then they will sit there and approve anything you say. What takes place that fools organizers is that in every situation there are some people who see in this something for themselves—credit, power, money, security, or whatever. They see they will latch on to the organizer and memorize all the gimmicks—"Give me a quickie course and I'll try to remember these things—tell me what to do—I want to be able to do it." They look good and the organization may get publicity and grants. *What you have really done is take your outside organizer and transferred his know-how to two or three people in the community who are on the make. They don't understand anything but the mechanics, and consequently they can't ever teach anybody anything because they don't know anything— therefore you can never have any change in leadership. That's what happens when you don't go through this process. And that's the kind of danger of this kind of organizing. You're just setting*

up a structure that tells people what to do. It's closer to them,
so you say that is democracy. But see, in a group of people you
are going to get all kinds of people, people who are ambitious,
people who should be leaders, people who shouldn't.

Building the Organization

It is best to build slowly and broadly. The organizer needs to
work with many people. She should dig for leadership. She
must create situations where people feel they are needed and
have a contribution to make. This may mean, for example,
spending a great deal of time with single individuals or small
groups of people as opposed to mass meetings, where those
members who talk best take over.

Organizers must never assume that the people who are the
most active at first are the best leaders for the long run. Rarely
are these activists the poor people in the organization. They
may, in fact, be the "community activists," adding on another
organization to belong to. There is certainly no guarantee they
understand the pulse of the community and are committed to
sharing leadership, developing leadership, and working with other people in a group cooperative spirit.

I met a young organizer with ACORN, John Kest, who had a
very interesting approach. He made it a priority to spend several
hours each evening talking with "secondary people"—members
who were not the primary leaders in the organization. In this
way, he avoided the mistake many organizers make of spending
all their time with the existing leadership. It is a lazy way of organizing, with some rather serious consequences: the organizer
loses his sense of rank-and-file concerns; the leaders' role is no
longer leadership of the people; rather, the leaders are viewed as
individuals with a special relationship to organizers, powerful by
virtue of their exclusive access to the organizers; a broader and
more diversified base of leadership is not developed.

To enable new people to take leadership positions, the structures of community organizations should be kept loose. Organizations which are heavy on patronage and offices become rigid
in structure and are dominated by old leadership. The people
furthest ahead get the leadership positions, and the rest of the

people, many of whom could provide new, energetic, creative leadership, are locked out.

Several organizations, for example, have tried to deal with this problem by building into their structure issue-related "action committees." These committees are directly linked to the issue campaigns of the organization and terminate when these campaigns are concluded. The important thing is that new leaders from these action committees are given decision-making positions on the organization's executive committee. They do not have to wait for the next annual convention to run for office. Throughout the year, new leadership is integrated with old leadership. Since the action committees are never permanent, there is a continuous flow of new leadership within the organization.

What it really gets down to is that the organizer must balance the short run with the long-run demands of building a strong organization. A case in point is in using the media.

It was part of the genius of Saul Alinsky that he clearly understood that we live in a media society and that organizers must make creative use of the media. Alinsky emphasized flashy tactics which would capture the attention of the media. Organizers who pursue this strategy (and it can be a very effective strategy) must rely on "colorful folks" who appeal to media people. The staff often goes with the toughest and most militant people, people who are not afraid and even like to speak in public. These are not necessarily leaders who have a real understanding of what is on people's minds and who are able to articulate these concerns for and with the membership.

Flashy tactics or "creative use of the media" or whatever one wants to call it is an important organizing strategy. Short-range demands dictate that organizers move in this direction. But long-range demands should at least make the organizer sensitive to some of the problems associated with this style of organizing. Dave Knotts pinpoints what is at stake:

> If you're going to put together any large-scale organization you have to go with the best talent available. We use flashy tactics because we are a media society. You haven't got the luxury of going back and dealing with people who are scared to death to stand up before a group and talk. You are forced, early on, to deal with the best. That's why you want to keep leadership fluid—you're

going with flashy stuff—you're going with the person who talks well—and *invariably, invariably, invariably* they're the wrong people. I've made that mistake so many times it is embarrassing. If the mistake is institutionalized in the structure of your organization, then you're stuck.

The mass meeting is an organizational event that likewise has to be carefully evaluated. Anxious to produce for funders and eager to gain publicity and recognition, organizers are quick to move toward mass meetings of one sort or another. As a show of strength, in dramatic confrontation with political or economic elites, the mass meeting can be a very effective strategy. My concern is with this event as it relates to the nature of community organizations. The large conventions, for example, almost always seem to be antidemocratic events dominated by the good talkers who make the speeches and get elected as officers of the organization. There is nothing very "grass roots" about most of the conventions I have attended or organized for. Myles Horton is unequivocal in his opposition to this event:

> I would eliminate the mass meeting from the organizing process. It has nothing to do with organizing. I think it is a publicity gimmick and a shortcut to find the glib people who stand out and talk. It is a weeding-out process that gets people. It is a lazy man's way of getting some people, and it is always the wrong people.
>
> I am serious about this. I was working with a group in the mountains a number of years ago and was beginning to get a base for a real grass-roots organization. And some high-powered organizer came in and convinced them they ought to have a mass meeting. I went up to the mass meeting to publicly withdraw from it— I'd been working here for two years. I said, "I don't want to be a party to this organization's death." They never had another grass-roots meeting—because they elected a bunch of glib officers. I knew it was going to happen. My experience is so completely clear on this—I want to stay away from it. *You are getting a synthetic organization—the talkers and the professionals. There is no more education or development. I don't want to be a part of it.*

A positive alternative to a mass meeting is to lay the groundwork through *grass-roots organizing.* The organizer works with lots of different people, often in small groups, and tries to get activity going at whatever level she can. From the beginning, the emphasis is on getting people to do things for themselves. She sticks with this process until there is some emerging leadership.

The creation of local organizing committees is a model that is often used to develop local leadership. Organizers do some of the initial "door knocking." Several residents who indicate strong interest, seem especially articulate, or have a following in the area are asked if they would form an organizing committee. The committee then makes the initial decisions on issues and conducts the community-wide canvassing and house meetings necessary to build a local chapter. After a formal meeting where officers are elected and more issues are decided on, the local organization takes action on various issue campaigns and strives to increase its numbers and power.

One organizer, who had considerable experience working with organizing committees, emphasized the importance of this model in developing local leadership: "We want to make sure our organization does not become a staff operation. Therefore, we generate organizing committees that really take responsibility. By the time of the first formal meeting, we already have a leadership."

I've seen this model work very well or fail miserably, depending on what's really happening in the process. The committee may or may not be seen as leadership by the people. They may grab all the power and "lead" in an authoritarian, top-down manner, or they may strive to share leadership and bring new people into leadership positions. They may be the talkers, the professional joiners, the moderate- or middle-income in the "low- and moderate-income people organizations," or they may be the poor as well as moderate-income people. They may be the people whom the organizer thinks of as good leaders because he can relate to them (inexperienced organizers often make this mistake), or they may be the people who are highly respected by their neighbors.

It is a tricky process. Organizers who view the task of building local chapters in terms of some kind of cost-benefit analysis and rapidly move from one stage to another may have an expansion timetable they can point to, but they have not used the organizing committee as a means of developing strong and diversified leadership.

One area that creates many problems for organizers is strategy *development*. Since most people are not used to thinking in conflict terms about situations, many organizers plunge right into making strategy for people. This is very different from the painstaking process of raising questions and making people think them through: (1) What are the problems in our community? (2) What do we feel most strongly about, and what should be our priorities? (3) What would it take to get a change on these problems? (4) Where does it make sense to start? (5) What is the political structure we are up against; what are the various routes of access to the decision-making apparatus?

If the premise is that the organizer is the outside expert who comes in to tell people what to do (if big shots can hire their lawyers, why can't poor people hire their organizers?), this is a legitimate sort of role for organizers—as long as everyone is "up front" about it. It is like a great deal of union organizing: there is a structure already set up with a constitutional framework, dues, and so forth, and there is a history which enables the organization to say, "If you follow this approach, we can guarantee you a certain amount of success. We can come in and organize you to deal with these problems if you want to be a part of this organization."

If you are trying to organize a community where the people think through their own problems through their own experiences and learn to make their own strategies and their own decisions, then "making strategy" for people will not do.

What do we really want to do? This is the primary question. For if we are serious about developing broad leadership and not just going with a few articulate people who are rarely at the bottom end of the income spectrum, we'll have to spend the necessary time. Among other things, *this means organizers should not give up on people*. Expectations can make a real difference. It is very much like it is in the schools. The teacher's expectation about a student is a critical factor in determining how much that student will learn. If the organizer assumes it is unrealistic to spend much time with Ms. Smith, a welfare mother who is down and out, she indeed won't develop as a leader. The high-powered organizer with a set timetable and all kinds of expansion goals has got to get this issue campaign going and that issue campaign going. He cannot go through the necessary process of leadership development. He cannot develop local people who really need the encouragement because he can't afford to "waste time" with them. Those organizers who believe in the ability of people to make decisions for themselves, whatever their income, and who are serious about the task of developing *people's* organizations, find that people respond and they develop far beyond our hopes.

Leadership development is a dynamic process that is of critical importance to the building of organizations and social movements. It is a process that can only take place at the grass-roots level. People come to see that their self-interest, in a broad sense, can best be served in a group. First, they get together in small groups; then they form organizations which ideally are as broad as possible. The next step, at certain times in history, is a social movement.

In my formative years there has only been one social movement—the Civil Rights Movement. I have only read or talked to people about the Industrial Union Movement of the 1930s and 1940s. Both of these social movements embodied goals that were challenging, ahead of their time, beyond the capacity of community organizations, and requiring large numbers of people working together. Many of us long for such a social movement today. But we cannot will or create social movements, however much we might like to.

Social movements are created by factors beyond our control. Only at certain times in history are there "crises," a particular set of economic and political conditions, which energize and activate people to very intense levels of political participation. On the other hand, people organizations are essential building blocks to a movement. They provide the space to meet with people and talk about goals and strategies. In the absence of a social movement, we have to do our best to build as broad and as strong and as progressive organizations as possible, organizations which are capable of renewing themselves in political struggle.

Whether we are successful or not largely depends on our ability to develop local leadership. It is only when people learn to work together that we will have change. This is the cement that makes strong organizations and makes a movement. Several months after OBRC officially closed its doors, I called Gayle Aldrich, a welfare mother, and Roger Tralle, a low-paid worker.

They had been active in OBRC and were neighbors of mine, so I was anxious to talk with them after having been out of town for over a year. I asked them what their plans were since OBRC no longer existed. Their answer: "We're going to build another organization!" Patti Fritz put it this way at a recent steering committee meeting: "I still have that damn OBRC consciousness." OBRC is gone, but many strong OBRC people remain—people who will never be the same as a result of their experience. Their strength and determination are what make grass-roots organizing so important.

Notes

Introduction

1. For further documentation and explication of this point, see Frances Fox Piven and Richard A. Cloward, *Regulating the Poor: The Functions of Public Welfare* (New York: Random House, 1971), pp. 258-259.
2. Rural Housing Alliance and Rural America, "Working Papers." Presented to the First National Conference on Rural America, Washington, D.C., April 14-17, 1975.
3. I do not use the BLS lower living standard to play a statistical game to exaggerate a claim. There is widespread dissatisfaction with the official government income poverty level. Poverty is defined in terms of income deficiency—the inability of an individual or family to purchase needed goods and services to assure adequate food, housing, clothing, medical care, and other necessities. The poverty formula as determined by the Social Security Administration is based on an estimated cost of food expenditures x 3 x the number of people in the family. It is assumed the average family spends one-third of its budget on food. The poverty index is figured on the Department of Agriculture's Economy Food Plan or Thrifty Food Plan. The USDA admits it is an emergency food diet that a family can live on for only a short period of time, that the plan assumes food has the same nutritional value through storage and preparation and people are nutritional experts in knowing exactly what to buy on this small allotment. Moreover, the price of food has risen dramatically over the past few years, but the USDA has not adjusted its food plan to meet this growing cost. There are many other major problems with this poverty index. The point is that we have established, by design, an unrealistic measurement of poverty which unfortunately serves as a measurement of social needs and as a criterion for eligibility for income assistance and area development programs. It is a political definition whereby we hide an important truth about ourselves as a country. For a thorough discussion of this point, see Herman P. Miller, *Rich Man, Poor Man*

(New York: Thomas Y. Crowell Co., 1971), and Bradley R. Schiller, *The Economics of Poverty and Discrimination* (Englewood Cliffs: Prentice-Hall, 1973).

4. See Rural Housing Alliance and Rural America, "Working Papers."

5. Mariellen Procopio and Frederick J. Perella, Jr., *Poverty Profile 1975.* Campaign for Human Development is the national social action arm of the Catholic Church.

6. James Agee and Walker Evans, *Let Us Now Praise Famous Men* (New York: Ballantine Books, Inc., 1941); Tony Dunbar, *Our Land Too* (New York: Random House, 1969); Si Kahn, *How People Got Power: Organizing Oppressed Communities for Action* (New York: McGraw-Hill, 1970); and the many studies of the eminent psychiatrist Robert Coles constitute a few exceptions.

7. As a part of our preliminary work to organizing in Rice County, we submitted a proposal to OEO for a rural legal assistance program in southern Minnesota. At this time, the agency sponsored only three rural programs in the United States. The California Legal Rural Assistance Program (CLRA) was the best known of these. It was under constant political pressure and seriously weakened by the Reagan and Nixon administrations.

8. Peter Bachrach and Morton Baratz, *Power and Poverty: Theory and Practice* (New York: Oxford University Press, 1970), pp. 50-51.

9. *Report of the National Advisory Commission on Civil Disorders, 1969* is an excellent example. And note the testimony of black psychologist Kenneth Clark, appearing before the commission: "I read that report. . . . of the 1919 riot in Chicago, and it is as if I were reading the report of the investigation committee of the Harlem riot of '43, the report of the McCone Commission on the Watts riot. I must again in candor say to you members of this Commission—it is a kind of Alice in Wonderland—with the same moving picture reshown over and over again, the same analysis, recommendations, and the same inaction." Two years earlier President Lyndon B. Johnson's own National Advisory Commission on Rural Poverty issued a perceptive study, *The People Left Behind* (1967). This report displeased the president and its distribution was severely limited.

10. Michael Parenti, "The Possibilities for Political Change," *Politics and Society*, vol. 1 (November 1970).

11. Peter Bachrach and Doug Bennett, "Education in Political Commitments," unpublished paper.

12. The director of the welfare department and chairman of the county bureau of commissioners were involved, for example, in the tenure controversy at Carleton. They supplied certain kinds of information (I don't know what kind) to the chairman of the political science department and were quoted as saying, "We're as anxious to get rid of him as you are."

Chapter 1

1. U.S. Census figures. As I noted previously, this official definition of poverty is highly suspect.
2. U.S. Census figures, 1970.
3. Ibid.
4. Ibid.
5. Ibid.
6. In 1970 I was appointed to the board of directors by the director and the board. A minister in Rice County had recommended me, and I assume my credentials as a professor-poverty expert were quite respectable.
7. Saul D. Alinsky, "The War on Poverty: Political Pornography," *Journal of Social Issues*, January 1965.
8. Saul D. Alinsky, *Rules for Radicals* (New York: Random House, 1971).
9. Carleton and St. Olaf colleges could have been a source of power by providing research skills and expertise but remained aloof. Their concern "in the community" was exclusively with businessmen and other professional people.
10. Lewis Lipsitz, "On Political Belief: The Grievances of the Poor," in Philip Green and Sanford Levinson, eds., *Power and Community: Dissenting Essays in Political Science* (New York: Random House, 1970).
11. The students understood this point much better than my colleagues. The research was attacked by various professors at Carleton on the grounds that there were no firm policy recommendations that the county commissioners and other local officials could find useful. The president of Carleton once opened a conversation with me this way: "If I were a county commissioner I would certainly want some recommendations to go on." The point of course was that the studies *were not for* the county commissioners.
12. The 236 program provided a subsidy to lending institutions to keep down interest rates so that nonprofit housing sponsors could keep down rents. But the rents were still much higher than public housing, and the majority of poor people in the county, including most of the aged, could not afford the rents.
13. This figure was calculated by comparing USDA eligibility requirements with the number of people in the county under the income limits as indicated in the 1970 census figures.
14. OBRC's relationship with the local press and media has been complicated throughout the past three years. At this point in time the organization was not threatening to local officials or businessmen. The *Daily News* editor told one reporter he normally wouldn't print such a story, but it was too sensational to pass up. Likewise, radio station KDHL was willing to carry a good story. There were certain advantages in this early stage of organizing when OBRC was "struggling for recognition." Once OBRC became a force to contend with in the community and a threat to those in power, its relations with local media

deteriorated to the point where the organization was "blacked out" from most news coverage. I will develop this point more fully in later chapters.

Chapter 2

1. The flat grant payment has seriously undercut welfare rights organizing. The welfare rights strategy was to organize mothers and immediately "take on" local county or city welfare departments. The strategy was very successful. Local welfare departments had discretionary power over utility, furniture, housing, clothing allowances. Most welfare mothers did not realize they were entitled to supplementary benefits in these areas and welfare departments did not notify them of their rights. Welfare rights organizing involved, in large part, getting mothers together and then confronting local welfare departments over benefits the women were entitled to as a matter of law. The flat grant system was instituted in many states as a strategy (an effective one) to combat welfare rights organizing.

Chapter 3

1. In the first year of organizing, we were very reluctant to work with liberal professionals in the community. For example, AFDC mothers could have received some support from professional people in lobbying for a higher flat grant payment. The professional people were more articulate and had experience in politics. Several liberal supporters personally knew our local legislators. This is precisely the reason we avoided their help. Welfare mothers were to *represent themselves*. They were the ones to do the strategizing, lobbying, speaking, and *learning*. Now, after a full year of organizing, we changed strategy. We were confident OBRC people would not be intimidated working with professional people who supported day care. The support of professionals was pivotal to success. It was an OBRC proposal and the organization could justifiably claim the victory.
2. This is an interesting variation of Michael Lipsky's view of political protest. Lipsky argues the essence of protest consists in activating third parties in the controversy in such a way as to put additional pressure on target institutions and help further protest goals. OBRC, located in a rural, small-town community, could not count on activating sympathetic third parties in the community. For one thing, the local media had become increasingly hostile. More important, there were no "cause" organizations or groups which the organization could count on. A strong conservative ideology prevailed throughout the community. So OBRC activated third parties *outside* the county in order to enlist support in its battle against local governments. See Michael Lipsky, "Protest as a Political Resource," *American Political Science Review*, December 1968, and *Protest in City Politics* (Chicago: Rand McNally, 1970).

Chapter 4

1. These two remarkable men point to the kind of contributions middle-class professionals can make to a poor people's organization like OBRC. By design, OBRC's leaders, rank-and-file members, and *organizers* came from the community (this point is more fully developed in the next two chapters). Joe Schmidt and Bill Moore were sensitive to the critical goal of developing local leadership and never attempted to "lead." But as "outsiders" trusted by people in the organization, they were able to offer at times more objective evaluations of the organization. Bill Moore had a solid grasp of community organizing, and his advice was indispensable to indigenous citizen organizers who never had any formal training.

2. OBRC, a "bottom-up" organization, needed the "expertise" of certain kinds of professionals. As noted above, Joe Schmidt and Bill Moore made (make) important contributions. But I think it is worth emphasizing the special need OBRC had (has) for research assistance to develop issue campaigns and consultation with skilled, professional organizers. Dave Knotts was a skilled and experienced organizer who had trained with Saul Alinsky. Unlike other professional organizers in the area, he respected the knowledge and skill OBRC people had developed through their own experience and did not attempt to impose an orthodoxy on them. Out of mutual respect, he was able to provide invaluable assistance to them on the dial-a-bus campaign. Unfortunately, his major responsibilities were with other organizations and his help was limited to this one instance. Other organizers were willing to work with OBRC on a continuing basis, but at a consulting fee the organization could hardly afford.

Chapter 5

1. For reasons discussed later in the chapter, little money was raised locally. The Christian Sharing Fund, the Youth Project (funding was technically for Phyllis Hanson and not OBRC), and Campaign for Human Development monies provided for almost the total operating budget of the organization. The CHD grant of $15,000 was the financial lifeline of OBRC.

2. Once OBRC became a threat in the community, it found it very difficult to get news coverage. The editor of the *Faribault Daily News* was (is) a conservative Republican who wanted his paper to appeal to his friends, who had no use for the low-income sector of the community. KDHL, the major radio station in Faribault, gave OBRC good coverage by way of some good announcers, all of whom were fired by the owner or quit due to personality problems with him. OBRC receives no coverage from KDHL now. The owner told the people that he did not like their parking "junkers" in front of his office and vowed he would not mention the OBRC name or use OBRC press releases on his station. He has kept his word. OBRC's relations with the paper are a bit more complicated. The organization has threatened to take the

paper before the Minnesota Press Council. The press council has no cease-and-desist power, but the hearing would draw considerable publicity (probably not local) and would be an embarrassment. Thus, the organization has been able to force some stories on the paper.

3. Center for Community Change and the Youth Project have their central offices located in Washington, D.C. (in the same building). The Youth Project was originally sponsored by Center for Community Change. Both are nonprofit organizations funded, in the main, by "liberal foundation" monies. They provide invaluable assistance to local community organizations. The Youth Project funds young people involved in social action work. The staff provides them with a great deal of professional consultation. Center for Community Change works both at the national and local level. In relation to national issues, it seeks to design more efficient and effective programs in jobs, income, and broad community development. At the local level it provides invaluable technical assistance, workshops, and links to other sources of aid for a broad range of groups and organizations throughout the country. These middle-class professional organizations perform a tremendous service for organizations like OBRC which do not have sophisticated research skills and are in need of crucial information about legislative programs which vitally affect their communities.

Chapter 6

1. James Q. Wilson, *Political Organizations* (New York: Basic Books, 1975), p. 13.
2. Ibid., pp. 33–34.
3. For a full theoretical development of this argument, see Mancur Olson, Jr., *The Logic of Collective Action* (Cambridge: Harvard University Press, 1965).
4. This year I am working on a comparative study of community organizing in various rural, small-town areas in the country. The organizers at one organization I visited were very much influenced by Mancur Olson's work, so much so that they dropped the political organizing campaigns which delivered "collective" benefits to members and nonmembers and focused solely on programs (food co-op, a community garden, etc.) where they could control benefits for members only. This was fine for maintenance, but the organization was not able to expand and grow in power.
5. What does "building for power" mean? Let me define it for the purpose of this argument as organizing for the attainment of OBRC's political goals as enunciated at the annual conventions.
6. A very important theoretical work on this subject is Peter Bachrach's *The Theory of Democratic Elitism: A Critique* (Boston: Little, Brown and Co., 1967).
7. For a very interesting account of precisely this kind of model, see Lawrence Neil Bailis, *Bread or Justice: Grassroots Organizing in the Welfare Rights Movement* (Lexington, Mass.: D. C. Heath and Co., 1975).

I have observed this model in operation in a number of different organizations. A fascinating account about a leadership training institute
with a very different philosophy is Frank Adams (with Myles Horton),
Unearthing Seeds of Fire: The Idea of Highlander (Winston-Salem:
John F. Blair, 1975).

8. I have in mind Wilson's definition of the problem of institutionalizing
an organization—"of ensuring its survival and successfully asserting its
special domain." See Wilson, *Political Organizations*, p. 208.

9. Articles have appeared in the *Arkansas Gazette, Washington Post,
Southern Voices, New York Times, Boston Globe, Harper's*, the *New
Republic, Miami Herald*, and the *Los Angeles Times* about ACORN.
For a recent and more detailed treatment of ACORN, see Andrew
Kopkind, "Acorn Calling: Door-to-Door Organizing in Arkansas,"
Working Papers, summer 1975.

Library of Congress Cataloging in Publication Data
Wellstone, Paul David.
How the rural poor got power.
Includes bibliographical references.
1. Political participation—Minnesota—Rice Co.
2. Rice Co., Minn.—Politics and government. 3. Rural
poor—Minnesota—Rice Co. 4. Organization for a Better
Rice County. I. Title.
JS451.M69R58 1978 320.9'776'555 77-22109
ISBN 0-87023-249-5